Amphibians and Reptiles

Rare and Endangered Biota of Florida
Ray E. Ashton, Jr., Series Editor

Florida Committee on Rare and Endangered Plants and Animals

Ray E. Ashton, Jr.
FCREPA Chair (1989–91)
   and Series Editor
Water and Air Research, Inc.
6821 SW Archer Road
Gainesville, Florida 32608

Paul E. Moler
FCREPA Chair (1992–93)
Chair, Special Committee
   on Amphibians and Reptiles
Wildlife Research Laboratory
Florida Game and
   Fresh Water Fish Commission
4005 S. Main Street
Gainesville, Florida 32601

Daniel F. Austin, Co-Chair
Special Committee on Plants
Department of Biological Sciences
Florida Atlantic University
Boca Raton, FL 33431

Mark Deyrup, Co-Chair
Special Committee on Invertebrates
Archbold Biological Station
Route 2, Box 180
Lake Placid, Florida 33852

L. Richard Franz, Co-Chair
Special Committee on Invertebrates
Florida Museum of Natural History
University of Florida
Gainesville, Florida 32611

Carter R. Gilbert
Chair, Special Committee on Fishes
Florida Museum of Natural History
University of Florida
Gainesville, Florida 32611

Stephen R. Humphrey
Chair, Special Committee on Mammals
Florida Museum of Natural History
University of Florida
Gainesville, Florida 32611

Herbert W. Kale II
FCREPA Chair (1985–86)
Co-Chair, Special Committee on Birds
Florida Audubon Society
1101 Audubon Way
Maitland, Florida 32751

James Rodgers
Co-Chair, Special Committee on Birds
Wildlife Research Laboratory
Florida Game and
   Fresh Water Fish Commission
4005 S. Main Street
Gainesville, Florida 32601

Allan Stout
FCREPA Chair (1987–88)
Department of Biological Sciences
University of Central Florida
Orlando, Florida 32816

Daniel B. Ward
FCREPA Chair (1983–84)
Co-Chair, Special Committee on Plants
Department of Botany
University of Florida
Gainesville, Florida 32611

Rare and Endangered Biota of Florida

VOLUME III.
AMPHIBIANS AND REPTILES

EDITED BY

PAUL E. MOLER

Chair, Special Committee on Amphibians and Reptiles
Florida Committee on Rare and Endangered
  Plants and Animals

UNIVERSITY PRESS OF FLORIDA
Gainesville, Tallahassee, Tampa, Boca Raton,
Pensacola, Orlando, Miami, Jacksonville

Special Committee on Amphibians and Reptiles

Paul E. Moler (Chair)
Florida Game and Fresh Water
    Fish Commission
4005 South Main Street
Gainesville, FL 32601

Ray E. Ashton, Jr.
Water and Air Research, Inc.
6821 SW Archer Rd.
Gainesville, Florida 32602

Steven P. Christman
Department of Natural Sciences
Florida Museum of Natural History
Gainesville, FL 32611

David Cook
Florida Game and
    Fresh Water Fish Commission
620 South Meridian Street
Tallahassee, FL 32304

Joan Diemer
Florida Game and
    Fresh Water Fish Commission
4005 South Main Street
Gainesville, FL 32601

Llewellyn M. Ehrhart
Department of Biological Sciences
University of Central Florida
P.O. Box 25000
Orlando, FL 32816

Richard Franz
Department of Natural Sciences
Florida Museum of Natural History
Gainesville, FL 32611

Dale R. Jackson
Florida Natural Areas Inventory
1018 Thomasville Road, Suite 200-C
Tallahassee, FL 32303

D. Bruce Means
Coastal Plains Institute
1313 North Duval Street
Tallahassee, FL 32303

Peter C. H. Pritchard
Florida Audubon Society
1101 Audubon Way
Maitland, FL 32751

This volume was made possible in part by grants from Florida Power and Light Company and Save the Manatee Club.

The University Press of Florida is the scholarly publishing agency of the State University System of Florida, comprised of Florida A & M University, Florida Atlantic University, Florida International University, Florida State University, University of Central Florida, University of Florida, University of North Florida, University of South Florida, and University of West Florida.

University Press of Florida
15 Northwest 15th Street
Gainesville, FL 32611

Contents

Amphibians

Threatened

Rare

Status Undetermined

Reptiles

Endangered

Threatened

Species of Special Concern

Rare

Foreword

In 1978, not long after I became executive director of the Florida Game and Fresh Water Fish Commission, I was privileged to be associated with the production of the initial six-volume Rare and Endangered Biota of Florida series. That series has enjoyed enormous popularity (each volume was reprinted at least once, most two or three times). It has served as the definitive reference compendium on endangered and threatened species in Florida and is widely recognized as among the most authoritative and comprehensive such works in the nation. I am proud the commission was integrally involved in that initial work, and likewise proud that we were involved in producing this revised series.

In the forewords to the initial volumes, I and my predecessor, Dr. O. E. Frye, Jr., acknowledged the momentum of endangered species conservation to that point, and how the series was a significant contribution in that regard, but admonished that we must not rest on our laurels—much remained to be done. Although much has indeed been done in the interim, I am disappointed that we have not approached the level of progress I had hoped we would attain by now. As the species accounts herein clearly demonstrate, many Florida species are perilously near extinction, and many of the factors leading to that dire circumstance are still with us. The composition of the current official state lists—42 endangered, 28 threatened, and 47 special concern animals, along with 199 endangered and 283 threatened plants—is compelling evidence in and of itself that our progress has been relatively minor (by comparison, there were 31 endangered and 54 threatened species in 1978). There are several reasons for this much-less-than-hoped-for progression, but primarily it has been related to insufficient funding at both the state and federal levels. And without proper funding, the necessary manpower and other resources cannot be emplaced to address many critical needs. So we face the dilemma of either addressing the needs of only a few species so as to maximize effect, or spreading our resources thinly among many species, minimizing the effects on an individual basis.

This is not to say, however, that we have not made some substantial strides forward in the last decade or so. Through an innovative translocation strategy, we have reestablished in Florida the previously extirpated Perdido Key beach mouse and significantly expanded the range of the Choctawhatchee beach mouse; because of stringent protection and rigorous application of "Habitat Management Guidelines for the Bald Eagle in the Southeast Region," Florida's bald eagle nesting population has grown to more than 550 pairs (as of the 1990–91 nesting season); the brown pelican and Pine Barrens treefrog have been delisted because of increasing populations and/or because our research efforts have provided new insight into those species' true status; nearly 50 manatee sanctuaries have been established in which boat speeds are restricted during the winter congregation period; our research since 1978 has resulted in more knowledge about endangered species biology, habitat needs, and the like, than during all previous time cumulatively; considerable endangered species habitat has been secured through CARL (Conservation and Recreation Lands), Save Our Coasts, Save Our Rivers, Save Our Everglades, and other land acquisition programs; and various information/education programs have resulted in a significant increase in public awareness and support for endangered species conservation. These few examples demonstrate what can be done with adequate resources and commitment, but in fact represent only the proverbial drop in the bucket in light of the total needs.

I hope this revised series reinvigorates our resolve and commitment to endangered and threatened species conservation and we will be able to cite a multitude of such examples by the time a third revision is necessary. These volumes provide an authoritative and comprehensive database from which to embark on such a course, and I congratulate and personally thank each researcher, writer, editor, and individual whose committed efforts have culminated in this exemplary work.

Colonel Robert M. Brantly, Executive Director
State of Florida Game and Fresh Water Fish Commission

Preface

"Thirty years ago Florida was one of the most extraordinary states in the Union, but being flat and quite park-like in character (a large part of the country consisted of open pinelands) it was an easy state for man to ruin, and he has ruined it with ruthless efficiency." This quote from Thomas Barbour's *That Vanishing Eden, A Naturalist's Florida,* written in 1944, is ever more appropriate today. He continues his lament—"A large part of Florida is now so devastated that many of her friends are disinclined to believe that she ever could have been the Paradise which I know once existed." Barbour was talking about the loss of natural habitat in Florida from 1915 to the early 1940s. Imagine what he would think today!

Within the FCREPA volumes, the emphasis is on specific plants and animals that the committee considers to be endangered, threatened to become endangered, or species of special concern (those species apparently in danger but about which we need more information). However, as one reads through the species accounts, there is a continuing theme of habitat loss or alteration by man. Since Barbour's days of study in Florida, the loss and degradation of natural habitats have accelerated beyond human comprehension. We are faced with the possible reality that the only thing which will cause a decline in the loss is that there will soon be no land left to develop.

We are also faced with the fact that we actually know very little about the fauna and flora of this state. When challenged to protect a species or develop regulations to prevent extinction, we are inevitably confronted with the fact that we know little about their life histories, let alone what is needed to preserve a population through biological time. We are also faced with the dilemma that there probably is not enough time or money to allow us to study these organisms, let alone experiment with management techniques. Our ecological knowledge of interspecific interactions and biological communities is even less. Yet we do know that once certain biological needs are not met, we lose another species and another community. The biological communities of this state are being compromised time and again by all levels of government, simply to serve the hunger for growth and development.

We are the first generation to realize that not only do we have local or regional environmental concerns but we now have to be aware of serious global degradations of our air and water. Global warming, acid rain, increased ultraviolet radiation, and degradation of our oceans are making us realize for the first time that our species may well be jeopardizing itself as well as the lowly gopher tortoise and tree snail. We are realizing that the world's biodiversity and the biological engine that drives many of the necessities of all life are being used up or changed by our overpopulated species. If we know so little about individual species and communities, how can we be prepared to understand the complexities of the biosphere, let alone the cause and effect of our actions.

Alarms have sounded in the minds of many people around the world, including Florida. The first step toward a solution to all of this is acknowledging that we are causing problems. Loss of uplands not only means loss of wildlife but also that we affect our water supplies, river systems, and ultimately the health of our coastal systems. Our state agencies are in the fledgling stages of creating regulations on development and the organized effort of protecting biological diversity and natural communities. Hopefully these agencies and the people of Florida will begin to recognize that we must increase our efforts to protect our environment and the creatures who inhabit it, not just to use for recreation but for the sake of preserving the machinery that makes our lives as living things possible.

It is these concerns that have been the driving force behind the volunteer-biologists who have unselfishly spent so many long hours putting together the information in these volumes. We hope that through the information provided here more biologists will turn their thoughts from the test tube to the laboratory in the field, funding agencies will realize the need for this basic knowledge, and government agencies will begin to think more on the biological community level and not the species or individual organism level. Most important, we hope that these volumes serve to educate the citizens of Florida so that we may all recognize the need to learn more and work together to make prudent decisions about our "Vanishing Eden."

Ray E. Ashton, Jr.
FCREPA Chair and Series Editor

A Brief History of FCREPA

The Florida Committee on Rare and Endangered Plants and Animals, FCREPA, was founded in 1973. The original group of 100 scientists, conservationists, and concerned citizens was organized by James Layne, Peter Pritchard, and Roy McDiarmid. The chairs of the Special Committees on Terrestrial Invertebrates, Marine Invertebrates, Plants, Reptiles and Amphibians, Fish, Birds, Mammals, and Liaison made up the first Endangered Species Advisory Board to the Florida Game and Fresh Water Fish Commission. These special committees were made up of concerned biologists who were living and/or working in the state of Florida. The first FCREPA meeting was called for biologists to discuss and evaluate the status of Florida's wildlife and to determine which species should be considered for special classification and concern. From this conference, five volumes—The Rare and Endangered Biota of Florida series—were produced. These were edited by Peter Pritchard of the Florida Audubon Society and Don Wood of the Florida Game and Fresh Water Fish Commission. Section editors for the first series included Roy McDiarmid, reptiles and amphibians; Herb Kale, birds; James Layne, mammals; Carter Gilbert, fish; Howard Weems, terrestrial invertebrates; Joe Simon, marine invertebrates; and Dan Ward, plants. Before its completion, the invertebrate volumes were combined under the editorship of Richard Franz.

Following the production of the FCREPA volumes by the University Presses of Florida in 1976, FCREPA continued to meet and support a special section of papers at the annual meeting of the Florida Academy of Sciences. The affiliation of FCREPA was organized under the guidance of Dan Ward, director of the herbarium at the University of Florida.

In the fall of 1986, it became obvious that the original publications were becoming dated and the demand for the publication was great (the volumes had been reprinted repeatedly). Then chair, Herbert Kale, vice president of the Florida Audubon Society, convened the second FCREPA conference at the youth camp in the Ocala National Forest. The committees on each group met and deliberated on the status of the species in their charge. It was decided at that meeting to rewrite the FCREPA series since considerable changes in our knowledge and in the state of the natural environment in Florida made much of the information produced more than 13 years before out of date. Editors for each of the volumes called together those knowledgeable individuals and potential contributors to the future volumes to discuss the status of the taxa covered in their volume. Their recommendations on the status (and the criteria used) of various species were discussed by everyone present at the 1986 meeting.

Under the direction of Jack Stout, University of Central Florida, and each of the section chairs and editors, the arduous task of preparing the new manuscripts was undertaken. Each section chair served as compiler and editor for each volume. Individual species accounts were prepared by biologists who were among the most qualified to write about the status of that species.

Ray Ashton, vertebrate zoologist, Water and Air Research, Inc. was appointed by the section chairs as managing editor of the series in 1988. Paul Moler, research biologist, Florida Game and Fresh Water Fish Commission, was voted as chair-elect (1992–1993). Four years of preparation and coordination, fund raising, and gentle prodding of the seven volunteer editors and the many contributors have produced the second FCREPA series.

Without the thousands of volunteer hours given by many outstanding Florida biologists, and the support from the Florida Game and Fresh Water Fish Commission, Save the Manatee Club, and Florida Power and Light Company, this effort would not have been possible. Royalties from the sales of these volumes and donations to the FCREPA effort are used to keep all the volumes in print and to fund future work.

Ray E. Ashton, Jr.
FCREPA Chair and Series Editor

Definitions of Status Categories

Categories used to designate the status of the organisms included in the Florida list of rare and endangered species are defined below. In the case of species or subspecies whose ranges extend outside the state, the category to which the form is assigned is based on the status of its population in Florida. Thus, a plant or animal whose range barely reaches the state ("peripheral species") may be classified as endangered, threatened, or rare as a member of the Florida biota, although it may be generally common elsewhere in its range.

In the following definitions, "species" is used in a general sense to include (1) full taxonomic species, (2) subspecies (animals) or varieties (plants), and (3) particular populations of a species or subspecies that do not have formal taxonomic status. This use of the term agrees with that of the Endangered Species Act of 1973.

Endangered.—Species in danger of extinction or extirpation if the deleterious factors affecting their populations continue to operate. These are forms whose numbers have already declined to such a critically low level or whose habitats have been so seriously reduced or degraded that without active assistance their survival in Florida is questionable.

Threatened.—Species that are likely to become endangered in the state within the foreseeable future if current trends continue. This category includes: (1) species in which most or all populations are decreasing because of overexploitation, habitat loss, or other factors; (2) species whose populations have already been heavily depleted by deleterious conditions and, while not actually endangered, are nevertheless in a critical state; and (3) species that may still be relatively abundant but are being subjected to serious adverse pressures throughout their range.

Rare.—Species that, although not presently endangered or threatened as defined above, are potentially at risk because they are found only within a restricted geographic area or habitat in the state or are sparsely distributed over a more extensive range.

Species of special concern.—Species that do not clearly fit into one of the preceding categories yet warrant special attention. Included in this category are: (1) species that, although they are perhaps presently relatively abundant and widespread in the state, are especially vulnerable to certain types of exploitation or environmental changes and have experienced long-term population declines; and (2) species whose status in Florida has a potential impact on endangered or threatened populations of the same or other species outside the state.

Status undetermined.—Species suspected of falling into one of the above categories for which available data are insufficient to provide an adequate basis for their assignment to a specific category.

Recently extirpated.—Species that have disappeared from Florida since 1600 but still exist elsewhere.

Recently extinct.—Species that have disappeared from the state since 1600 through extinction.

Major Terrestrial and Wetland Habitats

In discussing habitat needs of various organisms, it is often convenient to refer to classifications of plant communities as a starting reference point. A number of classifications that address Florida plant communities have been developed, usually with different purposes or different constraints imposed on the classifier (i.e., "differences must be discernible on aerial photography"). Because plants' and animals' habitat needs rarely fit these plant community classification schemes very closely, considerable additional description is usually necessary to adequately define an organism's habitat.

Commonly used plant classification schemes include the following:

Davis, John H. 1967. General map of natural vegetation of Florida. Agr. Exp. Sta., University of Florida, Gainesville.

Soil Conservation Service. 1980. General map ecological communities, state of Florida.

Florida Natural Areas Inventory. Undated. List of plant communities used by FNAI in collecting plant community data.

Florida Department of Transportation. 1985. Florida land use, cover and forms classification system.

Plant community types used in the narrative loosely follow the general map of natural vegetation of Florida by John H. Davis. Descriptions of each habitat are based on this map plus published sources and personal experience. Several of Davis' vegetation categories are grouped together for convenience and brevity. Marl prairies and Everglades sawgrass are combined with wet prairies and marshes while southern slash pine forests are included with flatwoods. Other categories are added, further subdivided or omitted in order to provide a brief overview of major plant communities in Florida. The narratives on Florida terrestrial and wetland plant communities are grouped as follows:

Upland plant communities
1. Coastal strand
2. Dry prairies
3. Pine flatwoods
4. Sand pine scrub
5. Longleaf pine–xerophytic oak woodlands (sandhill communities)
6. Mixed hardwood–pine
7. Hardwood hammocks
8. Tropical hammocks

Wetland plant communities
9. Coastal marshes
10. Freshwater marshes and wet prairies
11. Scrub cypress
12. Cypress swamps
13. Hardwood swamps
14. Mangrove swamps

1. Coastal Strand

The coastal strand includes beaches and the vegetation zones of beaches and adjacent dunes or rock. This vegetation type is most commonly associated with shorelines subjected to surf and high winds but may sometimes be found bordering calmer bays and sounds.

The vegetation of the beaches and foredunes is characterized by pioneer plants able to establish themselves in the shifting sand. Typical species include railroad vines, beach cordgrass, and sea oats. Inland from the foredune, saw palmetto and dwarf scrubby oaks are found and, in southern Florida, sea grape and other tropical vegetation as well. The vegetation tends to change from grassy to woody from the foredune inland to the more protected back dunes, and the composition of the vegetation of these back dunes is often similar to that of sand pine scrub habitat found inland on old dunes.

Strand communities are adapted to the severe stresses of shifting sands, a highly saline environment, and high winds. In some instances, salt spray plays a role similar to fire in other ecosystems by retarding succession indefinitely at a grass or shrubby stage.

Historically, impacts to coastal strand plant communities (sometimes the total loss of the community) have resulted from beachfront residential development; invasion by exotic vegetation, primarily Australian pine; and accelerated erosion of beaches due to maintenance of inlets or nearby residential and tourist development.

2. Dry Prairies

Dry prairies are vast, treeless plains, often intermediate between wet grassy areas and forested uplands. Scattered bayheads, cypress ponds, or cabbage palm hammocks often occur in prairie areas. The largest areas of dry prairies occur north and west of Lake Okeechobee.

This community is dominated by many species of grasses such as wiregrass and broomsedge. Palmettos are the most common shrubby plant over large areas, with fetterbush, staggerbush, and dwarf blueberry common in places. A number of sedges and herbs are also found on the dry prairies.

Relatively little has been published on the ecology of dry prairies. They have often been compared to flatwoods minus the overstory trees, and the similar vegetative groundcover would seem to justify this idea.

Fire is important in determining the nature of the vegetation and its suitability for different species of wildlife. Winter burning associated with cattle operations may have shifted this community from grasses and forbs to saw palmetto. Absence of fire may result in shrubby communities, while frequent growing season fires yield a more herbaceous environment.

Large areas of native dry prairies have been converted to improved pasture, and this trend is continuing. Eucalyptus plantations have also been established on some former dry prairie sites although this does not appear to be a continuing trend. Expansion of citrus production southward is probably responsible for most dry prairie losses at this time.

3. Pine Flatwoods

Pine flatwoods are characterized by one or more species of pine as the dominant tree species and occur on level areas. The soils of flatwoods are sandy with a moderate amount of organic matter in the top few centimeters and an acid, organic hardpan 0.3–1.0 m (1–3 ft) beneath the surface.

Three major types of flatwoods occur in Florida: **longleaf pine flatwoods** found on well-drained sites and characterized by longleaf pine as the dominant overstory tree; **slash pine flatwoods** with slash pine as the dominant overstory species and usually in areas of intermediate wetness; and **pond pine flatwoods** with the pond pine as the dominant tree species and typically occurring in poorly drained areas. South Florida slash pine tends to replace both slash pine and longleaf pine in central to southern peninsular Florida.

Southern slash pine forest is found on the sand flatlands and rocklands of extreme southern Florida and is characterized by an overstory of the south Florida variety of the slash pine. This association often has tropical components in its understory.

Considerable overlap in understory plants exists among the three major types of flatwoods, with many species found in all three communities. Generally, however, gallberry and saw palmetto dominate the understory in slash pine flatwoods; wiregrasses, blueberries, and runner oaks are especially prevalent in longleaf pine flatwoods; and several of the bay trees are characteristic of pond pine areas. Flatwoods also often include intermingled cypress domes, bayheads, and small titi swamps.

Pine flatwoods are the most widespread of major plant communities, occurring throughout the relatively level Pleistocene marine terraces in both peninsular and panhandle Florida. Their suitability for growing pine trees has resulted in vast areas being incorporated into industrial forests. Changes in both fire and moisture regimes have resulted in changes in plant species composition and wildlife values. In south Florida, residential development is rapidly eliminating this plant community (and all other upland communities).

4. Sand Pine Scrub

Sand pine scrub is a plant community found almost exclusively in Florida on relict dunes or other marine features created along present and former shorelines or other marine features. Sand pine scrub communities occur along the coasts on old dunes, in the Ocala National Forest, and along the Lake Wales Ridge extending through Polk and Highlands counties. The soil is composed of well-washed, sterile sands.

This community is typically two-layered, with sand pine occupying the top layer and various scrubby oaks and other shrub species making up a thick, often clumped, understory. Little herbaceous groundcover exists, and large areas of bare sand occur frequently. Groundcover plants, when present, frequently include gopher apple and Florida bluestem grass. Deermosses are often common. Typical understory plants include myrtle oak, inopina oak, sand live oak, Chapman's oak, rosemary, scrub holly, and silkbay.

Where sand pines are absent, this community is often referred to as evergreen oak scrub. **Scrubby flatwoods** is a scrub-like association often occurring on drier ridges in typical flatwoods or near coasts. The understory species of this vegetation type are similar to those of sand pine scrub, but the sand pine is replaced by slash pine or longleaf pine.

The sand pine scrub is essentially a fire-based community. Ground vegetation is extremely sparse and leaf fall is minimal, thus reducing the chance of frequent ground fires so important in the sandhill community. As the sand pines and scrub oaks mature, however, they retain most of their branches and build up large fuel supplies in the crowns. When a fire does occur, this fuel supply, in combination with the resinous needles and high stand density, ensures a hot, fast-burning fire. Such fires allow for regeneration of the sand pine community and associated oak scrub, which would otherwise pass into a xeric hardwood community.

Sand pine scrub and its ecologically important variations are seriously threatened. Residential development and especially citrus production have eliminated much of this plant community. In addition, isolation from fire has resulted in succession to xeric hardwood hammock with a relatively closed canopy, thereby reducing its value to most endemic plants and animals.

5. Longleaf Pine–Xerophytic Oak Woodlands (Sandhill Communities)

Sandhill communities (the **longleaf pine–turkey oak** association being one major subtype of this community) occur on well-drained, white to yellowish sands.

Longleaf pines form a scattered overstory in mature natural stands. In many areas, xeric oaks such as turkey oak, bluejack oak, southern red oak, and sand post oak, which were originally scattered or small understory trees, now form the overstory as the result of cutting of the pines and prevention of fire. In some areas of southern peninsular Florida, south Florida slash pine replaces longleaf pine in the overstory. Although tree species diversity in sandhills is low, there is a wide variety of herbaceous plants such as wiregrass, piney woods dropseed, golden aster, partridge pea, gopher apple, bracken fern, and pawpaw, which provide fairly complete groundcover.

Sandhills were second in area only to flatwoods in Florida's predevelopment landscape, occurring widely throughout the panhandle and the northern half of the peninsula.

Fire is a dominant factor in the ecology of this community. The interrelationships of the sandhill vegetation types, particularly the longleaf pine–wiregrass relationship, are dependent on frequent ground fires. The longleaf pine is sensitive to hardwood competition, and wiregrass plays a major role in preventing the germination of hardwood seeds while ensuring that there is sufficient fuel buildup on the floor of the community to carry a fire over large areas.

Very little longleaf pine sandhill remains. Commercial foresters have attempted to convert large areas to slash pine with poor success but have had better success converting sandhills to a closed canopy monoculture of sand pine. In many cases the wiregrass groundcover has been destroyed, making restoration of this community type problematic. Large areas have been converted to improved pasture or citrus. The well-drained soils make attractive development sites and the majority of sandhill community in peninsular Florida in private ownership has either been developed, is being developed, or is platted and subdivided for future development.

6. Mixed Hardwood–Pine

The mixed hardwood–pine community of Davis is the southernmost extension of the piedmont southern mixed hardwoods and occurs on the clay soils of the northern panhandle.

Younger growth may be primarily pine, with shortleaf and loblolly pine predominant. As succession proceeds the various hardwoods become dominant and constitute the natural climax vegetation of much of the area, especially wetter, yet well-drained sites. The overstory is characterized by a high species diversity and includes American beech, southern magnolia, white oak, sweetgum, mockernut hickory, pignut hickory, basswood, yellow poplar, white ash, and spruce pine. The understory includes many young overstory species plus dogwood, red mulberry, hop hornbeam, blue beech, and sweetleaf.

Historically, fire played a role in the function of this community by limiting its expansion into higher, better-drained sites. Later, agriculture served a similar function and limited this community to slopes and creek bottoms. The best examples, with the most diversity of tree species, tend, therefore, to occur in creek bottoms or on moist but well-drained slopes.

Residential subdivisions and other aspects of urbanization and conversion to loblolly pine plantations and agriculture are resulting in continued losses of this plant community. Locally significant losses result from stream or river impoundments, clay mining, and highway construction.

7. Hardwood Hammocks

The hardwood hammock community constitutes the climax vegetation of many areas of northern and central Florida. Hardwoods occur on fairly rich, sandy soils and are best developed in areas where limestone or phosphate outcrops occur. Hardwood forests are similar to the mixed hardwood and pine of the panhandle but generally lack the shortleaf pine, American beech, and other more northern species, have a lower overstory species diversity, and tend to have a higher proportion of evergreen species. Southern magnolia, sugarberry, live oak, laurel oak, American holly, blue beech, and hop hornbeam are characteristic species of this association. Variations in the species composition of hardwood hammocks are partially due to differences in soil moisture.

Major variations of this vegetative association include coastal hammocks, live oak–cabbage palm hammocks, and maritime hammocks. **Coastal hammocks** are relatively wet hardwood communities that occur in narrow bands along parts of the Gulf and Atlantic coasts and often extend to the edge of coastal marshes. **Live oak–cabbage palm hammocks** often border larger lakes and rivers and are scattered throughout the prairie region of central Florida. Either the oak or palm may almost completely dominate in any one area. **Maritime hammocks** occur behind sheltering beachfront dunes and are often dominated by live oak.

Notable examples of hardwood hammocks are in public ownership but residential development is widespread in better-drained hammocks within the ever-increasing range of urban centers. Historically, large areas of coastal hardwood hammocks have been site-prepared and planted to pine for pulpwood production. The current rate of loss due to this land use has apparently declined. Hammocks continue to be lost to agricultural conversion although the near-surface limestone of many hammocks sometimes makes them unattractive for agriculture.

8. Tropical Hammocks

Tropical hammocks are found on many of the tree islands in the Everglades and on many of the Florida Keys. Remnants of these habitats occur north to Palm Beach on the east coast and Sarasota on the west coast.

Tropical hammocks typically have very high plant diversity, containing over 35 species of trees and almost 65 species of shrubs and small trees. Typical tropical trees are the strangler fig, gumbo limbo, mastic, bustic, lancewood, the ironwoods, poisonwood, pigeon plum, and Jamaica dogwood. Vines, air plants, and ferns are often abundant. Tropical hammocks of the Florida Keys contain a number of plants that are extremely rare in the United States, including mahogany, lignum vitae, and thatch palms.

The tropical hardwood forest is the successional climax for much of the uplands of extreme south Florida. Because of susceptibility to frequent fires, this association is largely confined to islands or slightly wetter areas but may invade drier areas if fire is removed for any length of time.

Tropical hammocks have been largely lost to residential development in most areas of southern Florida. Relatively large areas remain on north Key Largo, where intensive efforts to buy or regulate this community have occurred.

9. Coastal Marshes

Coastal marshes occur on low wave-energy shorelines north of the range of the mangroves and are also interspersed with mangroves in many areas. Salt marshes may also extend into tidal rivers and occur as a narrow zone between the mangroves and freshwater marshes in the southern areas of the state.

Many areas within salt marshes are dominated by one plant such as saltgrass, smooth cordgrass, or blackrush. The species existing in any one area depends largely on the degree of inundation by tides.

Smooth cordgrass typically occupies the lower areas and often borders tidal creeks and pools. Blackrush occurs over vast areas, particularly along the Gulf coast, and is inundated less frequently, while the highest areas of the marsh are vegetated by saltgrass or such succulents as saltwort, glasswort, and sea ox-eye daisy.

The functioning of salt marshes centers primarily on tides and salinity. The harsh conditions associated with daily inundation, desiccation, and high salinities contribute to a low plant and animal species diversity. Those organisms that have adapted to this environment can be very productive, however. Tides also provide a close ecological relationship with adjacent estuaries.

Coastal marshes have been affected primarily by waterfront residential development. Current wetland regulatory programs appear to be successful in preventing major losses of this community for the time being, although scattered losses continue.

10. Freshwater Marshes and Wet Prairies

Freshwater marshes are herbaceous plant communities occurring on sites where the soil is usually saturated or covered with surface water for one or more months during the growing season.

Wet prairies are characterized by shallower water and more abundant grasses, and usually fewer of the tall emergents, such as bulrushes, than marshes. This category also includes the wet to dry marshes and prairies found on marl areas in south Florida.

Upwards of 15 separate types of marshes or wet prairies have been described in Florida. Major ones include sawgrass marshes; flag marshes dominated by pickerel weed, arrowhead, fire flags, and other nongrass herbs; cattail marshes; spike rush marshes; bulrush marshes; maidencane prairies; grass, rush, and sedge prairies; and switchgrass prairies dominated by taller grasses. Any single marsh may have different sections composed of these major types, and there is also almost complete intergradation among the types.

Fire and water fluctuations, the two major ecosystem managers of Florida, are important in the maintenance of marshes and wet prairies. Fire, especially when combined with seasonal flooding, serves to stress plants not adapted to these conditions and reduces competition from more upland species.

Historic major marsh systems include the Everglades, Upper St. Johns River, Kissimmee River floodplain, and Lake Apopka/Oklawaha marshes. Drainage for agriculture has been the dominant factor in marsh losses. Existing wetland regulatory programs and a relatively small amount of agriculturally suitable major marsh systems remaining in private ownership have reduced past rates of loss of these large systems. Major wetland acquisition and restoration projects are underway in the examples cited. Ephemeral, isolated, smaller marshes are more vulnerable to both agricultural and urban development and drainage or use as stormwater holding basins.

11. Scrub Cypress

Scrub cypress areas are found on frequently flooded rock and marl soils in south Florida. The largest areas occur in the Big Cypress region of eastern Collier County and northern Monroe County.

Scrub cypress forests are primarily marshes with scattered, dwarfed pond cypress. Much of the vegetation is similar to other relatively sterile marshes with scattered sawgrass, beakrushes, St. John's-wort and wax myrtle occurring commonly. Bromeliads, as well as orchids and other epiphytes, are often abundant on the cypress trees.

Most scrub cypress in the Big Cypress is in public ownership and does not appear threatened.

12. Cypress Swamps

Cypress swamps are usually located along river or lake margins or interspersed through other habitats such as flatwoods or dry prairies. In addition, they also occur as strands along shallow, usually linear drainage systems. These swamps have water at or above ground level for a considerable portion of the year.

Bald cypress is the dominant tree along lake and stream margins and may be the only tree that occurs in significant numbers in these locations. Other trees that are found within bald cypress swamps include water tupelo, Ogeechee tupelo, and Carolina ash. Pond cypress occurs in cypress heads or domes that are typically found in flatwoods or dry prairies. Associated trees and shrubs include slash pine, blackgum, red maple, wax myrtle, sweet bay, and buttonbush. Other plants include various ferns, epiphytes, poison ivy, greenbrier, and lizard's tail, with arrowhead, pickerel weed, sawgrass, and other marsh plants often found in the open water within cypress domes or strands.

Cypress swamps occur in submerged or saturated soils. Fire is an additional factor in drier cypress heads or domes. These factors are important in reducing competition and preventing the community from advancing to one dominated by evergreen hardwood trees (the bayhead community). There has apparently been a shift from cypress to hardwood swamps in areas where heavy harvesting of cypress has occurred in the past and the surviving hardwoods subsequently prevented cypress regeneration.

Bald cypress swamps are reasonably well protected by wetland regulations and the high cost of converting them to other land uses. Pond cypress swamps, while extremely widespread, have less protection because of their smaller size and more isolated nature. Cypress heads and ponds are susceptible to draining associated with industrial pine management, dredging for open water sites in residential development, and increased flooding when used to store stormwater runoff.

13. Hardwood Swamps

Deciduous hardwood swamps are found bordering rivers and lake basins where the forest floor is saturated or submerged during part of the year. Other names for this community include floodplain forest, bottomland hardwoods, and river swamp.

The wettest portions of these forests usually overlap with bald cypress swamps and consist largely of water tupelo, Carolina ash, and Ogeechee tupelo. In slightly higher areas this community is characterized by such hardwoods as pop ash, pumpkin ash, red maple, overcup oak, sweetgum, and water hickory. On terraces or other higher portions of the floodplain, the overstory includes a variety of more mesic species such as spruce pine, swamp chestnut oak, and diamond-leaf oak. Understory trees and shrubs include dahoon holly, buttonbush, blue beech, and hop horn-beam. Groundcover is sparse in most of these swamps.

Two distinctive additions to this major category are **bay swamps** (bay-heads or baygalls) and **titi swamps**. The former are broadleaf evergreen swamps occurring in shallow drainage ways and depressions, particularly in pine flatwoods. Loblolly bay, red bay, and sweet bay are the major tree species. Water levels are relatively stable, and the soil is usually an acidic peat. Titi swamps are dominated by one or more of three titi species and occur as strands or depressions in flatwoods or along the borders of some alluvial swamps in north Florida.

The periodic flooding of the river swamps is a dominant factor in the functioning of the system, and different communities will become established if these fluctuations are eliminated. All species within this community must be able to withstand or avoid the periodic stresses imposed by high water.

Hardwood swamps share common threats with cypress swamps. The wetter and the more contiguous with open waters, the stronger the regulatory protection. Bay swamps are occasionally mined for peat or lost in phosphate-mining operations, and receive comparatively less wetland regulation protection than other wetlands. The rate of loss is unknown.

14. Mangrove Swamps

Mangroves occur along low wave-energy shorelines on both coasts from Cedar Keys on the Gulf to St. Augustine on the Atlantic. Some of the best examples of mangrove forests are located in the Ten Thousand Islands area of southwest Florida.

Three species of mangroves dominate the composition of mangrove swamps. The red mangrove, with its stilt root system, is typically located on the outermost fringe with the most exposure to salt water. Further inland, but usually covered by water at high tides, are the black mangroves, with white mangroves yet farther inland. Buttonwood trees are often found above the reach of salt water. Other plants commonly found among the mangroves include saltwort, glasswort, and a variety of other salt-marsh species.

The mangrove community contributes to the productivity of bordering estuaries. Leaf fall from the mangroves provides food or substrate for countless organisms, ranging from bacteria to large fish such as the striped mullet. Detritus-feeding organisms support much of the estuarine trophic structure in mangrove areas including such gamefish as snook, tarpon, and spotted sea trout.

Mangrove swamps are largely in public ownership and the remainder are reasonably well protected by wetland regulations although losses due to marina and residential developments occur on a relatively small scale.

Prepared by: Brad Hartman, Florida Game and Fresh Water Fish Commission, Tallahassee, FL 32399-1600.

Introduction

It has now been 18 years since the Florida Committee on Rare and Endangered Plants and Animals (FCREPA) first met in 1973. That meeting ultimately led to the publication in 1978 of the *Rare and Endangered Biota of Florida* series.

This, the second edition of *Amphibians and Reptiles*, reflects a considerable increase in our knowledge of some of Florida's more sensitive herpetofauna. Seven species have been added to the list that appeared in the first edition: Florida Bog Frog, Pickerel Frog, Flatwoods Salamander, Eastern Tiger Salamander, Mimic Glass Lizard, South Florida Rainbow Snake, and Florida Pine Snake. The Florida Bog Frog and Mimic Glass Lizard are newly described species, and the Pickerel Frog has only recently been reported as possibly occurring in the state.

Two species, the Gopher Frog and River Cooter, were represented in the first edition by single subspecies. The listing of these two species has now been expanded to include all of their forms occurring in Florida.

Two species that appeared in the first edition have been deleted. The Alabama Redbelly Turtle (*Pseudemys alabamensis*) was previously listed as Status Undetermined based on reports of specimens from Wakulla and Franklin counties, Florida. These specimens are now considered to be Florida Redbelly Turtles (*Pseudemys nelsoni*), and the Alabama Redbelly Turtle is no longer thought to occur in Florida. The American Alligator was previously listed as Species of Special Concern, but the Committee feels that its removal from FCREPA classification is now warranted based upon (1) its remarkable recovery from the low population levels of the 1960s and (2) the regulatory mechanisms now in place to control harvest.

The classification of a number of other species has been revised. The Pine Barrens Treefrog was previously listed as Endangered based on its known occurrence at only 12 localities, but it is now known from approximately 150 sites within its limited range and is considered to be Rare. The Short-tailed Snake was previously listed as Endangered, but we now believe that Threatened more accurately reflects the status of this secretive snake. The Lower Keys population of the Red Rat Snake, previously listed as Threatened, has been downlisted to Species of Special Concern in recognition of the fact that the species appears to tolerate at least some types of low-intensity development. Another Keys form, the Florida Keys Mole Skink, has also been reclassified from Threatened to Species of Special Concern. The previous listing of the Suwannee Cooter (*Pseudemys concinna suwanniensis*) has been expanded to include all River Cooters occurring in Florida. Although the Suwannee Cooter was previously listed as Threatened, that subspecies appears to still maintain reasonable populations in several rivers, and Species of Special Concern is now regarded as the appropriate classification.

Two species, the Bluetail Mole Skink and the Lower Keys population of the Striped Mud Turtle, have been elevated from Threatened to Endangered status, and the Florida Scrub Lizard has been elevated from Rare to Threatened. The Bluetail Mole Skink is restricted to the southern portion of the Lake Wales Ridge, and recent surveys have found it to be rare in the few patches of scrub habitat remaining within its range. The Lower Keys population of the Striped Mud Turtle is considered by some to comprise a separate subspecies, the Key Mud Turtle (*Kinosternon baurii baurii*). However, arguments regarding the subspecific validity have diverted attention from the more critical need for conservation measures to assure survival of the form in the Lower Keys. Consequently, the Committee has chosen to list these turtles as the Lower Keys population, regardless of the ultimate resolution of their taxonomic status. The Florida Scrub Lizard is still locally numerous in areas of protected scrub habitat. However, rampant development is rapidly extirpating it from habitats on the Atlantic and Gulf coastal ridges. Inland, much of its former distribution has been converted to citrus groves and subdivisions, and prospects for its continued survival outside Ocala National Forest are not hopeful.

Finally, two species (Alligator Snapping Turtle and Southern Coal Skink) previously listed as Status Undetermined can now be assigned to other categories. The Southern Coal Skink is now known from 11 localities scattered widely across the Panhandle west of the Ochlockonee River. It is a secretive lizard that is easily overlooked, but suitable habitat is not uncommon and this species is now regarded as Rare. Recent data (D. R. Jackson, personal communication) suggest that the Alligator Snapping Turtle still occurs in good numbers in the Apalachicola River, and anecdotal information indicates that some other rivers may also support healthy populations. Nonetheless, the species is considered to be a Species of Special Concern because it is especially vulnerable to certain types of exploitation and has experienced long-term population declines throughout most of its range.

Throughout this volume, the term "species" is used in a general sense to include: (1) full taxonomic species, (2) subspecies, and (3) particular populations of species or subspecies that do not have formal taxonomic status. This use of the term agrees with that of the U. S. Endangered Species Act of 1973. However, this does create a minor problem of interpretation. A number of people have been tempted to compare the number of listed "species" with the total number of species occurring in the state in order to produce a single summary statistic showing the percentage of the state's species regarded as sensitive. This can be very misleading, but it is a trap to which even the 1978 first edition of this report succumbed. The reader is cautioned that no such simple comparison can be made. Of the 50 "species" listed herein, only 37 (74%) include all members of the particular taxonomic species occurring in the state. The remaining 13 listed "species" include only portions (subspecies or significant populations) of the taxonomic species to which they belong, and, with the exception of the Gulf Salt Marsh Snake, the listed populations represent no more than 5% of the species' total Florida distributions. Subspecies of two species (*Nerodia clarkii* and *Eumeces egregius*) appear a total of five times, thus further inflating the estimate of sensitive species when comparisons are made carelessly. The Committee considers 37 biological species, or 26.2% of the reptiles and amphibians occurring in Florida, to be sensitive in their entirety, and another 10 (7.1%) are regarded as sensitive in part. Thus, the Committee regards all or parts of 47 (33.6%) of the state's 141 species of native reptiles and amphibians to be vulnerable.

Habitat and Distributional Analysis

The major terrestrial and wetland habitats of Florida are considered briefly by Hartman (see previous section). In general, these habitats adequately describe the ecological distributions of Florida's rare and endangered amphibians and reptiles. However, the habitat requirements of certain species are more specific than Hartman's broad categories indicate. Two examples illustrate this point: certain types of titi swamps, described as a distinct variant of the hardwood swamps, are critical breeding sites for Pine Barrens Treefrogs and Florida Bog Frogs; the bayhead ponds that form the Florida habitat for the Many-lined Salamander also are recognized as a distinct variant of hardwood swamps.

In addition to the species found in the described terrestrial and wetland habitats, some rare and endangered amphibians and reptiles are found primarily in aquatic habitats that may or may not be independent of adjacent terrestrial and wetland habitats. To accommodate these species, we have added 7 additional habitats to Hartman's original 14, as follows: subterranean waters, seeps and sphagnum bogs, muck beds, ephemeral wetlands, ponds and lakes, streams and rivers, and the marine habitat. These will be further discussed below.

Xeric Habitats.—Several species of listed amphibians and reptiles are associated primarily with habitats that occur on the excessively drained soils characteristic of the central Florida ridges and certain coastal areas. Habitats referred to as sand pine scrub, sandhill, or Longleaf Pine–Turkey Oak are typical of these xeric areas. These habitats have a high degree of endemism but are rapidly being lost to agricultural, urban, and residential development. Species occurring only in xeric habitats of the Peninsula include the Bluetail Mole Skink, Short-tailed Snake, Sand Skink, and Florida Scrub Lizard. The Gopher Tortoise and Gopher Frog are also primarily associated with xeric habitats but are distributed throughout the Panhandle as well as the Peninsula. The proposed Florida Scrub National Wildlife Refuge would provide critically needed protection to several of the species restricted to xeric habitats.

Coastal Habitats.—The coastal brackish and marine areas provide habitat for several sensitive species of reptiles. Four listed reptiles (the American Crocodile, Atlantic Salt Marsh Snake, Gulf Salt Marsh Snake, and Mangrove Terrapin) are restricted to coastal salt marsh or mangrove swamp habitats. The establishment of Crocodile Lake National Wildlife Refuge on Key Largo has provided additional protection to the American Crocodile, and state acquisition of the Big Bend Preserve on the upper Gulf Coast has protected a major portion of the Florida distribution of the Gulf Salt Marsh Snake. Much of the distribution of the Mangrove Terrapin is protected within Key Deer and Great White Heron national wildlife refuges, but most of the habitat of the Atlantic Salt Marsh Snake receives only regulatory protection through state and federal dredge and fill permitting.

Five species of marine turtles are found in Florida waters. Three of these are considered to be Endangered, one is Threatened, and one is Rare. All of these except the Atlantic Ridley are known to nest along some Florida beaches. The proposed Archie Carr National Wildlife Refuge would provide protection to some of the more important nesting beaches, and it should be actively supported. Additionally, beaches on major rookeries should be closed to vehicles during the nesting season, and illumination of certain beaches should be restricted during the nesting season.

Freshwater Aquatic Habitats.—Several species of Florida amphibians are found only in specific types of aquatic sites. Only one member of Florida's herpetofauna, the Georgia Cave Salamander, is restricted to subterranean waters; it is known in Florida only from caves near Marianna, Jackson County. Two species, the Florida Bog Frog and Pine Barrens Treefrog, are found only in or near sphagnum bogs and acidic seepage habitats in the western Panhandle, and most Florida specimens of the Southern Coal Skink have also come from this habitat type. Muck beds form in hardwood swamps, usually in seeps or other areas with relatively stable water levels. The One-toed Amphiuma is restricted to muck beds of the upper Gulf Coast from Hernando County, Florida, to Mobile County, Alabama, and the enigmatic Gulf Hammock Dwarf Siren may also occupy this habitat. Finally, ephemeral wetlands, some of which Hartman includes under cypress swamps or freshwater marshes and wet prairies, are biologically very distinctive and support a unique assemblage of amphibians and invertebrates not found in permanent waters. These seasonal wetlands provide a critical habitat element for numerous amphibian species that breed nowhere else. These include Gopher Frogs, Flatwoods Salamanders, Striped Newts, and Eastern Tiger Salamanders. (For a further discussion of ephemeral wetlands, see Moler and Franz 1987.)

Five FCREPA listed species of freshwater turtles (River Cooter, Alligator Snapping Turtle, Barbour's Map Turtle, Alabama Map Turtle, and Gulf Coast Smooth Softshell) are restricted in Florida to the rivers of the upper Gulf Coast. Each of these species is harvested for food, and the two map turtles and the Alligator Snapping Turtle are also commonly collected as pets. Because they are restricted to riverine habitats, the accessibility of these five species makes them uniquely vulnerable to overexploitation. The status of these species should be closely monitored and regulations adjusted as necessary to assure adequate protection. The prohibition against commercial collecting, which already applies to River Cooters, Alligator Snapping Turtles, and Barbour's Map Turtles, should be extended to Alabama Map Turtles.

Atlantic Coastal Plain and Other Northern Components.—Many species included in this report are forms that are peripheral or marginal in the state. That is, the bulk of their range lies outside Florida. Most of these species are considered Rare. Forms associated with the Atlantic Coastal Plain fauna include the Pine Barrens Treefrog, Many-lined Salamander, Carpenter Frog, and Spotted Turtle. Most of the Florida distributions of the Many-lined Salamander and Carpenter Frog lie within Osceola National Forest, and the expansion of the forest boundaries through acquisition of the Pinhook Swamp will provide additional public holdings. Timber harvests in wetlands are especially apt to adversely impact populations of the Many-lined Salamander, and wetland stands should be protected from harvest.

Eglin Air Force Base, Blackwater River State Forest, and Conecuh National Forest (Alabama) support numerous local populations of the Pine Barrens Treefrog. The bog habitats on which this species depends are maintained by periodic fire. Due to the disruption of natural fire cycles resulting from fire suppression and habitat fragmentation, maintenance of these habitats will become increasingly dependent on fires prescribed for ecological habitat management.

Spotted Turtles are very secretive, and there is insufficient knowledge of their local distribution to allow for meaningful recommendations. However, this species is known to occur in both Osceola National Forest and Saint Marks National Wildlife Refuge.

Several other species have the major portions of their ranges to the north of Florida, with only peripheral populations in the state. These include the Seal Salamander, Four-toed Salamander, Pickerel Frog, and Southern Copperhead.

Lower Florida Keys.—Because of the restricted nature of the habitat (small islands) and because of the tremendous development of the Lower Keys, several unique Keys populations of reptiles are considered vulnerable. These include the Key Mud Turtle, Big Pine Key Ringneck Snake, Red Rat Snake, Florida Brown Snake, and Florida Ribbon Snake. The Florida Keys Mole Skink occurs in the Lower Keys but is also found in the Middle and Upper Keys. The Big Pine Key Ringneck Snake is a taxonomically distinct form endemic to the Lower Keys. Although portions of the Lower Keys are afforded protection in Key Deer National Wildlife Refuge, the refuge is badly fragmented by inholdings. Ongoing efforts to expand the refuge holdings should be encouraged. Several of the listed forms are very dependent on the small, freshwater pools that are scattered through the islands. These freshwater wetlands should receive maximum protection, and no further filling should be allowed.

Three other species have very restricted ranges and specific habitat requirements and deserve special mention. The Rim Rock Crowned Snake is known only from a few localities near Miami and on the Upper Keys south to Grassy Key and is considered Threatened. Special environmental consideration is needed in terms of maintenance of natural habitat and use of parks and green belts in open space design. The Georgia Blind Salamander is Rare and confined to subterranean waters of the Marianna Lowlands–Dougherty Plain physiographic region. It may be especially vulnerable to pesticide and other chemical pollution of subsurface waters. The Cedar Key Mole Skink is known only from the islands in the vicinity of Cedar Key. Efforts should be made to afford greater protection for the species in this area.

The species accounts that follow present detailed descriptions of each species, its range, habitat requirements, life history and ecology, together with its status classification and recommendations. A detailed Florida distribution map for each species, together with its total range, is also shown. Photographs of most species are provided; in most cases these are of Florida specimens.

This volume represents our best estimate of the current status of Florida's rare and endangered herpetofauna. Just as we have found it necessary to revise the information presented in the first edition of this work, we anticipate that the further passage of time will bring additional knowledge, necessitating further refinement. Recommendations for management and preservation of species are only as good as the available data. For many of the species treated in this volume, there is a clear need for more information on which to base management actions. It is hoped that this book will help to stimulate the work needed to gain that knowledge.

A total of 25 authors have contributed to the preparation of this revision. Several other individuals have provided the accompanying photographs; particular appreciation is extended to Barry Mansell, who generously supplied two-thirds of the included photographs. I also must acknowledge the cumulative contributions of those individuals who were involved in the original FCREPA deliberations and those who have provided continuing leadership in the ensuing 18 years. The series editor, Ray E. Ashton, Jr., has endured numerous delays and missed deadlines, with occasional patience. Without the efforts of all of these, this volume would not have been possible.

I would also like to especially thank the two previous chairs of the Special Committee on Amphibians and Reptiles, Roy W. McDiarmid and D. Bruce Means. In preparing the preceding introduction, I have excerpted extensively and shamelessly from Roy McDiarmid's excellent introduction to the first edition of this volume.

The distribution maps were prepared by John Wollinka. David Auth and Mark Hayes provided helpful comments on an early draft of the manuscript.

Finally, I note with sadness the passing of two original members of the Special Committee on Amphibians and Reptiles, Howard W. Campbell and Archie F. Carr, Jr. Duke and Archie both contributed greatly to our understanding of the herpetofauna of Florida, and they will be missed.

Paul E. Moler, Chair
Special Committee on Amphibians and Reptiles

Reference

Moler, P. E., and R. Franz. 1987. Wildlife values of small isolated wetlands in the southeastern Coastal Plain. Pp. 234–238 *in* R. R. Odom, K. A. Riddleberger, J. C. Ozier (eds.). Proc. 3rd SE Nongame and Endangered Wildlife Symp. GA Dept. Nat. Res., Atlanta.

Designations of Status

The following are the Florida amphibian and reptile species treated in this volume with their designations of status according to the current list (FCREPA). The U.S. Fish and Wildlife Service (Federal), the 1990 Florida Game and Fresh Water Fish Commission (State), and the previous FCREPA list (1978) designations of status follow.

Current FCREPA Status Species	1978 FCREPA	Federal	State
AMPHIBIANS			
Threatened			
Gopher Frog, *Rana capito* Le Conte	T*	C2	SSC
Rare			
Pine Barrens Treefrog, *Hyla andersonii* Baird	E	—	SSC
Carpenter Frog, *Rana virgatipes* Cope	R	—	—
Florida Bog Frog, *Rana okaloosae* Moler	—	C2	SSC
One-toed Amphiuma, *Amphiuma pholeter* Neill	R	—	—
Flatwoods Salamander, *Ambystoma cingulatum* (Cope)	—	C2	—
Seal Salamander, *Desmognathus monticola* Dunn	R	—	—

*Prior FCREPA listing applied to only one subspecies.

E = Endangered, T = Threatened, R = Rare, SSC = Species of Special Concern, SU = Status Undetermined, C2 = A candidate for listing with some evidence of vulnerability but for which not enough data exist to support listing, —No status.

Current FCREPA Status Species	1978 FCREPA	Federal	State
Rare (continued)			
Georgia Blind Salamander, *Haideotriton wallacei* Carr	R	C2	SSC
Four-toed Salamander, *Hemidactylium scutatum* (Schlegel)	R	—	—
Many-lined Salamander, *Stereochilus marginatus* (Hallowell)	R	—	—
Striped Newt, *Notophthalmus perstriatus* (Bishop)	R	—	—
Status Undetermined			
Pickerel Frog, *Rana palustris* LeConte	—	—	—
Eastern Tiger Salamander, *Ambystoma tigrinum tigrinum* (Green)	—	—	—
Gulf Hammock Dwarf Siren, *Pseudobranchus striatus lustricolus* Neill	SU	C2	—
REPTILES			
Endangered			
American Crocodile, *Crocodylus acutus* Cuvier	E	E	E
Green Turtle, *Chelonia mydas* (Linnaeus)	E	E	E
Hawksbill Turtle, *Eretmochelys imbricata* (Linnaeus)	E	E	E
Atlantic Ridley Turtle, *Lepidochelys kempii* (Garman)	E	E	E
Striped Mud Turtle, Lower Keys population, *Kinosternon baurii* (Garman)	T	—	E
Atlantic Salt Marsh Snake, *Nerodia clarkii taeniata* (Cope)	E	T	T
Bluetail Mole Skink, *Eumeces egregius lividus* Mount	T	T	T

E = Endangered, T = Threatened, R = Rare, SSC = Species of Special Concern, SU = Status Undetermined, C2 = A candidate for listing with some evidence of vulnerability but for which not enough data exist to support listing, —No status.

Current FCREPA Status

Species	1978 FCREPA	Federal	State
Threatened			
Gopher Tortoise, *Gopherus polyphemus* (Daudin)	T	C2	SSC
Loggerhead Sea Turtle, *Caretta caretta* (Linnaeus)	T	T	T
Sand Skink, *Neoseps reynoldsi* Stejneger	T	T	T
Florida Scrub Lizard, *Sceloporus woodi* Stejneger	R	C2	—
Big Pine Key Ringneck Snake, *Diadophis punctatus acricus* Paulson	T	C2	T
Short-tailed Snake, *Stilosoma extenuatum* Brown	E	C2	T
Florida Brown Snake, Lower Keys population, *Storeria dekayi victa* Hay	T	—	T
Rim Rock Crowned Snake, *Tantilla oolitica* Telford	T	C2	T
Florida Ribbon Snake, Lower Keys population, *Thamnophis sauritus sackeni* (Kennicott)	T	—	T
Species of Special Concern			
River Cooter, *Pseudemys concinna* (Le Conte)	T*	—	SSC
Alligator Snapping Turtle, *Macroclemys temminckii* (Harlan)	SU	C2	SSC
Florida Keys Mole Skink, *Eumeces egregius egregius* (Baird)	T	C2	SSC
Eastern Indigo Snake, *Drymarchon corais couperi* (Holbrook)	SSC	T	T
Red Rat Snake, Lower Keys population, *Elaphe guttata guttata* (Linnaeus)	T	—	SSC

*Prior FCREPA listing applied to only one subspecies.

E = Endangered, T = Threatened, R = Rare, SSC = Species of Special Concern, SU = Status Undetermined, C2 = A candidate for listing with some evidence of vulnerability but for which not enough data exist to support listing, —No status.

Current FCREPA Status Species	1978 FCREPA	Federal	State
Rare			
Spotted Turtle, *Clemmys guttata* (Schneider)	R	—	—
Barbour's Map Turtle, *Graptemys barbouri* Carr and Marchand	R	C2	SSC
Alabama Map Turtle, *Graptemys pulchra* Baur	R	—	—
Mangrove Terrapin, *Malaclemys terrapin rhizophorarum* Fowler	R	—	—
Gulf Coast Smooth Softshell, *Apalone mutica calvata* Webb	R	E	E
Leatherback Turtle, *Dermochelys coriacea* (Vandelli)	R	—	—
Southern Coal Skink, *Eumeces anthracinus pluvialis* Cope	SU	—	—
Cedar Key Mole Skink, *Eumeces egregius insularis* Mount	R	C2	—
Mole Snake, *Lampropeltis calligaster rhombomaculata* (Holbrook)	R	—	—
Apalachicola Common Kingsnake, *Lampropeltis getula* "goini" Neill and Allen	R	—	—
Gulf Salt Marsh Snake, *Nerodia clarkii clarkii* (Baird and Girard)	R	—	—
Southern Copperhead, *Agkistrodon contortrix contortrix* (Linnaeus)	R	—	—
Status Undetermined			
Mimic Glass Lizard, *Ophisaurus mimicus* Palmer	—	—	—
South Florida Rainbow Snake, *Farancia erytrogramma seminola* Neill	—	C2	—
Florida Pine Snake, *Pituophis melanoleucus mugitus* Barbour	—	C2	SSC

E = Endangered, T = Threatened, R = Rare, SSC = Species of Special Concern, SU = Status Undetermined, C2 = A candidate for listing with some evidence of vulnerability but for which not enough data exist to support listing, —No status.

Amphibians

Gopher Frog
Rana capito Le Conte
FAMILY RANIDAE
Order Anura

OTHER NAMES: Florida Crawfish Frog, White Frog.

DESCRIPTION: Relative to most ranid frogs, the Gopher Frog has a stubby body with short legs, an enormous head and mouth, and prominent eyes that are slightly larger than the tympanums. Distinct dorsolateral folds and tubercles (warts) are present on the dorsum. Males can be distinguished from females by their smaller size, enlarged thumbs, and paired lateral vocal sacs that inflate to large size. Two subspecies are reported from the state: the Florida Gopher Frog, *Rana capito aesopus,* and the Dusky Gopher Frog, *Rana capito sevosa* (west of Apalachicola River). Florida Gopher Frogs have a light ground color and a mostly unmarked venter. Dusky Gopher Frogs are darker with a spotted venter. In both races a series of round, dark spots form irregularly spaced rows along the dorsum and side; the limbs are distinctly barred.

RANGE: The distribution of the Gopher Frog in Florida appears to be contained within that of the Gopher Tortoise *(Gopherus polyphemus).* Unlike the Gopher Tortoise, the Gopher Frog appears to be absent from most coastal islands and dunes.

HABITAT: Most records of the species in Florida are from native, xeric, upland habitats, particularly Longleaf Pine–Turkey Oak sandhill associations which, not coincidentally, often support the densest populations of Gopher Tortoises. They also are known from pine flatwoods, sand pine scrub, xeric hammocks, and ruderal successional stages of these plant communities. Preferred breeding habitats include seasonally flooded, grassy ponds and cypress heads that lack fish populations. Populations of

Gopher Frog, *Rana capito*. Baker County, Florida (photograph by B.W. Mansell).

Gopher Frogs are known only from sites that support Gopher Tortoises. Even prime sandhill habitat, if more than a mile from suitable breeding sites, rarely supports Gopher Frogs.

LIFE HISTORY AND ECOLOGY: Most of what is known about the Gopher Frog is based on the biology of *R. c. aesopus,* but the habits of *R. c. sevosa* are believed to be similar. Although the Gopher Frog is seemingly dependent upon the burrows of the Gopher Tortoise for shelter and to some extent food, it occasionally occupies a variety of other retreats including the burrows of rodents and crayfish, as well as stump holes and other crevices. The Gopher Frog is the most frequently cited burrow commensal of the tortoise, and at one sandhill site accounted for 78% of the herpetofaunal captures. However, Gopher Frogs are rare or absent at many tortoise colonies. The author and his coworkers excavated or funnel trapped (4 trap-nights/burrow) Gopher Tortoise burrows at 18 central Florida sites during 1985–90. Gopher Frogs occurred at only 6 sites. At one 2,700 ha (6,750 ac) Pasco County study site, with an estimated population of 2,600 tortoises distributed among 4 upland habitats, in

1,182 trap-nights, Gopher Frogs were captured at only 2 of 13 sites in one community type (sandhill). The Gopher Frog is generally nocturnal but occasionally emerges to sit near the mouth of its burrow on dark, damp days. The diet consists mainly of invertebrates and anurans, including toads.

Throughout its range, *Rana capito* is an explosive breeder, with males

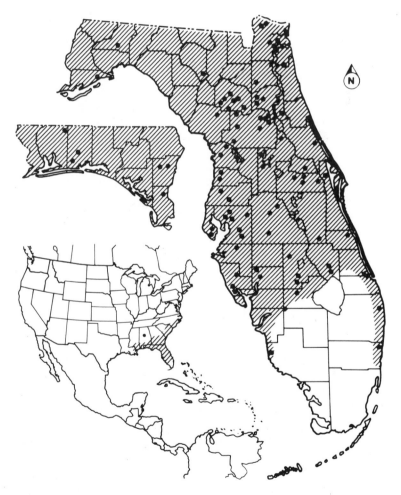

Distribution map of Gopher Frog (*Rana capito*). Dots indicate known localities.

typically calling only after heavy rains. The call is a very deep and distinctive snoring sound. Although Gopher Frogs in Florida have been recorded calling in every month of the year, most reproduction, especially in north Florida, occurs from February through April. In central and south Florida, where winter frontal systems are weaker, Gopher Frogs often breed in summer.

Gopher Frogs apparently disperse upwards of a mile from breeding ponds, and some individuals may use the same route and intermediate tortoise burrows upon returning. Female Gopher Frogs lay a mass of 3,000 to 7,000 eggs attached to vegetation. The tadpoles apparently transform in 3 to 5 months at a snout-vent length of 32–35 mm (1.3–1.4 in). With an average growth of 1.5 mm/month (0.06 in), Gopher Frogs may mature in their second year and may reach a maximum size of 108 mm (4.25 in) snout-vent length in 4–6 years.

SPECIALIZED OR UNIQUE CHARACTERISTICS: Among the 60 species of vertebrates known to inhabit Gopher Tortoise burrows, the Gopher Frog is seemingly the most dependent commensal species. This habit, coupled with its batrachophagous tendencies, makes it unique among the anurans of Florida.

BASIS OF CLASSIFICATION: The available evidence suggests that relative to the Gopher Tortoise (1) the geographic range of the Gopher Frog is more restricted, (2) even within suitable upland habitats, Gopher Frogs often are absent because adequate breeding sites are lacking, and (3) at sites where both upland and wetland life requisites are met, fewer Gopher Frogs are captured. Given the complex life cycle of the Gopher Frog, the documented causes of decline of the Gopher Tortoise in Florida, and the commensal relationship between the two species, it appears that the Gopher Frog is probably more imperiled than its host.

RECOMMENDATIONS: Any research or action that benefits the survivorship and management potential of the Gopher Tortoise ultimately will enhance populations of the Gopher Frog. When planning mitigation efforts for the Gopher Tortoise, more attention should be devoted to commensal species such as the Gopher Frog. From a conservation perspective, key research needs include (1) better defining the temporal and spatial relationship between upland habitat use and breeding ponds, (2) evaluating breeding pond requirements, (3) determining the dependence of the frog on tortoise burrows relative to alternative refugia, and (4) summarizing on a statewide basis the relative abundance of Gopher Frogs within tortoise colonies using documentation provided by the Gopher Tortoise relocation project and Development of Regional Impact grey literature.

Selected References

Altig, R., and R. Lohoefeer. 1983. *Rana arcolata*. Amer. Amphib. Rept.:324.1–324.4.

Carr, A. F. 1940. A contribution to the herpetology of Florida. Univ. Fla. Publ., Biol. Sci. Ser. 3:1–118.

Carr, A. F., and C. J. Goin. 1955. Guide to the reptiles, amphibians and freshwater fishes of Florida. University of Florida Press, Gainesville, Florida. 341 pp.

Conant, R. 1975. A field guide to the reptiles and amphibians of eastern and central North America. Houghton Mifflin Co., Boston. 429 pp.

Franz, R. 1984. The Florida Gopher Frog and the Florida Pine Snake as burrow associates of the Gopher Tortoise in northern Florida. Pp. 16–20 *in* D. R. Jackson and R. J. Bryant (eds.). The Gopher Tortoise and its community. Proc. 5th Ann. Mtg., Gopher Tortoise Council.

Jackson, D. R. and E. G. Milstrey. 1989. The fauna of Gopher Tortoise burrows. Pp. 86–98 *in* J. E. Diemer, D. R. Jackson, J. L. Landers, J. N. Layne, and D. A. Wood (eds.). Gopher Tortoise relocation symposium proceedings. Nongame Wildlife Program Tech. Report No. 5. Florida Game and Fresh Water Fish Commission, Tallahassee.

Wright, A. H. 1932. Life histories of the frogs of Okefenokee Swamp, Georgia. The Macmillan Co., New York. 497 pp.

Prepared by: J. Steve Godley, *Biological Research Associates, Inc., 3819 East 7th Avenue, Tampa, FL 33605.*

Pine Barrens Treefrog

Hyla andersonii Baird

FAMILY HYLIDAE

Order Anura

OTHER NAMES: Anderson's Treefrog

DESCRIPTION: Adults of the Pine Barrens Treefrog are small, green frogs (about 3.8 cm [1.5 in] long) with round, expanded toepads for climbing. The pea-green color of the back and upper surfaces of the legs changes to dark olive-green under certain conditions of stress or weather. A chocolate-brown to plum-colored lateral band extends along the sides from the nostril to the hind limb and is set off from the green dorsum by a narrow lemon-yellow border. The granulated skin of the belly is white. In the armpit, on the inside surfaces of the hind legs, and along the lower sides there are several bright yellow-orange spots that are usually concealed unless the frog is in motion. Females are slightly larger than males and have a white chin. The darker chin and throat of males inflates into a rounded vocal sac when calling. The call consists of a series of high pitched notes repeated rapidly in sequence about 0.4 seconds apart for several seconds duration. Recently transformed and young frogs are miniatures of the adults.

Tadpoles may reach 3.8 cm (1.5 in) in length and are dark olive with black spots scattered over the back. The belly is greenish yellow. The tail musculature, and to a lesser extent the tail crests, have well defined dark blotches and spots. These are coalesced along the upper sides of the tail musculature to form a distinctive black line with irregular borders that begins just behind the body and progresses uninterrupted about halfway down the tail (photograph in Means 1983).

RANGE: In Florida, the Pine Barrens Treefrog is known from about 150 localities in Santa Rosa, Okaloosa, Walton, and Holmes counties.

Pine Barrens Treefrog, *Hyla andersonii*. Okaloosa County, Florida (photograph by B.W. Mansell).

Twenty-two additional localities occur just north of the Florida border in Escambia, Covington, and Geneva counties, Alabama. Florida populations appear to be isolated by approximately 900 km (560 mi) from the next definitely known populations in North and South Carolina. These, in turn, are isolated from populations in the Pine Barrens of New Jersey. Together, these three small geographic areas make up the entire distribution of the species.

HABITAT: Florida habitats of this species are a special class of acid wetlands called hillside seepage bogs. Deep sands soak up rainwater, which percolates downward to an impervious clay subsoil then moves laterally until it seeps out along hillsides. Usually an open, grassy herb bog with carnivorous plants is developed at the seepage zone, which previously experienced periodic burning from natural fires that swept down from the adjacent Longleaf Pine forests immediately upslope. Herb bogs grade downslope into shrub bogs dominated by small, leathery leaved, evergreen shrub species. Almost always these include one or both titis *(Clif-*

tonia monophylla, Cyrilla racemiflora) and extensive *Sphagnum* moss. In varying proportions, other woody species associated with the Pine Barrens Treefrog are Sweet Bay Magnolia, Sweet Pepperbush, Fetterbush, Red Maple, Tulip Poplar, Black Gum, Mountain Laurel, St. John's worts, Sweet Gallberry, and others. In the absence of fire, these woody species invade herb bogs and may alter the hydrology of breeding pools through

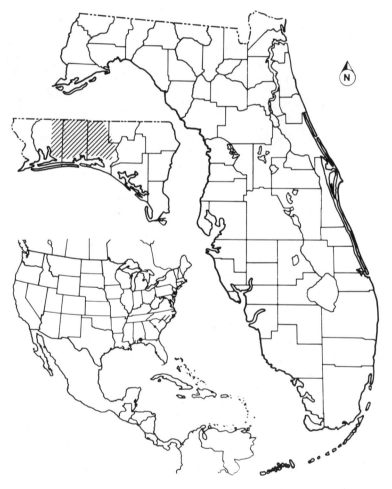

Distribution map of Pine Barrens Treefrog (*Hyla andersonii*).

increased evapotranspiration. Typical Pine Barrens Treefrog habitat includes both herb and shrub bog components. Adults forage in the evergreen shrubbery, and larvae develop in small pools of clear seepage water in the bogs. The pools are shallow (usually less than about 25 cm [10 in] deep) and contain a diverse flora of delicate wetland plants (*Sphagnum* spp., sedges, rushes, bladderwort, pipeworts, sundews, pitcher plants, and filamentous algae).

LIFE HISTORY AND ECOLOGY: Calling males of the Pine Barrens Treefrog have been heard as early as the first week in March and as late as the third week in September in Florida. Larvae have been collected from the last week in May to the last week in August. By the end of September, all larvae are probably transformed. Based on laboratory growth rates, larvae of one summer are capable of reaching adult size by the next, but this is not confirmed in the field. Males call from low perches (ground level to about 1.2 m [4 ft] high) in vegetation surrounding the breeding site.

Females deposit 200 or more eggs in batches of 4 to 9 while amplexed with a male who fertilizes the eggs as they are extruded. After hatching in 3 to 4 days, larvae begin an aquatic life eating algae and other plant matter. Tadpoles of both Florida and northern populations are very sensitive to their environment. Attempts to rear them in captivity in tap water or even water from the habitat have met with small success. Even captive Florida adults that are especially well cared for usually die after a few months or less. Choruses rarely exceed 10 males. A locality having audible males at one part of the breeding season may be silent at another, even though the species is calling elsewhere.

Knowledge presently available for Florida *Hyla andersonii* is based primarily on information gained at breeding sites found by locating calling males. This represents only a fraction of the life history and ecology of the species.

SPECIALIZED OR UNIQUE CHARACTERISTICS: In addition to being one of the most attractive of North American treefrogs, the Pine Barrens Treefrog has a remarkable distribution of disjunct populations, making it valuable to the study of biogeography. In addition, the Florida populations are significantly different from those along the Atlantic Seaboard in aspects of their morphology, ecology, and call structure. Such variation, coupled with geographic isolation, leads to species formation and, thus, is valuable to the study of evolution.

This species is highly specialized in its ecological preferences. Larvae seem to have a very narrow tolerance for aquatic environments, requiring a habitat type that is unique and rare in its own right. The ecology, distribution, and habitat of this species suggest that it was formerly more widespread during milder, wetter climates.

BASIS OF STATUS CLASSIFICATION: The Pine Barrens Treefrog is considered Rare in Florida because its range is confined to four panhandle counties. There is only a small part of the range in three adjacent Alabama counties. Also, population sizes may not be large locally, and the aquatic breeding habitat is rather ephemeral and subject to alteration by plant succession. A large percentage of Gulf Coast seepage bogs have been destroyed by man's interruption of the natural fires that kept out the shrub hardwoods.

RECOMMENDATIONS: Since the delicate wetland habitats are localized, small, and isolated within a small part of the state, habitat destruction poses the most serious threat to the continued existence of this species in Florida. State and federal agencies (Blackwater River State Forest, Eglin Air Force Base) should implement specific habitat management actions to insure the long-term protection of Pine Barrens Treefrog populations on public properties. Initiation of proper habitat management and further research into the biology of the Pine Barrens Treefrog should be undertaken to assure retention of this valuable living resource as a part of Florida's natural heritage.

Selected References

Christman, S. P. 1970. *Hyla andersonii* in Florida. Quart. J. Fla. Acad. Sci. 33(1):80.

Gosner, K. L., and I. H. Black. 1967. *Hyla andersonii.* Cat. Amer. Amphib. Rept.: 54.1–54.2.

Karlin, A. A., D. B. Means, S. I. Guttman, and D. Lambright. 1982. Systematics and the status of *Hyla andersonii* (Anura:Hylidae) in Florida. Copeia 1982(1): 175–178.

Means, D. B. 1983. The enigmatic Pine Barrens Treefrog. Fla. Wildlife 37(1): 16–19.

Means, D. B., and C. J. Longden. 1976. Aspects of the biology and zoogeography of the Pine Barrens Treefrog, *Hyla andersonii,* in northern Florida. Herpetologica 32:117–130.

Means, D. B., and P. E. Moler. 1979. The Pine Barrens Treefrog: Fire, seepage bogs, and management implications. Pp. 77–83 *in* R. R. Odom and L. Landers (eds.). Proc. Rare and Endangered Wildlife Symposium. Georgia Dept. Natural Resources, Game and Fish Division Tech. Bull. WL-4.

Moler, P. E. 1981. Notes on *Hyla andersonii* in Florida and Alabama. J. Herpetol. 15(4):441–444.

Tardell, J. H., R. C. Yates, and D. H. Schiller. 1981. New records and habitat observations of *Hyla andersonii* Baird (Anura: Hylidae) in Chesterfield and Marlboro counties, South Carolina. Brimleyana 6:153–158.

Prepared by: D. Bruce Means, *Coastal Plains Institute, 1313 North Duval Street, Tallahassee, FL 32303.*

Carpenter Frog
Rana virgatipes Cope
FAMILY RANIDAE
Order Anura

OTHER NAMES: Sphagnum Frog, Cope's Frog

DESCRIPTION: As an adult, the Carpenter Frog is a rather small ranid (3.8–6.3 cm [1.5-2.5 in] in body length) having a generally dark brown dorsum broken up by four light brown longitudinal stripes. The overall dark appearance is due to many dark brown to blackish spots that overlie a medium brown color between each pair of stripes. Two stripes are dorsolateral in position, falsely suggesting the presence of dorsolateral skin folds found in some other ranids. The remaining two stripes occur mid-laterally and separate the more uniform dorsal coloration from a variously unmarked to strongly dark brown mottled venter that is white or pale yellow in ground color. Males are obviously distinguishable from females only by the possession of paired vocal sacs found at the angle of the gape; when not inflated, these are grayish patches.

The large tadpole (90–100 mm [3.5–3.9 in]) is brown with black dots dorsally, grading on the sides of the belly into a yellowish color with buffy or greenish yellow spots. The middle of the belly is pale grayish yellow. The tail is grayish in color with a row of bold spots or a solid black line down the middle of the upper crest. A parallel line of dark pigment runs down the tail musculature to the tip.

RANGE: This is an exclusively Atlantic Coastal Plain species, ranging from the Pine Barrens of New Jersey to the Okefenokee Swamp of southeastern Georgia and northern Florida. Its Florida range as presently known is northern Baker and Columbia counties along the Georgia–Florida border.

Carpenter Frog, *Rana virgatipes*. Columbia County, Florida (photograph by B. W. Mansell).

HABITAT: In Florida and other Okefenokee Swamp localities, the Carpenter Frog is found in cypress and Black Tupelo swamps having sphagnous, boggy areas with water depths of 30 to 75 cm (11.8–29.5 in), cypress trunks and knees, patches of floating and rooted vegetation, and floating logs. It is also common to abundant in the open prairies and marshes. The water is darkly stained with organic acids and has a low pH.

LIFE HISTORY AND ECOLOGY: In Florida, the Carpenter Frog calls from the first week in March until the end of August, with eggs hatching 3 to 5 days after being laid. Most larvae grow during the fall and winter and transform in the early spring, but a few continue on into August. Those that transform early may be sexually mature by the end of the summer. Males mostly call from the water at the bases of cypress trunks, on knees or emergent logs and other vegetation. The call is a loud, double note repeated 3 to 5 times in succession. It resembles a carpenter hammering, hence the common name. Potential natural enemies include the Cottonmouth, Alligator, hawks, owls, raccoons, fish such as the Redfin Pickerel,

Bowfin, and centrarchids, the Two-toed Amphiuma, and larger ranid frogs. Although not known exactly, the diet of adult Carpenter Frogs probably consists of aquatic and flying insects, crayfish, spiders, and other arthropods.

SPECIALIZED OR UNIQUE CHARACTERISTICS: The Carpenter Frog shares the distinction with the Pine Barrens Treefrog and the Many-

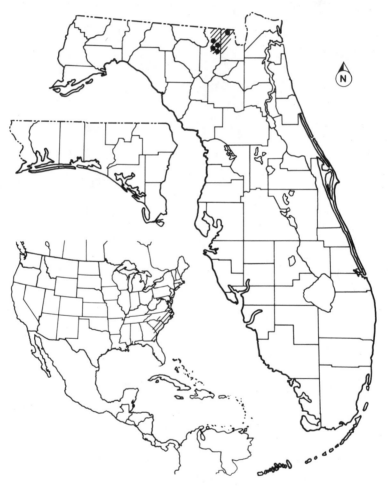

Distribution map of Carpenter Frog (*Rana virgatipes*). Dots indicate known localities.

Lined Salamander of being an Atlantic Coastal Plain derived endemic as-sociated with sphagnous, boggy habitats, highly acid in pH and swampy in nature. The tadpoles, and to a certain extent the adults, are probably important in the diet of certain game fish and wading birds. Florida pop-ulations represent the southernmost distributional limits of the species.

BASIS OF STATUS CLASSIFICATION: This species is considered Rare in Florida because it is known from a very small part of the state, and be-cause physiographic boundaries limit its probable occurrence elsewhere.

RECOMMENDATIONS: The ongoing addition of the Pinhook Swamp to Osceola National Forest will result in public ownership of virtually all Florida habitats known to support Carpenter Frogs. Also, since the Okefenokee Swamp is maintained as a National Wildlife Refuge, it is doubtful that the Carpenter Frog will ever become extirpated from the Florida herpetofauna. Only by draining or altering the wet, boggy habi-tat, or by polluting it with pesticides or other substances would this be likely. Hence, at this time, no further recommendations are deemed necessary.

Selected References

Gosner, K. L., and I. H. Black. 1968. *Rana virgatipes*. Cat. Amer. Amphib. Rept.:67.1–67.2.

Stevenson, H. M. 1970. Occurrence of the Carpenter Frog in Florida. Quart. J. Fla. Acad. Sci. 32(3):233–235.

Wright, A. H. 1932. Life-histories of the frogs of Okefenokee Swamp, Georgia. Macmillan Co., New York. 497 pp.

Wright, A. H., and A. A. Wright. 1949. Handbook of frogs and toads of the United States and Canada. Cornell University Press, Ithaca, New York. 640 pp.

Prepared by: D. Bruce Means, *Coastal Plains Institute, 1313 North Duval Street, Tallahassee, FL 32303;* and Steven P. Christman, *Department of Natural Sciences, Florida Museum of Natural History, Gainesville, FL 32611.*

Florida Bog Frog
Rana okaloosae Moler
FAMILY RANIDAE
Order Anura

OTHER NAMES: None

DESCRIPTION: The smallest North American member of the genus *Rana*, this species reaches a maximum snout-vent length of 48.8 mm (1 15/16 in). Dorsal coloration is yellowish green to yellowish brown; upper lip is greenish yellow. There are light spots on the lower jaw. There is a narrow but distinct dorsolateral ridge down each side of the back. The Florida Bog Frog is most reliably identified by the unique morphology of the rear foot. Webbing is extremely reduced; at least three phalanges of the fourth (longest) toe extend beyond the webbing, and at least two phalanges of all toes do so.

The tadpole is olive brown in color with numerous buff spots on the tail. The ventral surface is marked with numerous white spots, a character which distinguishes it from the otherwise similar tadpole of the Bronze Frog *(Rana clamitans)*, with which it is often found.

RANGE: The Florida Bog Frog is currently known from 23 localities in Walton, Okaloosa, and Santa Rosa counties, Florida. All but three of these localities are within the boundaries of Eglin Air Force Base. All known localities are in small streams tributary to the Yellow River or the East Bay River.

HABITAT: This species has been found only in or near shallow, non-stagnant, acid (pH 4.1–5.5) seeps and along shallow, boggy overflows of larger seepage streams, frequently in association with lush beds of sphagnum moss *(Sphagnum* spp.). Black titi *(Cliftonia monophylla)* is the predominant shrub/tree at most sites. Atlantic white cedar *(Chamaecypa-*

Florida Bog Frog, *Rana okaloosae*. Santa Rosa County, Florida (photograph by R. D. Babb).

ris thyoides) occurs at a number of sites and predominates at a few. In streams where, as a consequence of infrequent burning, streamside vegetation is comprised of a more mature hardwood forest, Florida Bog Frogs are typically found only at disturbed sites, such as utility right-of-way crossings.

LIFE HISTORY AND ECOLOGY: The voice is a series of 3–21 guttural *chucks* repeated at about five notes per second, but slowing audibly at the end. Males typically call while sitting in shallow water, often from small pools surrounded by sphagnum. They have been heard from mid-April to mid-September. Eggs are deposited as a surface film. Tadpoles apparently overwinter and transform the following spring or summer. Recently transformed frogs are about 21 mm (13/16 in) snout-vent length. The Florida Bog Frog is thought to reside year-round in the same areas used as breeding habitat. Two apparent *Rana okaloosae* × *R. clamitans* hybrids have been collected.

SPECIALIZED OR UNIQUE CHARACTERISTICS: The Florida Bog Frog

is endemic to Florida. It apparently has very narrow habitat tolerance and is known only from seepage habitats associated with a few steep head streams of western Florida.

BASIS OF STATUS CLASSIFICATION: This species was discovered in 1982. Intensive surveys have located it at only 23 sites associated with 20 small,

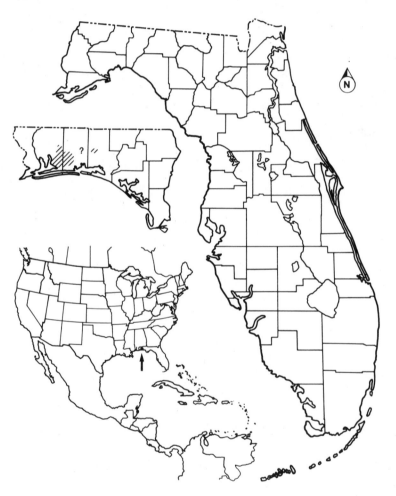

Distribution map of Florida Bog Frog (*Rana okaloosae*). Question mark indicates area of possible but undocumented occurrence.

cool, clear seepage streams. Three localities are based on single specimens, and these sites probably do not support viable populations. Several sites have been heavily impacted by siltation from road crossings, although frog populations in these areas often appear to be doing quite well. The steep walled valleys of the region facilitate the impoundment of streams, and residential developments in the area sometimes employ a series of dams to convert entire streams into a chain of lakes. Such impoundments constitute a threat to Florida Bog Frog habitats, especially in the three occupied streams which lie on private lands to the north of Eglin Air Force Base.

RECOMMENDATIONS: Probably the two greatest threats to the Florida Bog Frog are stream impoundment and habitat succession. Given the scarcity of sites supporting this species, it is imperative that streams where it occurs be afforded the maximum possible protection. Where appropriate, streamside vegetation should be managed to maintain the early successional shrub bog community on which the Florida Bog Frog depends. Such actions would additionally benefit other species, such as the Pine Barrens Treefrog *(Hyla andersonii)* and Panhandle Lily *(Lilium iridollae)*.

Our knowledge of this species is currently limited to distribution, seasonality, and some aspects of larval life history. Studies are needed to provide information on population size, structure, and turnover; age of sexual maturity; and potential competition with the Bronze Frog.

Selected References

Moler, P. E. 1985. A new species of frog (Ranidae: *Rana*) from northwestern Florida. Copeia 1985(2):379–383.

Prepared by: Paul E. Moler, *Florida Game and Fresh Water Fish Commission, 4005 South Main Street, Gainesville, FL 32601.*

One-toed Amphiuma
Amphiuma pholeter Neill
FAMILY AMPHIUMIDAE
Order Caudata

OTHER NAMES: None.

DESCRIPTION: The One-toed Amphiuma is a slender, eel-like amphibian that is uniformly dark brown in color (the ventral surface may be slightly lighter) and reaches a maximum length of about 30.5 cm (12 in). The small head is indistinct from the pencil-like body, which does not taper until past the vent, located about 3/4 the length of the individual. It is unique among salamanders in possessing two pairs of minute, single-toed legs. Males and females are indistinguishable externally except on magnified examination of the longitudinal vent, the interior of which is papillose in males. Also, the flesh surrounding the vent is swollen somewhat in males because of secretory glands lining the interior of the cloacal opening. There is a small oval gill opening on each side just behind the head, but no external gill, and the lidless eyes are flush with the skin of the head. The tail is slightly flattened laterally; the head is conical rather than slightly depressed as in *A. means,* with the apex rounded at the nose. Larvae have not yet been found. The absence of a rayed fin around the tail distinguishes the One-toed Amphiuma from the American Eel *(Anguilla rostrata).*

RANGE: The distribution records for the species, discovered in Levy County, Florida, remain essentially confined to northern Florida from the Gulf Hammock region in Hernando County northwest through the panhandle to at least the Yellow River. No specimens are yet known from the Escambia River drainage, but the species has been reported from both sides of Mobile Bay, in Mobile and Baldwin counties, Alabama. In Georgia, the One-toed Amphiuma is known only from the Ochlockonee River

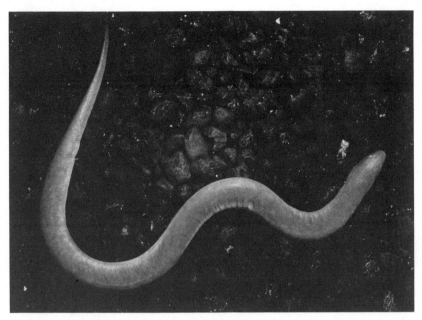

One-toed Amphiuma, *Amphiuma pholeter*. Jefferson County, Florida (photograph by B. W. Mansell).

drainage in Thomas and Grady counties. It is not known whether the One-toed Amphiuma ranges in Florida east of the central Florida ridge.

HABITAT: Probably the major reason this species was unrecognized prior to 1964 is its preference for deep, organic, liquid muck. The localities in which the One-toed Amphiuma is regularly found are muck beds in the floodplains of small, permanent or nearly permanent streams. The muck beds are derived primarily from hardwood litter, but many have a substantial contribution from cypress. In larger river floodplains, the habitat is usually found at the upper end of the high water regime at the confluence of tributary streams, where litter transported by the smaller stream accumulates in muck beds. The best muck sites seem to be those that are brown in color, relatively free of particulate organic matter, and soupy (totally saturated). Muck that has water standing on top of it or is not thoroughly saturated because water levels are lower than the surface of the muck has fewer One-toed Amphiumas.

LIFE HISTORY AND ECOLOGY: The results of several years of study of all aspects of the biology of the One-toed Amphiuma are not yet published (Means, in preparation). Field and laboratory observations indicate that egg laying probably takes place in June and July, when the female may lie coiled with the developing egg clutch in a manner similar to that in *Amphiuma means*. Young likely hatch in late summer and early fall. Very small young captured in the fall attained adult size in captivity in

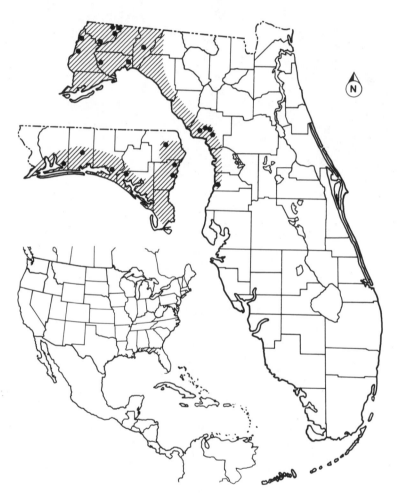

Distribution map of One-toed Amphiuma (*Amphiuma pholeter*). Dots indicate known localities.

two years, but might have grown faster in nature. It is not known whether this species has a larval stage. Hatchlings of *A. means* possess branched, external gills which can be resorbed very rapidly in the first few weeks after hatching. Because of the anaerobic conditions of the muck habitats preferred by *A. pholeter,* it is possible that hatchlings emerge from their egg capsules fully metamorphosed.

Muck beds inhabited by the One-toed Amphiuma are rich in invertebrate life; those found in the gut of *A. pholeter* included sphaeriid clams, earthworms of the genera *Diplocardia* and *Sparganophilus,* aquatic larvae of arthropods (dipterans and ephemeropterans), and terrestrial beetles. Possible predators include raccoons, feral pigs, Mud Snakes, Snapping Turtles, and Two-toed Amphiumas.

Although muck habitats are basically aquatic, the One-toed Amphiuma is an air breather, pushing the tip of its snout above the muck surface to respire. During droughts when individuals are trapped in muck that has lost its fluid consistency, healthy and active specimens have been excavated from burrows made by their bodies in the muck at least 12 inches deep and just above sandy, inorganic sediments. Torpid specimens have been excavated six inches deep in muck on cold days in winter.

SPECIALIZED OR UNIQUE CHARACTERISTICS: Amphiumas have been useful in biomedical research because of their extremely large somatic cells and large chromosomes with highly redundant DNA. The One-toed Amphiuma is one of only three living species of the family Amphiumidae, which extends at least 80 million years back into the upper Cretaceous. Amphiumas, alligators, gars, mudfish, sirens, and cypress are all species that have changed morphologically very little from their Cretaceous swampland ancestors. They are true relicts from the age of the dinosaurs. With the exception of a few localities just beyond the Florida border, the One-toed Amphiuma is almost exclusively a Florida animal. Its native wildlife value is thus increased by virtue of being irreplaceable once lost.

BASIS OF STATUS CLASSIFICATION: The small geographic range of the species, paucity of known localities, and unusual habitat type justify considering the One-toed Amphiuma to be Rare.

RECOMMENDATIONS: Research into the life history, ecology, behavior, and geographic distribution of the One-toed Amphiuma should be encouraged and funded. Anthropogenous chemical and physical impacts on the delicate wetlands supporting the species are poorly known and should be investigated. Sedimentation from runoff of silt and sand during road and home construction is a serious habitat threat. One-toed Amphiumas are known from so few localities that commercial collecting might be severely damaging. Commercial taking of specimens for the pet trade or for biomedical research should be prohibited or strictly regulated.

Selected References

Means, D. B. 1977. Aspects of the significance to terrestrial vertebrates of the Apalachicola River drainage basin, Florida. Pp. 23–67 *in* R. J. Livingston and E. A. Joyce (eds.). Proceedings of a Conference on the Apalachicola Drainage System. Fla. Marine Res. Publ. 26.

Neill, W. T. 1964. A new species of salamander, genus *Amphiuma,* from Florida. Herpetologica 20(1):62–66.

Stevenson, H. M. 1967. Additional specimens of *Amphiuma pholeter* from Florida. Herpetologica 23(2):134.

Prepared by: D. Bruce Means, *Coastal Plains Institute, 1313 North Duval Street, Tallahassee, FL 32303.*

Flatwoods Salamander
Ambystoma cingulatum (Cope)
FAMILY AMBYSTOMATIDAE
Order Caudata

OTHER NAMES: None

DESCRIPTION: The Flatwoods Salamander is a small headed, stocky salamander with a total length of about 13 cm (5.2 in). The body is silvery gray, with some individuals being nearly black. The back and tail are heavily mottled with black to dark brown, irregular blotches. The head and sides are spotted with similarly colored irregular spots. The underside is plain gray, with a few faint creamy blotches. The front and hind legs are nearly the same size. The aquatic larvae are quite unique in shape and pattern. The larvae are long and slender, with very slender legs and fragile tail fins. Bodies are black to brown with white to yellow longitudinal lines.

RANGE: Strictly a lower Coastal Plain species, the Flatwoods Salamander ranges west to Mobile County, Alabama (and probably adjoining Mississippi), and east through the lower Coastal Plain of Georgia to the southern half of South Carolina. The species is found throughout the Florida Panhandle and as far south as Marion County. The range seems to correspond to that of certain species of burrowing crayfish.

HABITAT: Flatwoods Salamanders are found in pine flatwoods—wire grass communities with adjoining cypress heads and naturally occurring ponds without large predatory fish.

LIFE HISTORY AND ECOLOGY: Little information is available about the life history of this species except during the breeding season. Adults can be seen moving en masse to cypress head ponds or small puddles that

Flatwoods Salamander, *Ambystoma cingulatum*. Santa Rosa County, Florida (photograph by B. W. Mansell).

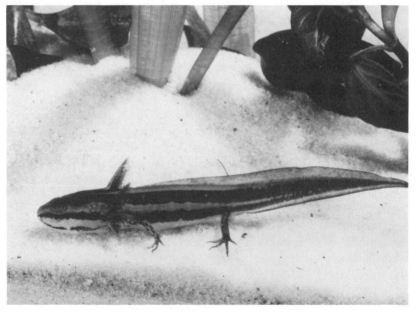

Flatwoods Salamander, *Ambystoma cingulatum* larva. Santa Rosa County, Florida (photograph by B. W. Mansell).

may be linked to these or similar bodies of water surrounded by pine flatwoods. Movements usually occur from October through January during rainy evenings when the barometric pressure is falling. Small clumps of eggs are laid attached to pine needles, twigs, and other vegetation at the edge or in shallow water. Eggs may be laid in small clumps of 1 to 35

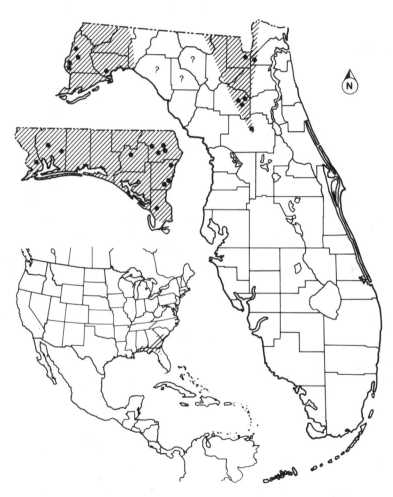

Distribution map of Flatwoods Salamander (*Ambystoma cingulatum*). Dots indicate known localities. Question marks indicate area of possible but undocumented occurrence.

eggs. A female is capable of laying more than 225 eggs in one season. Eggs hatch within 48 hr. Metamorphosis takes place about 90 days later, with most salamanders leaving the ponds by March or April.

In northeast Florida, adults have been observed moving in and out of the burrows of the crayfish *Procambarus pubischelae* prior to and after breeding. A closely related crayfish, *Procambarus hubbelli*, is found at Flatwoods Salamander breeding sites in Jackson and Santa Rosa counties. Movements of more than 1700 m have been recorded away from the breeding ponds and into surrounding pine flatwoods. Preliminary indications are that individuals have a large home range of more than 1500 m^2 (1815 yd^2) encompassing lowland pines that are frequently wet or temporarily flooded.

BASIS OF STATUS OF CLASSIFICATION: This species has a very limited range, and few records exist, indicating that it is not common anywhere. Its natural pine flatwoods—wiregrass habitat is diminishing rapidly due to development for agriculture and silviculture, cutting of cypress from cypress domes, and other uses. The extremely common practice of dropping surface water tables by extensive ditching and draining of pine flatwoods may have a disastrous effect on this and other fossorial amphibians. The wide use of pesticides in pinelands and neighboring farmlands may have a detrimental effect on this species, as might a constant winter-burn fire plan. Preliminary research shows that this species may require large tracts of land surrounding breeding sites to maintain viable populations.

RECOMMENDATIONS: Censusing of populations should be undertaken as soon as possible to determine the distribution and just how rare this species is in Florida. Further studies should be made of the post breeding movements and home ranges of subadult and adult animals.

Selected References

Anderson, J. D., and G. K. Williamson. 1976. Terrestrial mode of reproduction in *Ambystoma cingulatum*. Herpetologica 32(2):214–221.

Ashton, R. E., Jr., and P.S. Ashton. 1988. Handbook of reptiles and amphibians of Florida, Part III, The amphibians. Windward Press, Miami, Florida. 276 pp.

Martof, B. S. 1968. *Ambystoma cingulatum*. Cat. Amer. Amphib. Rept. 57.1–57.2.

Means, D. B. 1986. Flatwoods Salamander, *Ambystoma cingulatum* (Cope). Pp.

42–43 *in* R. H. Mount (ed.). Vertebrate animals of Alabama in need of special attention. Ala. Agr. Expt. Sta., Auburn Univ. 124 pp.

Prepared by: Ray E. Ashton, Jr., *Water and Air Research, Inc., 6821 SW Archer Road, Gainesville, FL 32602.*

Seal Salamander

Desmognathus monticola Dunn

FAMILY PLETHODONTIDAE

Order Caudata

OTHER NAMES: An earlier scientific name is *Salamandra phoca* Matthes. The common name, Seal Salamander, is derived from *phoca*, which means seal. Another common name is Appalachian Seal Salamander.

DESCRIPTION: Florida specimens of the Seal Salamander vary in size up to about 11.4 cm (4.5 in) total length. The body is lizard-like, but the skin is smooth and moist instead of dry and scaly. Large specimens are uniformly light brown with a few small dark dots dorsally; their bellies are white with a faint mottling of dark pigment. In juveniles and larvae there may be 10–12 paired spots down the back, light brown to tan in color, which may be set off from the brown dorsum by small patches of black; bellies are immaculate white. A distinctive row of small white spots occurs down the side of all individuals between the front and hind legs. Seal Salamanders possess a small groove running from the nostril to the margin of the upper lip and have 14 distinct vertical (costal) grooves on the sides of the body between the armpits and the anterior insertion of the hindlimb. Larvae (rarely larger than 2.5 cm [1 in] long) have three tiny stick-like, silvery-white gills on each side of the head; tails of larvae are flattened laterally, those of adults are more rounded.

RANGE: This species is known in Florida only from five small spring seepage ravines on the south side of Canoe Creek, west of the town of Bluff Springs, Escambia County. The Seal Salamander is basically a southern Appalachian species ranging from southeastern Pennsylvania to northern Georgia and Alabama. However, a number of populations are known from the Red Hills of the southern Alabama coastal plain, occur-

Seal Salamander, *Desmognathus monticola*. Escambia County, Florida (photograph by B. W. Mansell).

ring there disjunct from the main body of the geographic range of the species.

HABITAT: This salamander requires small stream habitats, usually as steep-walled ravines that have rocky stream bottoms and permanent moisture throughout the year (or at least retain moisture under the streambed or in friable stream banks). In Florida and southern Alabama, such habitats contain only crumbly sandstone, clay, or sometimes limestone rocks. The clear water of such streams is seepage in origin except during surface runoff from recent rains; near seepage sources water temperatures remain around 21° C (70° F) the year around. The vegetation in Florida habitats of the Seal Salamander is mixed deciduous and evergreen hardwoods on ravine slopes, including American Beech, Southern Magnolia, Laurel Oak, American Holly, Sweetgum, and others, and Tulip Poplar, Sweet Bay Magnolia, and Star Anise rooted in the wet soils of ravine bottoms.

LIFE HISTORY AND ECOLOGY: Aquatic and terrestrial arthropods in the leaf litter of the banks and stream bottom comprise most of the food of this species. A cluster of white eggs is laid attached to the undersurface of rocks in late summer and early fall and is attended until hatching by

the female coiled below. Larvae hatch in early fall and probably all un-
dergo metamorphosis by late spring or early summer. Sexual maturity is
probably attained by males in about 2.5 years and by females about one
year later. Courtship probably takes place in different pairs from fall to
spring.

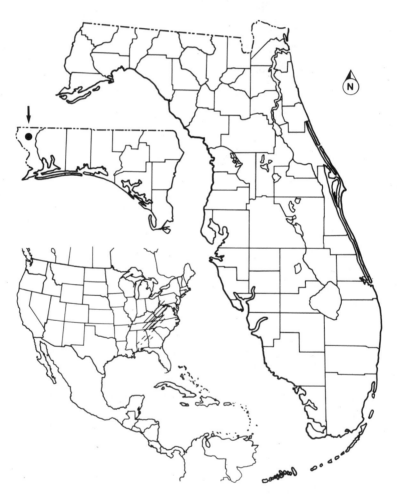

Distribution map of Seal Salamander (*Desmognathus monticola*). Dot indicates the
only known Florida locality.

Larvae are fully aquatic, living in shallow water over small gravel bars, along stream edges, and in seepage sites. Transformed juveniles live in shallow water at rocky stream edges, on seepage slopes, and in wet sites with larger gravel. Adults are found under rocks, in wet rocky sites, behind cracks in crumbly banks, and in burrows in the stream bank at or near the water's edge; they rest at night with their heads protruding from burrows or other hiding places to watch the surroundings for arthropods moving over the substrate.

Most of the energy that enters the habitat of the Seal Salamander arrives as leaf litter, twigs, and other dead organic material. Seal Salamanders are important carnivores, feeding on invertebrates that eat the litter, or on arthropod predators (spiders).

SPECIALIZED OR UNIQUE CHARACTERISTICS: This species is one of a limited number of animals and plants whose small southern populations are disjunct from major population centers in the southern Appalachians. In almost every case the southern relict populations are morphologically distinct from their northern conspecifics. This fact, and possible population consequences due to differences in latitude and altitude, make this species valuable for study of evolution and comparative ecology.

BASIS OF STATUS CLASSIFICATION: The Seal Salamander is essentially known from a single locality (five adjacent ravines a few hundred meters apart) in the northern part of the westernmost county of Florida. The nearest known neighboring population occurs at least 48 km (30 mi) to the north across a probable physiographic barrier (R. Mount, personal communication). The Florida population may thus be isolated from populations already considered relict. At the least, the Florida population represents the southernmost extent of the geographic range of the species.

RECOMMENDATIONS: Public ownership of the locality and maintenance as a wildlife refuge is the only long-term assurance against loss of this northern relict species from the state's natural heritage.

Selected References

Conant, R. 1975. A field guide to reptiles and amphibians of eastern and central North America. Houghton Mifflin Co., Boston, 429 pp.

Dunn, E. R. 1916. Two new salamanders of the genus *Desmognathus*. Proc. Biol. Soc. Washington 29:73–76.

Folkerts, G. W. 1968. The genus *Desmognathus* Baird (Amphibia; Plethodontidae) in Alabama. Ph.D. diss., Auburn University, Auburn, Alabama. 129 pp.

Means, D. B., and C. J. Longden. 1970. Observations on the occurrence of *Desmognathus monticola* in Florida. Herpetologica 26:396–399.

Prepared by: D. Bruce Means, *Coastal Plains Institute, 1313 North Duval Street, Tallahassee, FL 32303.*

Georgia Blind Salamander
Haideotriton wallacei Carr
FAMILY PLETHODONTIDAE
Order Caudata

OTHER NAMES: Haideotriton, Blind Cave Salamander. This blind cave species has the name "Georgia" Blind Salamander because for 19 years a deep well at Albany, Dougherty County, Georgia, was the only published locality. Although a cave in Grady County, Georgia, is also known to harbor it, the Georgia Blind Salamander primarily is known from about 15 caves near Marianna, Jackson County, Florida.

DESCRIPTION: The Georgia Blind Salamander is an aquatic troglobite (found only in subterranean waters and possessing specialized adaptations for cave life in the dark zone). Most specimens range between 2.5 and 5.0 cm (1–2 in) in total length and are juveniles, but adults may exceed 7.6 cm (3 in). The entire body is slightly translucent, pinkish- to silverish-white in color, usually having a faint wash of dark pigment in the form of small specks or almost imperceptible blotches. The legs are relatively long and slender. The head is depressed somewhat with tiny dark eyespots buried beneath the skin and a snout (truncated at the tip) that is longer than in most salamanders. The tail is flattened laterally and finned for use in aquatic propulsion. Bright red external gills on each side set off the head from the narrower neck region. The smallest individuals are essentially the same, proportionally, except that the dark pigment in the eyespots and over the dorsum tends to be more pronounced. Twelve to 13 costal grooves are rather prominent along the sides.

RANGE: This remarkable salamander is confined to subterranean waters in limestone sediments, probably throughout the Marianna Lowlands–Dougherty Plain physiographic region (principally Jackson County).

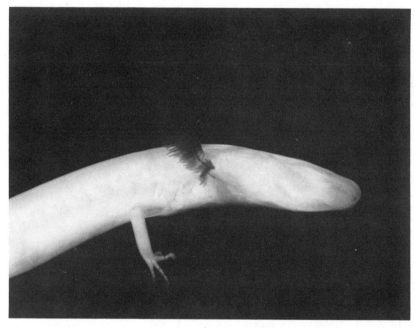

Georgia Blind Salamander, *Haideotriton wallacei*. Jackson County, Florida (photograph by B. W. Mansell).

Wherever air in caves permits access to groundwater in this part of Florida, the salamander has usually been found. The Georgia Blind Salamander occurs sympatrically with a number of troglobitic crustaceans, especially the Dougherty Plain Cave Crayfish *(Cambarus cryptodytes)*.

HABITAT: In those caves where this species can be studied in its natural habitat, the Georgia Blind Salamander is found where underground water is exposed as subterranean streams or clear pools. The pools may be connected to deeper subterranean water or they may be stranded on the cave floor due to a drop in the water table. *Haideotriton* often is seen resting on bottom sediments in these pools and streams; individuals also are seen underwater clinging to limestone sidewalls, where they move over ledges or rough, vertical faces.

LIFE HISTORY AND ECOLOGY: The reproductive cycle is unknown except that gravid females have been collected in the third week in May and the second week in November. Generally, those individuals collected from caves are mostly immature. Observations made with SCUBA in caves suggest that younger, smaller individuals tend to be concentrated near the interface of water–air–cave floor in shallow water (where they would be more accessible to collection); older, mature individuals are more frequent on the floor of solution tunnels in deeper water (D. B. Means, personal observation). Food of the Georgia Blind Salamander primarily con-

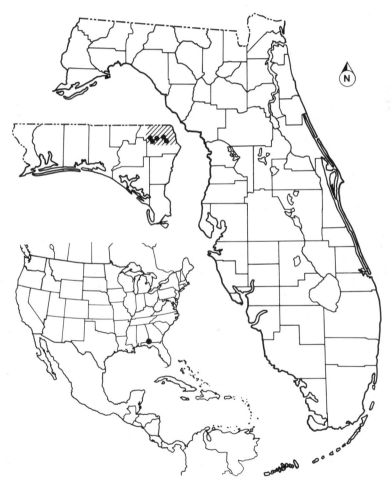

Distribution map of Georgia Blind Salamander (*Haideotriton wallacei*). Dots indicate known localities on Florida map. On inset, dot indicates range.

sists of small troglobitic crustaceans. Its predators may include Dougherty Plain Cave Crayfish *(Cambarus cryptodytes)*, the American Eel *(Anguilla rostrata)*, Brown Bullhead *(Ictalurus nebulosus)*, Florida Chub *(Notropis harperi)*, and each other.

SPECIALIZED OR UNIQUE CHARACTERISTICS: As a fully cave-adapted species, the Georgia Blind Salamander possesses many morphological, physiological, and behavioral specializations not found in terrestrial or aquatic animals. This species might be a good biological indicator of water quality. It is one of the very few vertebrates inhabiting one of the earth's simplest, most discretely definable ecosystem types. Because of this, the Georgia Blind Salamander has great scientific value for the study of community ecology, evolution, and zoogeography. Also, because the geographic range is so small and most populations are known from Florida, it can almost be considered an endemic. This makes the continued existence of the species highly dependent on its preservation in Florida. All but scientific collecting is prohibited by Florida statute.

BASIS OF STATUS CLASSIFICATION: That this species is commonly found in caves does not necessarily imply that caves are the major habitat of the Georgia Blind Salamander. Underground solution channels, especially in recharge areas around sinkholes, may support populations equally. However, it makes ecological sense that density of individuals will be greatest near greatest food abundances. Food of all the aquatic troglobites may well be highest in caves, sinkholes, and other areas where the energy (in the form of plant detritus, bat guano, etc.) that supports the ecosystem first enters. Since those caves and sinkhole localities where this species is known to occur number fewer than about 15 in Florida, and 17 overall, it merits Rare status.

RECOMMENDATIONS: The most serious human threat to the Georgia Blind Salamander is alteration of its aquatic habitat by pollution from agricultural practices or by changes in the water table. The latter effect can be produced either by stream impoundment, which elevates the water table above ground level (e.g., Jim Woodruff Dam), or by depressing the water table below its present subsurface level because of demand from wells and, especially, center-pivot irrigation. At least two sites are under the protection of Marianna Caverns State Park. Other cave localities are on adjacent private property, or within a few miles of the park.

Selected References

Brandon, R. A. 1967. *Haideotriton* and *H. wallacei*. Cat. Amer. Amphib. Rept.:39.1–39.2.

Carr, A. F. 1939. *Haideotriton wallacei*, a new subterranean salamander from Georgia. Occ. Pap. Boston Soc. Nat. Hist. 8:333–336.

Lee, D. S. 1969. A food study of the salamander *Haideotriton wallacei* Carr. Herpetologica 25:175–177.

Means, D. B. 1977. Aspects of the significance to terrestrial vertebrates of the Apalachicola River drainage basin, Florida. Pp. 23–67 *in* R. J. Livingston and E. A. Joyce (eds.). Proceedings of a conference on the Apalachicola drainage system. Fla. Marine Res. Publ. 26.

Peck, S. B. 1973. Feeding efficiency in the Cave Salamander, *Haideotriton wallacei*. Int. J. Speleol. 5:15–19.

Pylka, J. M., and R. D. Warren. 1958. A population of *Haideotriton* in Florida. Copeia 1958:334–336.

Prepared by: D. Bruce Means, *Coastal Plains Institute, 1313 North Duval Street, Tallahassee, FL 32303.*

Four-toed Salamander

Hemidactylium scutatum (Schlegel)

FAMILY PLETHODONTIDAE

Order Caudata

OTHER NAMES: None.

DESCRIPTION: Three characteristics serve to identify this small (adults about 6.3 cm [2.5 in] in length), lungless salamander from all others: it has a constriction at the base of the tail, four toes on all feet, and an enamel-white ventral surface that is dotted with intensely black, distinct spots. The back is rusty to reddish-brown and may have numerous small black specks; the top of the tail is yellowish-brown and speckled with black. Larvae are as yet unknown from Florida, but are small (1.3 to 2.5 cm [0.5 to 1.0 in] long) and have the dorsal tail fin extending onto the back.

RANGE: In Florida, the Four-toed Salamander is known only from a few specimens collected from the upper Ochlockonee River drainage and from Alaqua and Basin creeks drainage basins in Walton County. Another individual was taken from near the confluence of the Chattahoochee and Flint rivers in southwestern Georgia. The distribution of the species is a classic example of disjunction. The main body of its range is primarily the Appalachian Mountains, Piedmont, Appalachian Plateau, and Great Lakes regions of the eastern United States. But disjunct outlier populations occur throughout the surrounding physiographic regions from the Atlantic Coastal Plain to the Interior Highlands.

HABITAT: Florida specimens of the Four-toed Salamander have been found on sphagnous seepage terraces of mature stream floodplains (2 localities), under small wood debris, and under a soggy log in sparse wood-

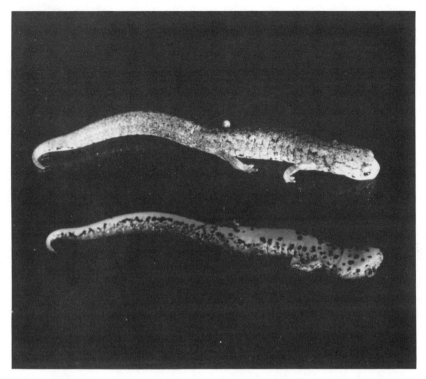

Four-toed Salamander, *Hemidactylium scutatum*. Walton County, Florida (photograph by B. W. Mansell).

land (1 locality) near the shore of Lake Talquin (a man-made impound-ment of the Ochlockonee River). In general, the habitat of this species is bottomland hardwood forests near sphagnous, boggy areas. Such habi-tats in Florida are mostly found in floodplains.

LIFE HISTORY AND ECOLOGY: Eggs are probably laid in March or April in Florida along edges of boggy streams (with the female coiled under them), where they are only an inch or two above water and most likely nestled in moist, mossy vegetation. Upon hatching, they wriggle down to water to take up an estimated 6-week-long aquatic larval life before transforming into small terrestrial juveniles. Adults live under debris on the moist woodland floor, possibly taking refuge in densely matted mosses, litter, and roots, or in friable soil a few inches below the surface during dry periods and in winter. The food of adults consists largely of arthropods of the soil litter.

SPECIALIZED OR UNIQUE CHARACTERISTICS: The Four-toed Salamander is one of a number of species of animals and plants whose disjunct
Florida populations are probably relicts of a formerly more continuous
geographic distribution. Most of these species are presently more com-

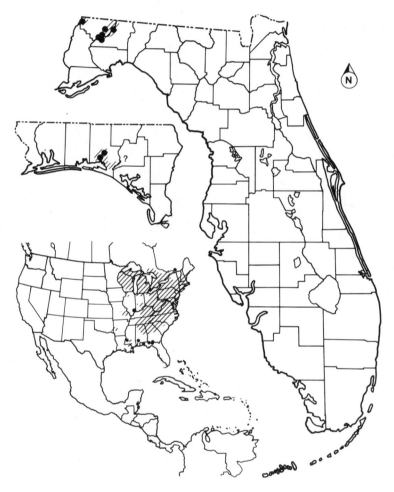

Distribution map of Four-toed Salamander (*Hemidactylium scutatum*). Dots
indicate known localities. Question mark indicates area of possible but
undocumented occurrence.

monly found to the north (usually in the southern Appalachians). All evidence seems to point to the expansion of their ranges during glacial periods, followed by contraction and subsequent isolation into relict populations during warmer and drier interglacial stages. Study of relict populations can lead to advances in the understanding of evolution, ecology, and biogeography.

BASIS OF STATUS CLASSIFICATION: Where this species lives in the northeastern United States, it occurs in much greater local densities than appears to be the rule for Florida populations. The half-dozen Florida localities have produced fewer than 10 specimens from the state. Such small numbers force the conclusion that the Four-toed Salamander is rare in Florida.

RECOMMENDATIONS: Basic study is needed on this species in Florida before much can be said about insuring its survival as part of the native fauna. The impoundment of Lakes Talquin and Seminole almost certainly reduced the range of the species in this state, unbeknownst to anyone at the time. Any further disturbance of the Ochlockonee and Apalachicola river valleys (by impoundment, sedimentation from construction activities, or from channelization) would probably have a deleterious effect on the remaining populations of the Four-toed Salamander.

Selected References

Fugler, C. M., and G. W. Folkerts. 1967. A second record of *Hemidactylium* from Florida. Herpetologica 23(1):60.

Grobman, A. B. 1954. Florida State Museum: Report of the director for 1953–54. Gainesville, Florida. p.11.

Neill, W. T. 1963. *Hemidactylium*. Cat. Amer. Amphib. Rept.:1.1.

Neill, W. T. 1963. *Hemidactylium scutatum*. Cat. Amer. Amphib. Rept.:2.1–2.2.

Stevenson, H. M. 1958. A record of *Hemidactylium scutatum* in Florida. Copeia 1958(1):49.

Prepared by: D. Bruce Means, *Coastal Plains Institute, 1313 North Duval Street, Tallahassee, FL 32303.*

Many-lined Salamander

Stereochilus marginatus (Hallowell)
FAMILY PLETHODONTIDAE
Order Caudata

OTHER NAMES: Margined Salamander.

DESCRIPTION: The Many-lined Salamander is a small, brownish, rather nondescript, aquatic salamander. The ground color is dull yellow to yellowish brown, and there are several rows of indistinct, narrow, longitudinal lines on each side of the body, which usually break up on the tail, presenting a mesh-like appearance. The belly is somewhat lighter yellow with scattered, dark specks. Adults reach a total length of about 10 cm (4 in), and, although they are aquatic, lack external gills. Larvae are similar but have external bushy gills.

RANGE: In Florida, the Many-lined Salamander is known only from Columbia, Baker, Union, and Nassau counties, near the Okefenokee Swamp. Elsewhere, it ranges on the Coastal Plain as far north as southeastern Virginia. Northeastern Florida is, thus, at the periphery of the species' range.

HABITAT: *Stereochilus marginatus* occurs in acidic ponds and sluggish streams, especially where cypress and sphagnum are present. They have been found in Bald Cypress swamps, bayheads, and gum swamps, where they spend most of their time submerged in the shallow waters and hidden in sphagnum moss or leaf litter. In Florida, the Many-lined Salamander is known only from acidic (pH 4–5) bayhead ponds and sluggish streams surrounded by pine flatwoods and scattered Bald Cypress stands. Adults and larvae apparently have similar habitat requirements.

Many-lined Salamander, *Stereochilus marginatus* late larva. Nassau County, Florida (photograph by B. W. Mansell).

LIFE HISTORY AND ECOLOGY: Both adults and larvae are almost entirely aquatic. Mating takes place in the fall, eggs are laid in the winter, and hatching occurs in the spring. Females lay 50–60 eggs in small clumps, often above the water line in rotting logs. When the eggs hatch, the larvae wriggle into the water, where they develop for 2–3 years before metamorphosing into adults. The Many-lined Salamander feeds on small invertebrates, primarily isopods, amphipods, and chironomid larvae.

SPECIALIZED OR UNIQUE CHARACTERISTICS: The Many-lined Salamander reaches the end of its geographic distribution in extreme northeastern Florida. It is an element of the Atlantic Coastal Plain biota, which includes several other endemic plants and animals, many of which do not quite range into Florida. *Stereochilus* is believed to be evolutionarily one of the most primitive members of the family Plethodontidae, and is unusual among aquatic salamanders in that it lacks gills.

BASIS OF STATUS CLASSIFICATION: Because Florida populations of *Stereochilus* are at the very periphery of the natural range of the species, they are subject to fluctuation and possible extirpation. Extensive draining of sphagnum ponds and logging of bayheads and cypress stands in north-

eastern Florida would probably eliminate the species from the state. The
Many-lined Salamander occurs in Osceola National Forest, where it must
be considered vulnerable to destructive logging practices. Clear-cutting
in and adjacent to wetlands, chemical herbicide spraying, road construction, drainage pattern alterations, and mechanical site preparation altera-

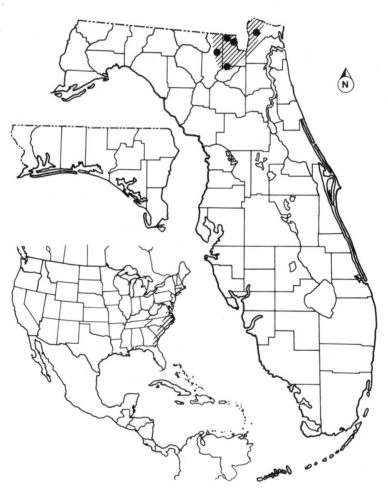

Distribution map of Many-lined Salamander (*Stereochilus marginatus*). Dots
indicate known localities.

tions all pose unquantified threats to the survival of *Stereochilus* in Osceola National Forest and in the private timber-lands nearby. *Stereochilus* probably occurs in the tiny (less than 5600 ha [14,000 ac]) Big Gum Swamp National Wilderness Area, where it may be safe from commercial timber operations.

RECOMMENDATIONS: In order to maintain any populations of *Stereochilus* in Florida, it may be necessary to protect some of their habitat in Osceola National Forest. Current and proposed commercial timber management in Osceola National Forest may well lead to the extirpation of the Many-lined Salamander in Florida.

Selected References

Bruce, R. C. 1971. Life cycle and population structure of the salamander *Stereochilus marginatus* in North Carolina. Copeia 1971 (2):234–246.

Christman, S. P., and H. I. Kochman. 1975. The southern distribution of the Many-lined Salamander, *Stereochilus marginatus*. Fla. Sci. 38 (3):140–141.

Foard, T., and D. L. Auth. 1990. Food habits and gut parasites of the salamander *Stereochilus marginatus*. J. Herpetol. 24(4):428–431.

Rabb, G. B. 1956. Some observations on the salamander, *Stereochilus marginatus*. Copeia 1956 (2):119.

Rabb, G. B. 1966. *Stereochilus marginatus*. Cat. Amer. Amphib. Rept.:25.1–25.2

Prepared by: Steven P. Christman, *Department of Natural Sciences, Florida Museum of Natural History, Gainesville, FL 32611.*

Striped Newt

Notophthalmus perstriatus (Bishop)

FAMILY SALAMANDRIDAE

Order Caudata

OTHER NAMES: None.

DESCRIPTION: The adult Striped Newt is a small (6–10 cm [2.4–3.9 in]), aquatic, olive or greenish brown salamander with a pair of parallel red stripes running down the back and terminating on the tail. The belly is yellow with black specks. The skin is rough-textured, not slimy as in most salamanders. The larvae are smooth-skinned, olive to brown in color with a series of lighter dashes along each side, and have well-developed bushy gills. In the terrestrial red eft stage, Striped Newts are rough-skinned and dull orange or reddish brown, still with the parallel red stripes on the back. One population in the Ocala National Forest is believed to omit the red eft stage and reach sexual maturity without losing the external gills; adults from this population look like large larvae.

RANGE: The Striped Newt is known only from southeastern Georgia and northern Florida, west to Tallahassee and south to Orlando. The type locality is in Georgia.

HABITAT: Striped Newts are restricted to isolated wetlands of two distinctly different types: sinkhole ponds in High Pine (=Sandhills) and cypress and bay ponds in Pine Flatwoods communities. Only rarely do Striped Newts occur in the same ponds as the common Eastern Newt, and they do not typically occur in permanent ponds, which usually harbor predatory fishes. The terrestrial red eft stage often wanders far and is a typical element of the High Pine communities of northern Florida.

LIFE HISTORY AND ECOLOGY: Adult Striped Newts feed on aquatic

Striped Newt, *Notophthalmus perstriatus*. Alachua County, Florida (photograph by B. W. Mansell).

dipteran (fly) larvae as well as almost anything of appropriate size, including even frog eggs. Terrestrial efts are seldom found, but during fall and winter rains they move to and from ponds, often crossing roads. Breeding takes place in early spring, when males develop a fleshy tail fin and black, horny pads along the underside of the hind legs. Hatchlings appear in April from eggs deposited in March. Larvae can be found in ponds from April to December.

SPECIALIZED OR UNIQUE CHARACTERISTICS: The Striped Newt is almost totally restricted to Florida, just barely ranging into southeastern Georgia. Although other newts have been extensively studied, very little is known about this rare and unusual element of the North Florida piney woods.

BASIS OF STATUS CLASSIFICATION: The distribution of Striped Newts appears to be spotty and sporadic. They are not found continuously throughout their range and are absent from many areas where seemingly

suitable habitat exists. Striped Newts are restricted to small isolated wetlands and ponds, and, thus, are especially vulnerable to extirpation during development. Populations in the Ocala National Forest are vulnerable
to extirpation by fisheries management activities (i.e., blasting deep pot-
holes in intermittent isolated ponds) designed to maintain permanent
populations of bass and bluegill.

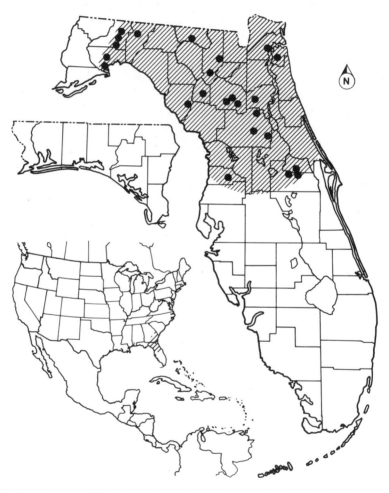

Distribution map of Striped Newt (*Notophthalmus perstriatus*). Dots indicate
known localities.

RECOMMENDATIONS: More research is needed on this uncommon and enigmatic salamander. It appears that small isolated wetlands are required for its existence, and, therefore, these should not be destroyed. U.S. Forest Service and Florida Game and Fresh Water Fish Commission activities that destroy temporary ponds and replace them with permanent fishing ponds should be halted. It is also possible that some of these small, isolated populations could be over-collected, and, therefore, commercial sale of Striped Newts should be prohibited.

Selected References

Bishop, S. O. 1941. Notes on salamanders with descriptions of several new forms. Occ. Pap. Mus. Zool. Univ. Michigan 451:1–21.
Christman, S. P., and L. R. Franz. 1973. Feeding habits of the Striped Newt, *Notophthalmus perstriatus*. J. Herpetol. 7(2):133–135.
Mecham, J. S. 1967. *Notophthalmus perstriatus*. Cat. Amer. Amphib. Rept.: 38.1–38.2.

Prepared by: Steven P. Christman, *Department of Natural Sciences, Florida Museum of Natural History, Gainesville, FL 32611;* and D. Bruce Means, *Coastal Plains Institute, 1313 North Duval Street, Tallahassee, FL 32303.*

Pickerel Frog
Rana palustris LeConte
FAMILY RANIDAE
Order Anura

OTHER NAMES: Marsh Frog, Spring Frog.

DESCRIPTION: The Pickerel Frog is a medium sized ranid with a maximum snout-vent length of about 80 mm (3 1/8 in). There is a dorsolateral ridge down each side of the back extending to the groin. The ground color is grayish. Two parallel rows of squarish, dark blotches lie between the dorsolateral ridges, and there are other blotches on the sides. The hidden surfaces of the legs are yellow. The only Florida species with which the Pickerel Frog might be confused is the Southern Leopard Frog, which has rounded blotches and a light spot in the center of the tympanum.

RANGE: *Rana palustris* is found from eastern Texas east to South Carolina and north to southeastern Canada and is rare and local in the southeastern Coastal Plain, possibly only occurring in Florida in the vicinity of Pensacola, Escambia County. The nearest known population inhabits the mouth of a cave near Brooklyn, Conecuh County, Alabama, approximately 100 km (62 mi) northeast of Pensacola; that population is thought to be disjunct from the continuous distribution of the species.

HABITAT: Pickerel Frogs are typically found in sphagnum bogs and cool, clear streams. Some populations in Texas and the Carolinas occupy warm, floodplain swamps, habitats quite different from those usually associated with this species.

LIFE HISTORY AND ECOLOGY: This species breeds during winter and early spring, typically in small streams or woodland pools. The call is a

Pickerel Frog, *Rana palustris*. Watauga County, North Carolina (photograph by R. W. Van Devender).

low-pitched croak, which has been likened to a snore or the sound produced by tearing fabric. Males sometimes call from underwater, and the call has little carrying power.

In other parts of its range, outside the breeding season, the Pickerel Frog is often found in wet meadows. However, if this species does occur in Florida, it may limit its activities to relatively cool ravine streams.

SPECIALIZED OR UNIQUE CHARACTERISTICS: Pickerel frogs produce a noxious skin secretion which is toxic to many reptiles and other amphibians. Local, disjunct populations in the southeastern portion of the range likely are relicts of a more extensive distribution during times of cooler climates associated with Pleistocene glacial periods.

BASIS OF STATUS CLASSIFICATION: Ashton and Ashton (1988) first noted that seven Pickerel Frogs (USNM 292511-17) in the collection of the U.S. National Museum were reportedly collected in the vicinity of Pensacola, Escambia County, Florida. Although the specimens are undated, the original catalogue number (USNM 3502) suggests that the specimens are quite old. The current records of USNM provide no further locality data, but R. E. Ashton (personal communication) stated that he had found indication that the precise locality was "1 mi NW Pensacola, N of US 90." That area today is part of urban Pensacola, and it is un-

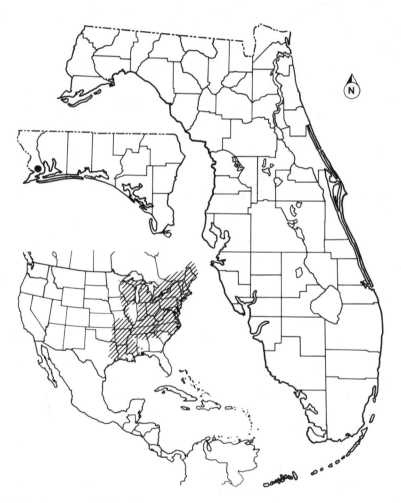

Distribution map of Pickerel Frog (*Rana palustris*). Dot indicates the only reported Florida locality.

likely that Pickerel Frogs survive there. It is not certain that Pickerel Frogs did occur in the Pensacola area, but, if so, they might still be found in some of the cooler ravines of the western Panhandle.

RECOMMENDATIONS: Suitable habitats in the western Panhandle should be surveyed for the presence of Pickerel Frogs. Only if a population were found could management recommendations be adequately formulated.

Selected References

Ashton, R. E., Jr., and P. S. Ashton. 1988. Handbook of reptiles and amphibians of Florida, Part III, The amphibians. Windward Press, Miami, Florida. 276 pp.

Mount, R. H. 1975. The reptiles and amphibians of Alabama. Auburn Univ. Agric. Exp. Stn., Auburn, Alabama. 347 pp.

Wright, A. H., and A. A. Wright. 1949. Handbook of frogs and toads of the United States and Canada. Cornell University Press, Ithaca, New York. 640 pp.

Prepared by: Paul E. Moler, *Florida Game and Fresh Water Fish Commission, 4005 South Main Street, Gainesville, FL 32601.*

Eastern Tiger Salamander

Ambystoma tigrinum tigrinum (Green)

FAMILY AMBYSTOMATIDAE

Order Caudata

OTHER NAMES: None.

DESCRIPTION: Adult Tiger Salamanders are large (7.5–16 cm [3–6.5 in] snout-vent length) salamanders with wide heads and prominent eyes. These colorful animals have a series of irregularly shaped olive- or yellowish-brown, tan, or cream-colored blotches atop a dark brown to black dorsal ground color. The blotches extend down the sides. The belly is usually yellow to olive and marked by patches of darker pigment. There are 11–14 costal grooves. Mature males in breeding condition have a conspicuous swelling around the vent. The combination of large size and distinctive coloration make these animals perhaps the most immediately recognizable salamander in Florida.

The eggs and larvae, while less distinctive than the adults, can also be readily identified with practice. The ova range in diameter from 0.2 to 0.5 cm (0.08–0.2 in) and are surrounded by three gelatinous envelopes. Total length of the larvae at hatching ranges from 1.0 to 1.7 cm (0.4–0.67 in). Larvae do not have balancers (unlike many other ambystomatid larvae) and have from 13 to 21 rakers (average around 17) on the anterior face of the third gill arch. Larger, fully limbed larvae are distinguishable from other ambystomatid larvae in Florida because, unlike the adults, Tiger Salamander larvae are the least distinctively colored. These animals are gray to brown and lack the distinctive markings of other species such as Marbled Salamander larvae (*Ambystoma opacum*, a series of white dots along the bottom edge of the sides), Mole Salamander larvae (*Ambystoma talpoideum*, a pair of lines along the lateral edge of the venter), or Flatwoods Salamander larvae (*Ambystoma cingulatum*, bold longitudinal stripes).

Eastern Tiger Salamander, *Ambystoma tigrinum tigrinum*. Santa Rosa County, Florida (photograph by B. W. Mansell).

Eastern Tiger Salamander, *Ambystoma t. tigrinum* larva. Santa Rosa County, Florida (photograph by B. W. Mansell).

RANGE: The Tiger Salamander is known to occur in north and north central Florida from Santa Rosa County in the west as far as Hernando County to the south. The Eastern Tiger Salamander extends throughout the Atlantic Coastal Plain (once as far north as Long Island, New York)

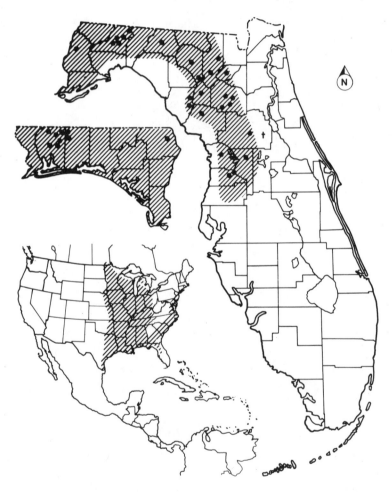

Distribution map of Eastern Tiger Salamander (*Ambystoma tigrinum tigrinum*). Cross indicates a locality from which the species has apparently been extirpated. Dots indicate known localities.

and through the Midwest from west of the Appalachian Mountains to the middle of the Great Plains. It does not occur in the highlands, and it is not known from the lower Mississippi delta. Fossil records in Florida date from the upper Pliocene.

HABITAT: The fossorial adults appear to inhabit both pine and hardwood forests and mixed woods. The extent to which adults actually live in open areas or areas of mixed woods and fields is unknown. Breeding occurs in a variety of ponds, from depressions in flatwoods to farm ponds in pastures. Successful breeding depends on the absence of fish from the pond; entire cohorts of larvae are extirpated by even small populations of predatory fish. The preferred type of pond appears to be a shallow depression of large surface area with a significant amount of herbaceous, emergent vegetation. These ponds are usually classified as "isolated wetlands" because they are rarely connected by surface flow to any stream or river.

LIFE HISTORY AND ECOLOGY: Adults emerge from their subterranean existence in winter and migrate to breeding sites during nights of heavy rainfall. Males often arrive at the ponds before females and usually stay in the pond longer. Studies of marked individuals indicate that the median residence time in the pond is 13 days for males, and somewhat less for females. Females appear to move only on a very few nights, compared to males. Females depart the pond at the first opportunity after depositing their eggs; males appear to depart only after they have gone several nights without encountering any females. Breeding migrations are made in direct response to rain and are, therefore, somewhat unpredictable, but they usually occur in north Florida anytime from December through early February. Adults are rarely encountered outside of the breeding season.

Eggs are deposited either singly or, more commonly, in a spherical or cylindrical gelatinous mass attached to herbaceous vegetation. The eggs are preyed upon by adult newts as well as some aquatic Hemiptera. Larvae are predaceous on zooplankton, insects, and tadpoles. The larvae have distinctive activity patterns, especially while they are small. They stay hidden during the day amidst litter on the bottom of the pond and move into the water column to forage at night. Larger larvae tend to move higher in the water column than smaller larvae. Larvae grow very rapidly and may transform at 6–9 cm (2.4–3.5 in) snout-vent length after periods ranging from 60–100 days, depending upon water temperature, food levels, population density, etc.

Upon completion of metamorphosis the juveniles leave the pond on rainy nights and disperse. It takes at least two years for the transformed juveniles to attain sexual maturity. It is not clear to what extent a juvenile ultimately returns to the pond from which it emerged. Adults, once they have bred in a pond, return faithfully to that same pond every year. They will return to the site of the pond even if the pond is no longer there due to human impact. Studies of other salamanders of this type indicate that it is likely that a large fraction of juveniles do indeed return to their natal pond, thus making populations of this species strongly localized.

Population studies indicate that this species has a pattern of "boom and bust" fluctuations in numbers that is typical of pond-dwelling amphibians. In some years there is no successful breeding; no juveniles emerge from a pond despite initial egg numbers in the tens of thousands. In other years there can be as many as 24 juveniles emerging per ovipositing female. These variations in breeding success induce large fluctuations in adult numbers in subsequent years as well as substantial fluctuations in age-structure. Adults appear to live for several years after attaining maturity, and this compensates to some extent for the wide annual variation in breeding success. Populations are known to have been extirpated by the introduction of fish such as bluegill into the breeding ponds.

SPECIALIZED OR UNIQUE CHARACTERISTICS: The Eastern Tiger Salamander is a subspecies of a taxon that is enormously variable in coloration, life history, and morphology. In recent years there has been considerable speculation about whether this is indeed one species or a series of closely related species. There can be considerable variation even within one of the subspecies. Thus this species has emerged in recent years as a valuable study system for the processes of local adaptation and incipient speciation. In the temporary pond community in which the larvae are embedded, this species is in many ways a "keystone" species. As a predator it exerts strong effects on prey populations and exerts substantial indirect effects on the structure of the entire community. Communities with and without Tiger Salamander larvae are very different in the species of tadpole, insect, and zooplankton present and the relative abundances of the members of the community.

The basis for habitat selection by breeding adults is not clear. Where these salamanders occur, they breed in a distinct subset of what appear to be suitable ponds. It is not clear whether this represents true habitat selection for characteristics that are not apparent to biologists or the artifacts of history. Given the strong fidelity of breeding adults to a pond and the "boom and bust" pattern of population fluctuations, biologists may be observing a subset of what were once more numerous individual populations.

BASIS OF STATUS CLASSIFICATION: The fidelity of adults to ponds makes the status of these populations critically dependent on the breeding locations. These locations are all "isolated wetlands" that vary seasonally in size and have little to no status for regulatory protection. Smaller sites tend to be under development pressure, and larger sites are under pressure from either direct development atop them or transformation by adjacent development into either fish-stocked ponds or stormwater catchment areas. Adults will not move to another pond if "their" pond disappears. Many breeding sites are known to have been eliminated in the last decade. Migrating adults move directly to ponds across roads, and increased traffic pressure from adjacent, developed areas has caused increased mortality in many areas. This species is facing a substantial threat from the increasing levels of human impact on its environment.

RECOMMENDATIONS: Habitat destruction poses the most severe threat to this species. Better recognition and protection of isolated wetlands is necessary to preserve these animals; the fidelity of adults to breeding sites is likely to preclude the effectiveness of mitigation for this species. The present status of the populations of this species across its range is not clear, and some work should be undertaken to assess that status as well as the extent of local differentiation across the range in Florida. So little is known about the secretive, long-lived adults that little can be recommended about adult habitat. It does appear certain, however, that without better protection of the breeding sites, this species will become only a memory in this state.

Selected References

Anderson, J. D., D. D. Hassinger, and G. H. Dalrymple. 1971. Natural mortality of eggs and larvae of *Ambystoma t. tigrinum*. Ecology 52:1107–1112.

Gehlbach, F. R. 1967. *Ambystoma tigrinum*. Cat. Amer. Amphib. Rept.:52.1–52.4.

Hassinger, D. D., J. D. Anderson, and G. H. Dalrymple. 1970. The early life history and ecology of *Ambystoma tigrinum* and *Ambystoma opacum* in New Jersey. Am. Midl. Nat. 84:474–495.

Keen, W. H., J. Travis, and J. Juilianna. 1984. Larval growth in three sympatric

Ambystoma salamander species: Species differences and the effects of temperature. Can. J. Zool. 62:1043–1047.

Semlitsch, R. D. 1983. Structure and dynamics of two breeding populations of the Eastern Tiger Salamander, *Ambystoma tigrinum*. Copeia 1983:608–616.

Prepared by: Joseph Travis, *Department of Biological Science, Florida State University, Tallahassee, FL 32306-2043.*

Gulf Hammock Dwarf Siren

Pseudobranchus striatus lustricolus Neill

FAMILY SIRENIDAE

Order Caudata

OTHER NAMES: None.

DESCRIPTION: The family Sirenidae includes a group of permanently aquatic salamanders possessing external gills and lacking the rear legs and pelvic girdle. The smaller dwarf sirens (*Pseudobranchus*) are distinguished from the true sirens (*Siren*) by having only three (rather than four) toes on each forelimb and by retaining a striped color pattern throughout life (among Florida *Siren,* only the larvae of the Greater Siren are striped). The Gulf Hammock Dwarf Siren is distinguished from other *Pseudobranchus* by the combination of three distinct, light dorsal stripes, a very broad orange-brown lateral stripe, and a silvery-white ventrolateral stripe. The venter is black mottled with white. Maximum reported length is 215.7 mm (8.5 in).

RANGE: The Gulf Hammock Dwarf Siren has been reliably reported from only three localities in Levy and Citrus counties. It may be more or less restricted to wetlands within the narrow strip of hydric hardwood hammock situated near the Gulf Coast. Other *Pseudobranchus* have been collected from Lake Rousseau, Levy County, and at several sites within the pine flatwoods east of the Gulf Hammock, but these specimens show little or no *lustricolus* influence.

HABITAT: Neill (1951) reported the Gulf Hammock Dwarf Siren to occur in stagnant bogs associated with cypress and flatwoods ponds, drainage ditches, and smaller floodplain lakes.

LIFE HISTORY AND ECOLOGY: Little information is available on the biology of the Gulf Hammock Dwarf Siren. Neill (1951) suggested that individuals typically live in "foul-smelling, blackish muck of decaying organic material," where they remain positioned vertically below the surface of the muck, surfacing only for an occasional gulp of air.

The biology of other *Pseudobranchus* is better known. Dwarf sirens are frequently found in mucky soils around the periphery of marshes and ponds and among the roots of the introduced Water Hyacinth (*Eichhornia crassipes*). They feed on small oligochaete worms, chironomid larvae, and other small aquatic invertebrates. The eggs are laid singly, scattered among the aquatic vegetation, but the reproductive biology of dwarf sirens is especially poorly known. It is not known with certainty whether fertilization is internal or external, but *Pseudobranchus* lacks the glands and anatomical structures normally possessed by salamanders exhibiting internal fertilization.

SPECIALIZED OR UNIQUE CHARACTERISTICS: The family Sirenidae is highly specialized for an aquatic existence, but sirens and dwarf sirens can survive periodic drying of their habitats by retreating into the mud, where they form cocoons and remain dormant until water returns. Because of their low vagility and their ability to survive in ponds that periodically dry, populations of sirenids are sometimes very localized and inbred. Recent studies have shown a remarkable variation in chromosome number within this group, and sirenids may prove important in our understanding of the mechanisms of chromosomal evolution and population genetics.

BASIS OF STATUS CLASSIFICATION: The Gulf Hammock Dwarf Siren was described in 1951 on the basis of 11 specimens taken at three localities in Levy and Citrus counties; it has not been collected since, despite repeated efforts to do so. Both the Narrow-striped Dwarf Siren (*Pseudobranchus striatus axanthus*) and the Slender Dwarf Siren (*Pseudobranchus striatus spheniscus*) have been collected from areas very near sites from which *P. s. lustricolus* has been reported, and the systematic relationship of *lustricolus* to the other dwarf sirens remains unclear.

RECOMMENDATIONS: Efforts to locate this elusive and enigmatic salamander should continue. Should specimens become available, biochemical and karyological techniques should be employed to clarify the systematic relationship of *lustricolus* to other *Pseudobranchus*. Investigations into the ecological requirements of the Gulf Hammock Dwarf Siren are needed, but these must necessarily await its rediscovery.

Selected References

Kezer, J. 1982. Chromosome variation in the dwarf siren, *Pseudobranchus striatus.* 25th Ann. Mtg. Soc. Study Amphib. and Rept. 1982:81 (Abstr.).
Martof, B.S. 1972. *Pseudobranchus striatus.* Cat. Amer. Amphib. Rept.: 128.1–128.2.

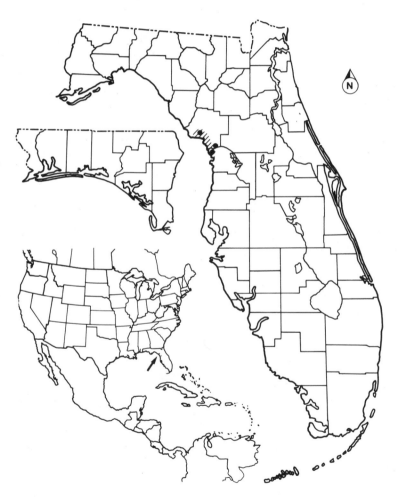

Distribution map of Gulf Hammock Dwarf Siren (*Pseudobranchus striatus lustricolus*). Dots indicate known localities.

Moler, P. E. 1988. Correction of the type locality of the Gulf Hammock Dwarf
    Siren, *Pseudobranchus striatus lustricolus*. Fla. Field Nat. 16:12–13.
Moler, P. E., and J. Kezer. 1992. Karyology and systematics of the salamander
    genus *Pseudobranchus* (Sirenidae). Copeia. In press.
Neill, W. T. 1951. A new subspecies of salamander, genus *Pseudobranchus,* from
    the Gulf Hammock region of Florida. Publ. Res. Div. Ross Allen's Rept. Inst.
    1(4):39–46.

Prepared by: Paul E. Moler, *Florida Game and Fresh Water Fish Commission, 4005 South Main Street, Gainesville, FL 32601.*

Reptiles

American Crocodile

Crocodylus acutus Cuvier

FAMILY CROCODYLIDAE

Order Crocodilia

OTHER NAMES: Florida Crocodile.

DESCRIPTION: The American Crocodile is a large reptile with a typical crocodilian build. It is grayish brown and mottled with black. The back is covered with several rows of large, keeled scales; the lateral rows tend to be irregular, with numerous scales missing or out of line. The neck is only lightly armored, with expanses of bare skin lying between the 6–12 nuchal scales. The belly is covered with smooth, soft, rectangular, whitish scales, each marked posteriorly with a small pore. The snout is tapered, and the fourth tooth of the lower jaw is exposed by an indentation in the lateral margin of the upper jaw. The tail comprises approximately one-half the total length. A row of heavy scutes projects dorsolaterally from each side of the front half of the tail; these two rows converge midway down the tail. The posterior half of the tail is flattened laterally and capped with a single row of projecting scutes.

Adults average 2.2 to 3.4 m (7.2–11.1 ft) in length. The largest modern specimen measured in Florida was 3.77 m (12.4 ft) long, but a specimen of about 4.72 m (15.5 ft) was reported in the late 1800s.

The American Crocodile bears a superficial resemblance to the familiar American Alligator, although the two species are only distantly related. From the American Alligator, the American Crocodile can be distinguished by its brown rather than black color, its narrower snout with the fourth tooth of the lower jaw projecting outside the upper jaw, and by the presence of a distinct pore near the posterior margin of each ventral scale. Crocodiles often bask with the mouth held open wide, a behavior only rarely seen in alligators.

American Crocodile, *Crocodylus acutus*. Monroe County, Florida (photograph by P. E. Moler).

RANGE: The American Crocodile occurs primarily in coastal swamps and rivers in extreme southern Florida, in Cuba, Jamaica, Hispaniola, along the Caribbean Coast from Venezuela north at least to the Yucatan Peninsula, and along the Pacific Coast from Sinaloa, Mexico, south to the Rio Tumbes of Peru. Because of the potential for confusion with Morelet's Crocodile *(Crocodylus moreletii),* reports of the occurrence of the American Crocodile along the Gulf Coast of Mexico require confirmation.

In Florida, crocodiles originally occurred as far north on the Atlantic Coast as Lake Worth, Palm Beach County. Southern Biscayne Bay, Dade County, now appears to be the northern limit, although individual crocodiles occasionally wander farther north. On the west coast, crocodile sightings have always been rare, but crocodiles still occur as far north as Sanibel Island, although no breeding has been documented on the southwest coast. The documented recent breeding range of the American Crocodile includes the mainland shoreline from southern Biscayne Bay (Turkey Point) west to Cape Sable, as well as North Key Largo and some of the islands in Florida Bay. Although crocodiles are occasionally sighted in the Lower Florida Keys, there is no indication that these represent a resident breeding population.

HABITAT: Through much of its range, the American Crocodile is largely confined to coastal estuarine swamps or landlocked saline lakes. In Central America, it is found also in large inland freshwater lakes, such as

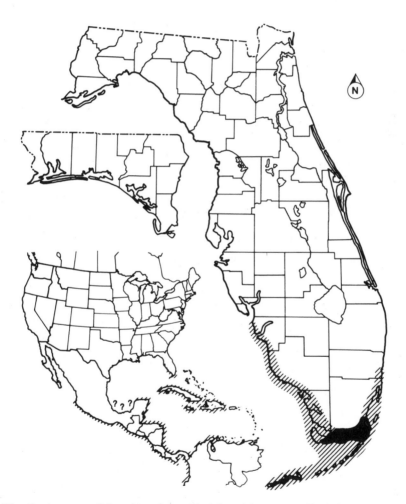

Distribution map of American Crocodile (*Crocodylus acutus*). Shaded area indicates known nesting distribution.

Gatun Lake, Panama, and Lake Nicaragua. In Florida, it occurs primarily in mangrove swamps, but it occasionally wanders a few miles inland.

LIFE HISTORY AND ECOLOGY: Most crocodilians are opportunistic predators, taking whatever they can catch. The Nile Crocodile (*Crocodylus niloticus*) and the Indo-Pacific Estuarine Crocodile (*Crocodylus porosus*) are notorious for taking large prey, including man. However, the American Crocodile seldom takes anything larger than a raccoon, rabbit, or cormorant. The diet consists primarily of crabs, fish, snakes, turtles, birds, and small mammals. Contrary to popular lore, the American Crocodile is not more aggressive than the American Alligator.

Courtship and mating occur in late winter and early spring. Nesting occurs about a month later, usually in late April or early May. Nests are built above the vegetation line on beaches, stream banks, or canal levees. Many nest sites are used recurrently, presumably by the same female. One Key Largo nest site has been used annually from 1978 to the present (1992) with the exception of one year. Occasionally, a female simply picks a suitable site, digs a hole, and deposits the eggs, but more typically she scrapes together a mound of the surrounding soil, which may be sand, marl, or peat, depending upon the area. She then digs a hole in the mound and deposits 20–50 eggs. Average clutch size is about 35. Incubation takes 85–90 days, roughly three weeks longer than in the American Alligator. The female remains near the nest through the incubation period but does not normally defend the nest against man. Whether the nest is defended against other possible predators is not known. Compared to other crocodilians, the American Crocodile seems to suffer relatively little nest depredation, averaging only about 15% of total nest production. Hatching success is mediocre, however. In some lower lying areas, storm tides may flood the egg cavity, thus drowning the embryos. In years characterized by low spring/early summer rainfall, high levels of late embryonic mortality are seen, presumably caused by desiccation of the embryos. Nests in peat soils seem to be especially susceptible to desiccation.

At hatching time, the female opens the nest and carries the young to the water in her mouth. The young are not able to dig out on their own and will die if not released from the nest. Unlike the alligator, the female American Crocodile does not remain with her young after they have hatched.

The hatchlings are about 25 cm (10 in) in length and 50 gm (1.75 oz) in mass. At least in sheltered areas, they remain together loosely for four to five weeks and then disperse. In areas subject to wind and wave action they may disperse sooner. After the first few weeks of life, American Crocodiles are largely solitary. Hatchlings feed primarily on small fish but may also take snakes, crabs, spiders, and insects. Initial growth is rapid, and by four months of age the young average about 45 cm (17.7 in) in length and 300 gm (10.5 oz) in mass. There is little or no growth during the cooler winter months, but rapid growth resumes in late March or early April. By one year of age, young crocodiles average about 65 cm (25.6 in) in length.

Although larger crocodiles are capable of tolerating high salinity levels for extended periods, laboratory studies have demonstrated that hatchlings are sensitive to prolonged exposure to high salinities. Nonetheless, in the wild, hatchling crocodiles seem to tolerate ambient salinities higher than those which they tolerate in the laboratory. It is now known that young crocodiles are able to drink from the temporary lens of fresh water which floats on the heavier salt water following a shower. Thus, only in years of limited rainfall do the young seem to be particularly susceptible to osmoregulatory problems. In years of reduced late summer/fall rainfall, hatchling growth rates are typically depressed.

Females reach sexual maturity at a size of about 2.20 m (7.25 ft) and an age of about 11–13 years.

SPECIALIZED OR UNIQUE CHARACTERISTICS: The American Crocodile is a tropical species, which reaches the northern limit of its distribution in extreme southern Florida.

BASIS OF STATUS CLASSIFICATION: Although the American Crocodile originally occurred on the Atlantic Coast as far north as Lake Worth, except for an occasional wanderer, it no longer occurs on the Atlantic Coast north of central Biscayne Bay. Also, it has been largely eliminated from the Florida Keys south of Key Largo. The species was likely never very numerous in Florida, but today the population probably numbers no more than 500 non-hatchlings, including only about 30 breeding females. All known nesting occurs along the mainland shoreline from Turkey Point to Cape Sable, on Key Largo, or on some of the smaller islands in northeastern Florida Bay. Despite the fact that most of the breeding range in Florida is protected in Everglades National Park, Crocodile Lake National Wildlife Refuge, and at Florida Power and Light's Turkey Point electrical generating facility, the very restricted distribution of the species in the United States makes it vulnerable to catastrophic loss through disease or hurricane destruction of both individuals and habitat.

Elsewhere in its range, the species has been severely reduced in numbers due to malicious killing, hunting for skins, and loss of habitat. The species is considered to be Endangered throughout its distribution.

RECOMMENDATIONS: Given the very limited distribution of the American Crocodile in Florida, it is critical that no further reduction in habitat quantity or quality be allowed. Within habitats occupied by crocodiles, such activities as swimming, diving, and jet skiing should be discouraged, not because crocodiles are particularly aggressive, but because people are highly intolerant of crocodiles in proximity to recreation areas.

The greatest identifiable cause of mortality among larger crocodiles is U.S. Highway 1, which accounts for 3–4 roadkill fatalities annually. U.S. 1 cuts through the heart of the crocodile breeding range. For a stretch of 12 km (7.2 mi) the only corridors joining the wetlands on the two sides of the road are three pairs of usually submerged culverts. Most of the fatalities occur when crocodiles attempt to cross the highway adjacent to these submerged culverts. All of these culverts need to be replaced with bridges or box culverts with sufficient clearance to allow for their utilization by crocodiles.

The American Crocodile is a large and potentially dangerous predator. Nonetheless, its popular reputation as a highly aggressive animal is without basis. Given the considerable human presence within the range of the American Crocodile, there is a need for a rational and well-managed public educational effort to inform the residents of south Florida about the status and biology of the crocodile. Ultimately, survival of this species in Florida will almost certainly depend upon an informed, enlightened, and tolerant public.

Selected References

Dimock, A. W. 1918. The Florida Crocodile. Amer. Mus. J. 18(6):447–452.

Dimock, A. W., and J. Dimock, 1908. Florida enchantments. Outing Publishing Co., New York. 319 pp.

Gaby, R., M. P. McMahon, F. J. Mazzotti, W. N. Gillies, and J. R. Wilcox. 1985. Ecology and status of a population of *Crocodylus acutus* (Reptilia; Crocodilidae) at a power plant site in Florida. J. Herpetol. 19:189–198.

Jacobsen, M. T. 1983. Crocodilians and islands: Status of the American Alligator and the American Crocodile in the lower Florida Keys. Fla. Field Nat. 11(1):1–24.

Kushlan, J. A., and F. J. Mazzotti. 1989. Historic and present distribution of the American Crocodile in Florida. J. Herpetol. 23(1):1–7.

Kushlan, J. A., and F. J. Mazzotti. 1989. Population biology of the American Crocodile. J. Herpetol. 23(1):7–21.

Mazzotti, F. J. 1983. The ecology of *Crocodylus acutus* in Florida. Ph.D. diss., The Pennsylvania State University, University Park, Pennsylvania. 161 pp.

Mazzotti, F. J., J. A. Kushlan, and A. Dunbar-Cooper. 1988. Desiccation and cryptic nest flooding as probable causes of egg mortality in the American Crocodile, *Crocodylus acutus,* in Everglades National Park, Florida. Fla. Sci. 51(2):65–72.

Ogden, J. C. 1978. Status and nesting biology of the American Crocodile, *Crocodylus acutus* (Reptilia, Crocodilidae) in Florida. J. Herpetol. 12(2):183–196.

Ogden, J. C., and C. Singletary. 1973. Night of the crocodile. Audubon 75(3):32–37.

U.S. Fish and Wildlife Service. 1984. American Crocodile recovery plan (revised). U.S. Fish and Wildlife Service, Atlanta, Georgia. 37 pp.

Prepared by: Paul E. Moler, *Florida Game and Fresh Water Fish Commission, 4005 South Main Street, Gainesville, FL 32601.*

Green Turtle
Chelonia mydas (Linnaeus)
FAMILY CHELONIIDAE
Order Testudines

OTHER NAMES: Edible Turtle, Greenback Turtle, Soup Turtle.

DESCRIPTION: Hatchlings are solid black to dark gray above with a white margin circumscribing the posterior carapace and the trailing edge of the flippers. The plastron is creamy-white. The juvenile carapace is brownish to green, with light and dark streaks radiating within each scute. Although a faint juvenile pattern may be seen in some adults, the carapace is primarily olive with numerous black spots. The Green Turtle has four pairs of costal scutes and one pair of prefrontal scales. Mature females measure from 0.88 to 1.17 m (35–46 in) in straight carapace length and weigh 104 to 177 kg (220–389 lb).

RANGE: The Green Turtle generally ranges throughout the tropics and subtropics, worldwide. Of approximately 30 known major nesting areas, only two (at Tortuguero, Costa Rica, and Aves Island) are on the rim of the Western Atlantic north of South America. In U.S. Atlantic waters Green Turtles are known from New England to Texas and from Puerto Rico and the Virgin Islands. Nearly all of the species' nesting in the United States occurs in Florida, and most of that occurs along the east-central and southeastern coast from Volusia to Dade County. Greatest nesting densities occur at Melbourne Beach, Hutchinson Island, and Jupiter Island. There is only one recent nesting record from the entire Gulf Coast of Florida (at Eglin AFB, Santa Rosa County, in 1987), but there is an important population of immature Green Turtles in the area from Homosassa Bay to the Cedar Keys. Other significant populations of immature Green Turtles forage in the Indian River Lagoon system and Florida Bay.

Green Turtle, *Chelonia mydas* (photograph by P. C. H. Pritchard).

LIFE HISTORY AND ECOLOGY: Hatchlings (ca 30 g at hatching) emerge from beach nests, swim immediately offshore, and are thought to become associated with floating pelagic vegetation. Juveniles first appear along Florida coastal waters at one to three years of age. Juveniles 2–60 kg (4–130 lb) forage as herbivores in shallow coastal waters before abandoning this developmental habitat as sub-adults. It is unclear whether these turtles recruit to the Florida nesting adult population. Adult females nest on Florida beaches from May to September. Females deposit up to six clutches averaging 136 eggs each and return to the same stretch of beach at predominately two-year intervals. Foraging grounds of adults and sub-adults are unknown.

SPECIALIZED OR UNIQUE CHARACTERISTICS: This is the only herbivorous sea turtle and one of very few truly large marine herbivores. It has been exploited commercially for its meat (turtle steaks and the stock for Green Turtle soup) more than any of the others, and in recent years it has been the source of skins and oil for the leather and cosmetics trade.

BASIS OF STATUS CLASSIFICATION: Although the historical status of the Green Turtle in Florida is highly speculative, it seems likely that it was formerly more abundant than now. The suggestions of an upward trend in recent nesting numbers is very tentative and insufficient to confirm recovery in this population. Recent nesting numbers indicate that there are probably no more than 375 adult females nesting in Florida.

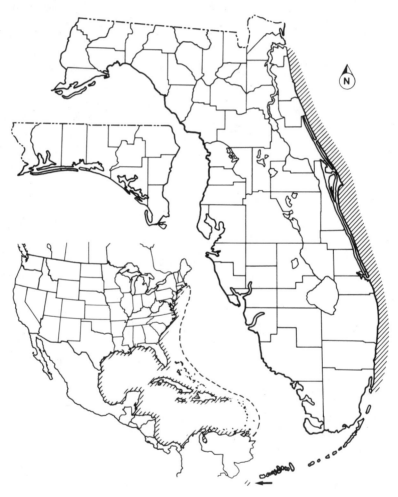

Distribution map of Green Turtle (*Chelonia mydas*). Florida map shows Florida nesting distribution. Inset map shows total distribution.

Population estimates for the year-round resident juveniles inhabiting both coasts and the Keys are lacking. Current threats include incidental capture by fishing nets, poaching, collisions with power boats, entanglement in synthetic debris, contact with chemical pollutants, and the degradation of nesting beach habitat.

RECOMMENDATIONS: Green Turtles are fully protected under state and federal law. It is imperative that the laws be strictly enforced. There is an urgent need for tighter regulation of gill net fisheries, near-shore and off-shore, that are now known to take significant numbers of Green Turtles incidental to the capture of pompano and other finfish. Many coastal counties and municipalities have lighting ordinances that are directed primarily at protecting loggerheads. Inclusive ordinances should be passed where there are none, and many of the existing ones should be improved to accommodate the wariness of adult Green Turtles and the peculiar photic responses of Green Turtle hatchlings. Manipulative techniques, such as "head-starting" and broad-scale nest translocation, remain unproven in effecting population recovery and should be used only in special cases, with frequent professional review. Green Turtle nesting beaches should be monitored for the frequency of nest depredation, and contingency plans for the removal of mammalian predators should be made for scenarios in which depredation becomes excessive.

Every effort should be made to maintain the natural attributes of the good, high-energy nesting beaches of southeast Florida. At the time of this writing initiatives have been launched within both state and federal governments to acquire, as a National Wildlife Refuge, beach and dune lands in south Brevard and north Indian River counties, where approximately 40% of Florida Green Turtle nesting occurs. Creation of the refuge (which would be named for Florida's late, pre-eminent herpetologist, Dr. Archie Carr) is of utmost urgency because population growth and beach-front development are proceeding at an explosive rate in that area. Failure of the refuge proposals will clearly result in the loss of this beach as a Green Turtle nesting ground by the year 2000.

Selected References:

Carr, A. F., and R. M. Ingle. 1959. The green turtle in Florida. Bull. Mar. Sci. Gulf Carib. 9(3):315–320.

Dodd, C. K. 1981. Nesting of the green turtle, *Chelonia mydas* (L.), in Florida: Historic review and present trends. Brimleyana 7:39–54.

Ehrhart, L. M. 1983. Marine turtles of the Indian River Lagoon system. Fla. Sci. 46(3/4):337–346.

Hirth, H. F. 1971. Synopsis of biological data on the green turtle, *Chelonia mydas*. F. A. O. Fisheries Synopsis No. 85.

Mendonca, M. T., and L. M. Ehrhart. 1982. Activity, population size and structure of immature *Chelonia mydas* and *Caretta caretta* in Mosquito Lagoon, Florida. Copeia 1982(1):161–167.

Prepared by: Llewellyn M. Ehrhart, *Department of Biological Sciences, University of Central Florida, P.O. Box 25000, Orlando, FL 32816;* and Blair E. Witherington, *Department of Zoology, University of Florida, Gainesville, FL 32610.*

Hawksbill Turtle

Eretmochelys imbricata (Linnaeus)

FAMILY CHELONIIDAE

Order Testudines

OTHER NAMES: None.

DESCRIPTION: The Hawksbill is a small to medium-sized sea turtle; adult females in the Caribbean range from 62.5 to 94.0 cm (24.6–37.0 in) straight carapace length. The diagnostic features of the species are two pairs of prefrontal scales, posteriorly overlapping scutes on the carapace (except in very young and very old animals), four pairs of costal scutes, two claws on each flipper, and a sharply pointed, beak-like mouth. The carapace is often distinctively patterned with radiating streaks of yellow, reddish brown, brown, and black.

RANGE: The Hawksbill Turtle has a circumtropical range. It is widely distributed in the Caribbean and western Atlantic, normally occurring from Florida southward along the Central American mainland to Brazil and throughout the Bahamas and the Greater and Lesser Antilles. Although historical records of nesting in Florida are rare, increased surveillance of beaches by volunteers and researchers during the 1980s has resulted in the documentation of one or two Hawksbill nests nearly every year. It is likely that at least several more go unnoticed. Documented nesting records exist for the following counties: Volusia, Brevard, Martin, Palm Beach, Broward, Dade, and Monroe (Boca Grande Key). According to stranding and museum records, the known range of the Hawksbill in Florida extends north to Duval County on the east coast and to Levy County on the west coast.

HABITAT: Hawksbills are most typically associated with coral reefs but

Hawksbill Turtle, *Eretmochelys imbricata*. Panama (photograph by A. Meylan).

also occupy other hard-bottom habitats such as limestone ledges and outcroppings.

LIFE HISTORY AND ECOLOGY: Association with hard bottoms is most likely linked to the Hawksbill's nearly exclusive diet of demosponges. Although other benthic organisms are consumed, choristid and hadromerid sponges appear to be the principal food of this species throughout the Caribbean (Meylan 1988). Limited data from Florida show comparable findings. With rare exception, Hawksbills observed in Florida waters are immature. Approximately half of all Hawksbill strandings recorded in Florida since 1980 have involved animals less than 20 cm (7.9 in) carapace length (Florida DNR Sea Turtle Stranding and Salvage Network data base). Hawksbills of this size class are rarely sighted alive in coastal waters in Florida, and it is likely that many of these strandings involve turtles from offshore habitats. They may, in fact, be post-hatchlings from nesting beaches in Mexico and the Caribbean that are being transported through Florida waters by the Gulf Stream current. Sightings of larger, but still immature, Hawksbills are regularly made on reefs in the Palm Beach area; infrequent observations have also been made in hard-bottom communities off Brevard, Broward, and Monroe counties. Hawksbills nest diffusely throughout their circumtropical range, with few known aggregations (Witzell 1983). Females may nest several times within a season, usually at 15- to 18-day intervals. Nesting in subsequent seasons is usually non-annual. A female tagged on Jupiter Island, Florida, in 1974 was observed a second time in 1974, once in 1977, and three times in

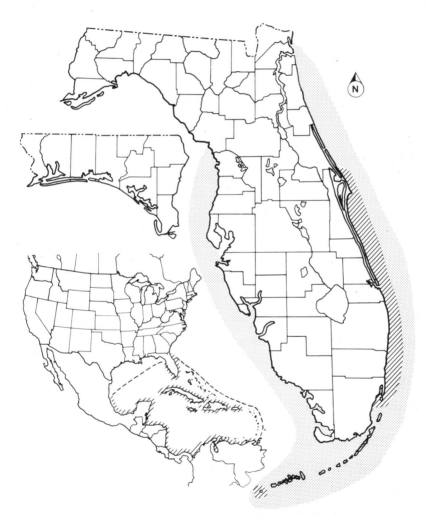

Distribution map of Hawksbill Turtle (*Eretmochelys imbricata*). Crosshatching indicates Florida nesting distribution.

1979 (Lund 1985). The turtle exhibited a high degree of site fidelity, as is typical of this species; all five nests were located within a 2.8 km (1.7 mi) stretch of beach, with two nests less than 100 m (330 ft) apart. Because of the typically diffuse nesting distribution of the Hawksbill, comparatively few animals have been tagged and subsequently recaptured, and the assumption is often made that individuals of this species do not undertake long-distance migrations. This assumption may be erroneous; the few recaptures of tagged Hawksbills that have been recorded around the world indicate that they can and do travel large distances.

SPECIALIZED OR UNIQUE CHARACTERISTICS: With the exception of a small number of highly evolved marine fish, no other vertebrate shares the highly spongivorous feeding habit of the Hawksbill. The Hawksbill is also unique in being the source of true tortoiseshell, which is derived from the epidermal scutes overlaying the bones of the carapace and plastron. This highly decorative material has been used for centuries in jewelry, ceremonial articles, and inlay work.

BASIS OF STATUS CLASSIFICATION: The Hawksbill is perhaps second only to the Atlantic Ridley in terms of endangerment. Although widespread subsistence use of eggs and meat is a threat to the species, exploitation for tortoiseshell is undoubtedly the principal cause for decline throughout the world (Groombridge 1982). In the Caribbean, lucrative fisheries for lobsters and reef fish have resulted in significant incidental take of the Hawksbill. The tendency of Hawksbills to nest diffusely throughout their range has made it difficult to protect them through the establishment of nesting preserves. In Florida, pollution of offshore waters by petroleum products (especially oil tanker discharges) is a serious threat to early life-history stages. Entanglement in persistent marine debris, especially monofilament line and nets, is also a well-documented source of mortality.

RECOMMENDATIONS: In a worldwide perspective, ending the international trade in tortoiseshell is the most important step in improving the survival outlook of the Hawksbill. Japan accounts for most of the world market, and international efforts must be made to persuade this country to end its trade. In Florida, protection of reef habitats and comprehensive efforts to curb marine pollution are critical to the long-term survival of the Hawksbill.

Selected References

Groombridge, B. 1982. The IUCN amphibia-reptilia red data book. Part I. IUCN, Gland, Switzerland. 426 pp.

Lund, P. F. 1985. Hawksbill Turtle *(Eretmochelys imbricata)* nesting on the east coast of Florida. J. Herpetol. 19(1):164–166.

Meylan, A. 1988. Spongivory in Hawksbill Turtles: A diet of glass. Science 239: 393–395.

Witzell, W. N. 1983. Synopsis of biological data on the Hawksbill Turtle *Eretmochelys imbricata* (Linnaeus, 1766). F. A. O. Fisheries Synopsis No. 137, Rome. 78 pp.

Prepared by: Anne Meylan, *Florida Marine Research Institute, 100 Eighth Avenue, SE, St. Petersburg, FL 33701–5095.*

Atlantic Ridley Turtle

Lepidochelys kempii (Garman)

FAMILY CHELONIIDAE

Order Testudines

OTHER NAMES: Tortuga Lora (Spanish).

DESCRIPTION: The Atlantic Ridley Turtle is a small species of sea turtle with an extremely broad carapace, not tapered posteriorly, that is sometimes wider than it is long. The small orbit located high on the head above the deep upper jaw (supralabial scale) creates a parrot-like appearance—thus the Spanish vernacular name. Mature females average about 64 cm (25.2 in) carapace length (range 58–75 cm [22.8–29.5 in]) and range in weight from 32 to 49 kg (70–108 lb). Dorsal coloration of the adult is grey to olive-green with a yellowish plastron. Hatchlings are uniformly dark (black when wet), with the plastron becoming lighter (white) after several months. This dark color phase persists well after the pelagic life stage. There is a transition from the juvenile coloration to the adult beginning at about 28 cm (11 in) carapace length.

RANGE: Adult Atlantic Ridleys are generally believed to be restricted to the Gulf of Mexico, with the exception of a few records of adult-sized individuals from the east coast of Florida. Whether or not the latter were sexually mature is not known; however, a single unsuccessful nesting attempt occurred in Palm Beach County in May 1989. Immature Ridleys range widely throughout the Gulf of Mexico and in the North Atlantic from Florida northward to Nova Scotia and eastward to Bermuda, the Azores, and Europe. The fate of the Atlantic expatriates remains an enigma—some succumb to the cold winter waters of the North Atlantic, while others manage to survive by migrating south or offshore to warmer waters, or perhaps hibernating. The question remains whether or not these "survivors" return to the Gulf of Mexico to breed.

100

Atlantic Ridley Turtle, *Lepidochelys kempii* (photograph by P. C. H. Pritchard).

LIFE HISTORY AND ECOLOGY: Atlantic Ridleys are associated with a wide range of coastal benthic habitats, usually sand or mud bottoms, that support an abundant fauna of crustaceans and other invertebrates. Their primary prey consists of portunid crabs, especially the genus *Callinectes*. However, other crab species are consumed, along with molluscs and other benthic species.

The smallest post-pelagic individuals recorded are about 20 cm (7.9 in) in carapace length and are usually found in the shallow coastal waters, bays, and sounds in waters less than 2 m (6.6 ft) deep. However, movements to deeper, warmer water in the winter months have been reported. Adults and older subadults are found in deeper water but appear to be restricted to the inshore zone or shallow banks further offshore. Seasonal and reproductive migrations also appear to be restricted to coastal rather than pelagic routes.

Almost the entire nesting effort takes place on a few kilometers of beach at Rancho Nuevo, Tamaulipas, Mexico (lat 23° 10', long 97° 50'). Some scattered nesting does take place to the north and south of Rancho Nuevo in Mexico. In the United States, a few Ridleys have been recorded nesting in south Texas, primarily on south Padre Island. Recently, one Ridley nested successfully in Pinellas County, Florida, on Madeira Beach in May 1989, and 24 hatchlings were produced. The significance of this

rare event, and the east coast nesting attempt, is not known. A synchronized, aggregated nesting effort, locally called an "arribada," was the normal reproductive behavior for this species before the breeding population
declined to the low levels observed today.

The Ridley nests annually and deposits 1–3 clutches of about 110
eggs each per season. In 1947, it was estimated that about 40,000 fe-

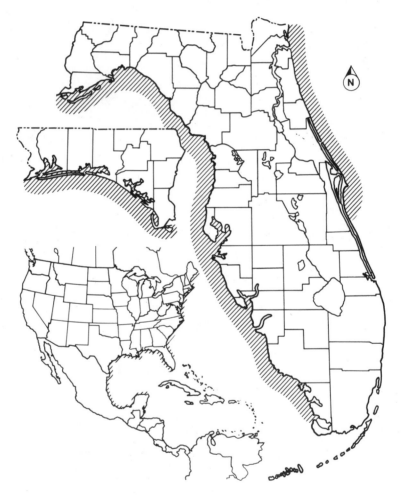

Distribution map of Atlantic Ridley Turtle (*Lepidochelys kempii*).

males emerged in a single day to nest along a one mile section of beach. Today, fewer than 500–600 females nest in a season, and fewer than 200 nest at one time. Decades of extensive exploitation of eggs caused the initial decrease in the population along with the directed take of the adults. Drowning in shrimp trawls also took its toll and is believed to be the most serious threat to this species' continued existence. This latter mortality imposes a chronic drain on the survivors, because Atlantic Ridley foraging habitat overlaps that of the commercial shrimp grounds. Tagging studies conducted at Rancho Nuevo revealed that the two most important foraging areas for the adults were in Campeche Bay, Mexico, and Louisiana coastal waters. The majority of recaptures were reported by shrimp fishermen.

Nothing is known about the distribution or occurrence of Atlantic Ridley hatchlings in the pelagic stage in the Gulf of Mexico (the two smallest post-hatchlings recorded were from the Atlantic). The coastal benthic zone of the northern Gulf of Mexico is an important developmental habitat for young Ridleys after leaving the pelagic environment. Older subadults are found in the eastern Gulf at Cedar Key, Florida. In the Atlantic, subadult Ridleys appear to be highly migratory—foraging as far north as Chesapeake Bay in the spring, summer, and fall, then migrating south in winter to Cape Canaveral, Florida. In New England, small Ridleys are frequently found cold-stunned in winter in Long Island Sound and Cape Cod Bay. Some apparently survive and forage in the sounds and bays throughout the year, but their ultimate fate is unknown.

SPECIALIZED OR UNIQUE CHARACTERISTICS: The restricted range of the adult population (Gulf of Mexico) and synchronized, aggregated nesting during daylight hours focused on a small area of the beach are special characteristics of the Atlantic Ridley Turtle. Unfortunately, the "arribada" is no longer the spectacular event it once was.

BASIS OF STATUS CLASSIFICATION: There has been a dramatic decline of the nesting assemblage from an estimated 40,000 females in 1947 to only 1000–2000 in the 1970s. The total world population today is estimated to include fewer than 600 adult females. Reasons for the decline were intensive egg collecting, taking of females, and shrimp trawl mortality on the foraging grounds. Drowning of turtles in shrimp trawls is believed to be the single most important factor responsible for the continued decline of females and the prevention of recruitment of subadults into the breeding stock.

RECOMMENDATIONS: Recommendations to insure the long-term survival of the Atlantic Ridley Turtle are (1) continue and expand the nesting beach protection effort at Rancho Nuevo and the other minor nesting beaches south of Tampico, (2) enforce the use of turtle excluder devices (TEDs) in the United States, (3) require TEDs in other areas and seasons when data become available to support such measures, and (4) assist Mexico to develop and implement its own TED regulations through technology transfer and other cooperative measures.

Selected References

Caillouet, C. W., Jr., and A. M. Landry, Jr. (eds.). 1989. Proc. first international symposium of Kemp's Ridley Sea Turtle biology, conservation and management. October 1–4, 1985, Galveston, Texas. Texas A & M Sea Grant Program. TAMU–SG–105. 260 pp.

Carr, A. F. 1980. Some problems of sea turtle ecology. Amer. Zool. 20(3):489–497.

Groombridge, B. 1982. The IUCN amphibia–reptilia red data book. Part I. IUCN, Gland, Switzerland. 426 pp.

Pritchard, P. C. H., and R. Marquez M. 1973. Kemp's Ridley Turtle or Atlantic Ridley, *Lepidochelys kempii*. IUCN Monograph No. 2: Marine Turtle Series. Morges. 30 pp.

Prepared by: Larry H. Ogren, *National Marine Fisheries Service, Panama City Laboratory, 3500 Delwood Beach Road, Panama City, FL 32408.*

Striped Mud Turtle,
Lower Keys population

Kinosternon baurii (Garman)

FAMILY KINOSTERNIDAE

Order Testudines

OTHER NAMES: Key Mud Turtle.

DESCRIPTION: Adults average 90 to 100 mm (3.5–3.9 in) in carapace length (CL). The carapace is dark with three dorsal light lines barely evident or virtually obscured by dark pigment. The mandible is dark, lacking distinct yellow streaks or blotches. The plastron is narrow; when measured at the abdominal-femoral suture, it constitutes 34–38% CL in males and 37–43% CL in females. There is a need for a definitive study of the biochemical taxonomy of the populations of *K. baurii*. This is the only native, pond-dwelling chelonian within its range. Some of the larger ponds have introduced specimens of mainland "sliders." Diamondback terrapins *(Malaclemys)* occur only in sea water.

RANGE: *K. baurii* as a species is restricted to peninsular Florida, the Florida Keys, and extreme southeastern Georgia and South Carolina. The distinctive population occupying the lower Florida Keys is considered by some to constitute a separate subspecies, *K. b. baurii* (Lazell 1989). The Lower Keys consist of islands stretching from Big Pine Key to Key West. The primary barrier separating the two populations on Big Pine and Key Vaca is a sea water gap (spanned by the "seven mile bridge") with strong tidal currents surging between the Gulf of Mexico and the Atlantic Ocean. In addition to this physical barrier, there are significant geological differences between the surface limestone formations of the Lower and Upper Keys. The Lower Keys consist of Miami oolitic limestone, whereas the Upper Keys are composed of Key Largo limestone. Specimens of *K. baurii* are known from most of the islands between Big Pine and Key West.

105

Striped Mud Turtle, *Kinosternon baurii*. Big Pine Key, Monroe County, Florida
(photograph by B. W. Mansell).

The largest populations may be in pockets of especially favorable habitat
on some of the smaller islands, such as Summerland Key, rather than on
the largest island, Big Pine Key.

HABITAT: *K. baurii* is an aquatic turtle which also utilizes terrestrial retreats when ponds dry up or become too saline. It is restricted to small,
usually temporary ponds which have salinities below 15 ppt. Turtles leave
the water if salinities rise above this level. Such brackish situations are
due to a mixing of rainfall-derived groundwater with the sea water which
underlies the islands. Suitable ponds must be deep enough to penetrate
into the fresh ground water "lens." They are usually found in or along
the edge of elevated hardwood hammocks. Exceptionally dense turtle
populations have been found in some artificially constructed "mosquito
control ditches" which penetrate into the underground freshwater table
and retain water longer than most natural hammock ponds. Typical vegetation around the ponds is dominated by Buttonwood *(Conocarpus)*. Red
and Black Mangroves *(Rhizopohora* and *Avicennia)* sometimes occur, as
does cattail *(Typha)* in disturbed sites. The most critical abiotic features
of the required habitat seem to be the drying cycles and salinities of the
ponds.

LIFE HISTORY AND ECOLOGY: There has been only one study to date of the ecology of the Lower Keys population of *K. baurii,* and it focused on aspects of physiological ecology related to salinity tolerance. Turtles are active year-round whenever water below about 15 ppt is found in ponds. They are quite faithful to a "home" pond; only 3 of 59 individual

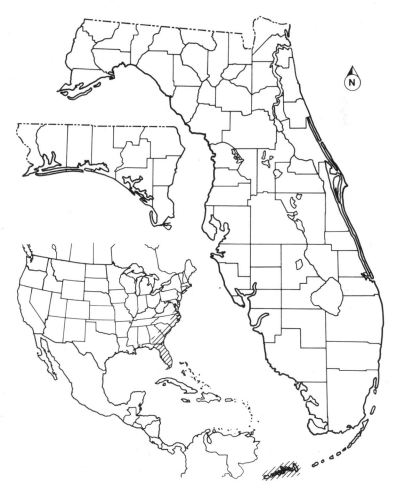

Distribution map of Striped Mud Turtle (*Kinosternon baurii*). (Lower Keys population only)

turtles recaptured 136 times were found in more than a single pond. This appears to reflect a strong selective pressure to remain where conditions have proven to be favorable in the past. Hammock ponds often contain very little animal life, except for a few insects. Mangrove ponds which are subject to occasional tidal inundation contain fish. Mosquito control ditches often have a more diverse freshwater community, including fish, crayfish, amphibians, and insects. The only field observation of feeding by mud turtles was consumption of mosquito larvae which had congregated into a clump. Turtles appear to be avid scavengers, since they are attracted to meat in traps. Although they are not easily seen against the dark pond bottoms, they are active diurnally and can often be picked up by hand while they are foraging. Isotope tracking of turtles has shown that certain terrestrial retreats (under rock ledges or among tree roots) are used repeatedly when ponds dry up or become too saline. Few hatchlings or small individuals are captured in the wild. Clutch size appears to be small, as in other mud turtles, and adults are long-lived. In ponds on Big Pine Key where alligators occur, many turtles have apparent tooth marks on their shells. The densest local population known (59 turtles) occurs in a small area (52 m^2 [63 yd^2]) of mosquito control ditches on Summerland Key. Several hundred were estimated to inhabit the area of Summerland Key south of U. S. Highway 1. On undisturbed Johnston Key, the population estimate was about 50.

SPECIALIZED OR UNIQUE CHARACTERISTICS: As is apparently the case with many species of mud turtles, this population is highly specialized for life in temporary ponds. Such ponds provide a refuge from certain types of predation and competition. However, temporary ponds are a rather rigorous habitat. The environmental unpredictability of ponds calls for a suite of adaptations that are unique for temporary ponds, or even for subsets of ponds based on their particular drying cycle and salinity. It appears that *K. baurii* is highly dependent on certain specific characteristics of temporary ponds in the Lower Keys. The most significant abiotic factor limiting this turtle seems to be salinity. It avoids salinities above 15 ppt. Physiological tests show that it has only a limited capacity to tolerate immersion in sea water. However, salinity tolerance of Lower Keys populations may be superior to that of populations from the southernmost mainland. *K. baurii* is the most obvious "indicator species" occurring in the fast-disappearing freshwater pond–marsh habitats of the Lower Keys. It is also an especially interesting illustration of behavioral osmoregulation in reptiles. As such, it demonstrates what may be the earliest stage in the evolution of adaptations for a marine life (Dunson and Mazzotti 1989).

BASIS OF STATUS CLASSIFICATION: The Lower Keys are subject to intensive development, especially of the hammock pond habitat essential for survival of Striped Mud Turtles. Reasonable populations apparently remain on some islands, but the greatest numbers are on privately owned land. The largest island, Big Pine Key, does not hold substantial numbers of turtles, even in superficially suitable habitat. While this may in part be due to the occurrence of predation by alligators, it may also presage a more general effect of the large-scale disruption of the natural habitat. Future filling in of mosquito control ditches to accommodate management recommendations for Key Deer will have a negative impact on the population of this turtle if suitable natural habitat is not available.

RECOMMENDATIONS: A thorough survey of all suitable habitat and measurement of population sizes in the Lower Keys are needed to evaluate the proportion in public and private ownership. At present, it appears that a large percentage of the population occurs on private lands, where extirpation is only a matter of time. It would be valuable also to clear up the continued controversy over the subspecific designation. This could probably be settled by carrying out a comparison of allozymes. Aside from its intrinsic importance, protection of the Lower Keys population could be valuable as a means of enhancing protection of its general habitat, the hardwood hammock.

Selected References

Duellman, W. E., and A. Schwartz. 1958. Amphibians and reptiles of southern Florida. Bull. Fla. State Mus. 3(5):181–324.

Dunson, W. A. 1979. Salinity tolerance and osmoregulation of the Key Mud Turtle, *Kinosternon b. baurii.* Copeia 1979(3):548–552.

Dunson, W. A. 1981. Behavioral osmoregulation in the Key Mud Turtle, *Kinosternon b. baurii.* J. Herpetol. 15(2):163–173.

Dunson, W. A., and F. Mazzotti. 1989. Salinity as a limiting factor in the distribution of reptiles in Florida Bay: A theory for the estuarine origin of marine snakes and turtles. Bull. Mar. Sci. 44(1):229–244.

Ernst, C. H. 1974. *Kinosternon baurii* (Garman). Cat. Amer. Amphib. Rept. 161.1–161.2.

Iverson, J. B. 1978. Variation in Striped Mud Turtles, *Kinosternon baurii* (Reptilia, Testudines, Kinosternidae). J. Herpetol. 12(2):135–142.

Lazell, J. D. 1989. Wildlife of the Florida Keys. Island Press. Washington, D. C. 253 pp.

Uzzell, T. M., Jr., and A. Schwartz. 1955. The status of the turtle *Kinosternon bauri palmarum* Stejneger with notes on variation in the species. J. Elisha Mitchell Soc. 71(1):28–35.

Prepared by: W. A. Dunson, *Department of Biology, The Pennsylvania State University, University Park, PA 16802.*

Atlantic Salt Marsh Snake
Nerodia clarkii taeniata (Cope)
FAMILY COLUBRIDAE
Order Squamata, Suborder Serpentes

OTHER NAMES: Eastern Florida Water Snake, East Coast Striped Water Snake, Salt Water Snake.

DESCRIPTION: The Atlantic Salt Marsh Snake is a relatively small, slender, rough-scaled water snake with a pattern of longitudinal stripes that are variously broken into blotches. The dorsal ground color is pale olive, with a median pair of dark-brown dorsolateral stripes enclosing a light mid-dorsal stripe. The dark stripes tend to be broken posteriorly into a longitudinal series of blotches, and the light stripe is often interrupted by dark crossbars. There is also a row of dark blotches along the lower sides, usually merging to form stripes in the neck region. The belly is typically black with a central row of large whitish or yellowish spots. The Atlantic Salt Marsh Snake seldom exceeds 61 cm (2 ft) in total length.

RANGE: Salt Marsh Snakes *(Nerodia clarkii clarkii, N. clarkii compressicauda,* and *N. clarkii taeniata)* occur in saline coastal habitats from the vicinity of Corpus Christi, Texas, to the Atlantic Coast of central Florida, including the Florida Keys and the north coast of Cuba. The Atlantic Salt Marsh Snake is found only on the east coast of central Florida.

Although historically reported from scattered localities in Volusia, Brevard, and Indian River counties, *N. c. taeniata* appears to be restricted to a limited coastal strip in Volusia County. It intergrades with the Mangrove Salt Marsh Snake *(N. c. compressicauda)* southward through Brevard and Indian River counties, however, and the occurrence of partially striped patterns throughout this area is not unusual. The type locality is National Gardens, in Volusia County.

Atlantic Salt Marsh Snake, *Nerodia clarkii taeniata*. Volusia County, Florida (photograph by B. W. Mansell).

HABITAT: The Atlantic Salt Marsh Snake inhabits coastal salt marshes and mangrove swamps ranging in salinity from brackish to full-strength seawater. It has been observed along tidal creeks, ditches, and pools in association with glassworts *(Salicornia)* and Black Mangrove *(Avicennia germinans)*.

LIFE HISTORY AND ECOLOGY: The Atlantic Salt Marsh Snake has been observed most often at night during low tidal stages, when it apparently feeds on small fishes that become trapped in the shallow water. There is evidence that it may seek shelter in Fiddler Crab *(Uca)* burrows, especially during the day. It has, however, been found active by day, suggesting that its activity patterns may be influenced by several factors, including tidal cycles and seasonality. Like all *Nerodia*, the Atlantic Salt Marsh Snake is viviparous. One captive female had a litter of nine (eight alive and one stillborn) in late August; another gave birth to three young in October. Although additional data are lacking, the life history of *N. c. taeniata* may be similar to that of the Gulf Salt Marsh Snake *(N. c. clarkii)*, which it resembles in appearance and behavior.

SPECIALIZED OR UNIQUE CHARACTERISTICS: Salt Marsh Snakes are among the few North American reptiles that have successfully exploited estuarine habitats. They differ from the Southern Water Snake *(Nerodia fasciata)*, a closely related freshwater species, in a suite of characters re-

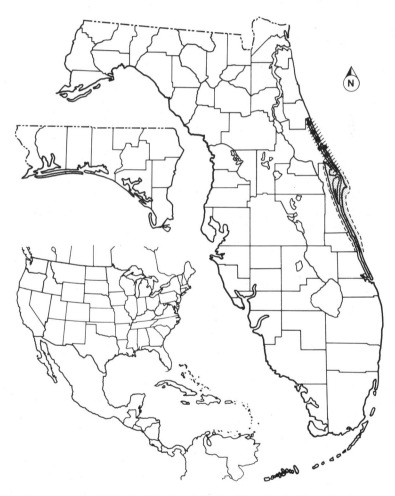

Distribution map of Atlantic Salt Marsh Snake (*Nerodia clarkii taeniata*). Stippling indicates zone of intergradation with Mangrove Water Snake (*N. c. compressicauda*).

lated to their ecological specialization. Some systematists consider Salt
Marsh Snakes to be conspecific with *N. fasciata* due to reproductive
compatibility and hybridization in brackish areas where their ranges
overlap.

The Atlantic Salt Marsh Snake has the smallest range and is the least
known race of *N. clarkii*. Water snakes from various localities along the
U.S. Gulf Coast, however, may have a dorsal pattern of stripes and
blotches similar to *N. c. taeniata*. This is often the result of hybridization
between the longitudinally-striped Gulf Salt Marsh Snake *(N. c. clarkii)*
and adjacent crossbanded races. There is a striking similarity between *N.
c. taeniata* and the *clarkii* × *compressicauda* intergrades from nearly the
same latitude on the Florida Gulf Coast. This suggests that *taeniata*
could actually be the product of past hybridization involving *clarkii* and
compressicauda ancestors. Although *N. c. clarkii* now occurs only along the
Gulf Coast, *clarkii* and *compressicauda* may have had adjacent distributions
near the present range of *taeniata* during the Pleistocene, due to chang-
ing sea levels. The Atlantic Salt Marsh Snake may therefore be a relict
population of hybrids derived from a striped ancestor that no longer occurs in the area. It has also been suggested that the Atlantic Salt Marsh
Snake is not a valid subspecies, but merely a population of *N. c. compressicauda* that is partially striped due to the local prevalence of marsh instead
of mangroves.

BASIS OF STATUS CLASSIFICATION: Progressive development along the
coast of Volusia County threatens to eliminate most of the remaining
habitat of the Atlantic Salt Marsh Snake. Wetland alteration through
draining, diking, and impounding can promote hybridization with an adjacent freshwater species, the Southern Water Snake. This can lead to
genetic swamping of *N. c. taeniata* by the extensive *N. fasciata* gene pool,
causing the Atlantic Salt Marsh Snake to lose its genetic identity. It can
remain genetically distinct only if hybridization is limited to narrow zones
of ecological transition between freshwater and saline habitats.

The present distribution of the Atlantic Salt Marsh Snake is much
more restricted than previously believed. Water snakes throughout the
historical range of *N. c. taeniata* often show various degrees of interme-
diacy between the Atlantic Salt Marsh Snake, the Southern Water Snake,
and the Mangrove Salt Marsh Snake *(N. c. compressicauda)*. The striped
taeniata phenotype appears to be most prevalent in the northern portion
of the range, while crossbanding or uniform coloration, presumably from
compressicauda influence, increases toward the south. Surveys on the Mer-

ritt Island National Wildlife Refuge (northern Brevard and southern Volusia counties) in 1979 and 1980 found little evidence of *N. c. taeniata*, with most snakes closely resembling *N. c. compressicauda*. At present, the Atlantic Salt Marsh Snake is consistently found only along the coast of Volusia County, near New Smyrna Beach. Salt Marsh Snakes from farther south in Brevard and Indian River counties, although occasionally striped, appear to comprise a zone of intergradation with *N. c. compressicauda*.

RECOMMENDATIONS: Much additional study is needed to clarify the taxonomic and population status of the Atlantic Salt Marsh Snake. Whether or not it is a valid subspecies, the Atlantic Salt Marsh Snake is a relict of historical and/or ecological processes unique to Florida and should be preserved. Further disturbance of estuarine wetlands in Volusia County must be strongly discouraged. The belt of mangrove swamps and salt marshes along the Halifax and Indian rivers in Volusia County should be protected as critical habitat. This area extends from approximately 8 km (5 mi) north of Ponce de Leon Inlet southward to the vicinity of Oak Hill and includes part of the Canaveral National Seashore. This habitat should be intensively surveyed for *N. c. taeniata* with an emphasis on obtaining a density estimate. Salt marshes in northern Volusia and southern Flagler counties, near the original type locality, should be searched for undiscovered striped populations. Additional surveys should be conducted south of Volusia County, especially along the barrier islands, to determine the southern extent of the striped *taeniata* phenotype.

Selected References

Carr, A. F., and C. J. Goin. 1942. Rehabilitation of *Natrix sipedon taeniata* Cope. Proc. New England Zool. Club 21:47–54.

Cope, E. D. 1895. On some new North American snakes. Amer. Nat. 29:676–680.

Dunson, W. A. 1979. Occurrence of partially striped forms of the mangrove snake *Nerodia fasciata compressicauda* Kennicott and comments on the status of *N. f. taeniata* Cope. Fla. Sci. 42(2):102–112.

Hebrard, J. J., and R. C. Lee. 1981. A large collection of brackish water snakes from the central Atlantic coast of Florida. Copeia 1981(4):886–889.

Kochman, H. I. 1977. Differentiation and hybridization in the *Natrix fasciata* complex (Reptilia: Serpentes): A nonmorphological approach. M.S. thesis, University of Florida, Gainesville. 105 pp.

Lawson, R., A. J. Meier, P. G. Frank, and P. E. Moler. 1991. Allozyme variation and systematics of the *Nerodia fasciata-Nerodia clarkii* complex of water snakes (Serpentes:Colubridae). Copeia 1991(3):638–659.

Neill, W. T. 1958. The occurrence of amphibians and reptiles in saltwater areas, and a bibliography. Bull. Mar. Sci. Gulf Carib. 8(1):1–97.

Prepared by: Howard I. Kochman, *U.S. Fish and Wildlife Service, National Ecology Research Center, 412 NE 16th Avenue, Room 250, Gainesville, FL 32601;* and Steven P. Christman, *Department of Natural Sciences, Florida Museum of Natural History, University of Florida, Gainesville, FL 32611.*

Bluetail Mole Skink

Eumeces egregius lividus Mount

FAMILY SCINCIDAE

Order Squamata, Suborder Sauria

OTHER NAMES: Blue-tailed Red-tailed Skink, Brown Red-tailed Skink, Red-tailed Skink.

DESCRIPTION: The Bluetail Mole Skink is a small, shiny, brownish lizard, usually with a bluish tail. The unregenerated tail in juveniles and young adults is bright blue. Older adults and adults with regenerated tails usually have a light pinkish or salmon-colored tail. The legs of the Mole Skink are slightly reduced and not used when the animal is "swimming" in loose sand, but they are still functional when the lizard is walking on the surface. The ground color is some shade of light brown with a pair of dorsolateral lighter stripes that widen or diverge posteriorly. During the late winter breeding season, males develop a colorful orange pattern on their sides. There are usually seven supralabials on each side of the head. The total length is about 12.7 cm (5 in), with the tail making up slightly more than one-half.

Large adults and individuals with regenerated tails cannot be distinguished from the wide-ranging and parapatric subspecies, *E. e. onocrepis*. In these cases, identification must be based on locality.

RANGE: The Bluetail Mole Skink occurs only on the Lake Wales Ridge in Polk, Highlands, and Osceola counties, Florida, its total range encompassing less than 20,000 ha (50,000 ac). Mole Skinks of the subspecies *E. e. onocrepis* occur in appropriate habitat throughout Central Florida off the Lake Wales Ridge, and, in areas of contact, apparently hybridize with *lividus*. Specimens examined from Vineland in Orange County were referable to *E. e. onocrepis*. All of the localities from which *lividus* is known are above 30 m (100 ft) in elevation. The Bluetail Mole Skink is

117

Bluetail Mole Skink, *Eumeces egregius lividus*. Highlands County, Florida (photograph by
B. W. Mansell).

known to still occur at its type locality north of Avon Park in Polk
County. Other subspecies of *E. egregius* range throughout Florida and
northward into southern Georgia and southeastern Alabama.

HABITAT: The Bluetail Mole Skink is confined to the well-drained, sandy
uplands of the Lake Wales Ridge, occurring in Sand Pine Scrub, Rosemary Scrub, Oak Scrub, Turkey Oak Barrens, High Pine (either Longleaf
or South Florida Slash Pine), and Xeric Hammock. It is most frequently
found just under the sand at a depth of 2.5 to 5 cm (1–2 in) under pine
needles, leaves, fallen logs, or palmetto fronds. Optimum *lividus* habitat
appears to be Rosemary Scrub and Oak Scrub, where the lizards move
freely between the surface and subsurface in the loose sands. They are less
commonly found in High Pine and the "Turkey Oak Barrens" that remain after High Pine communities have been lumbered.

LIFE HISTORY AND ECOLOGY: Nothing is known of the life history of
this subspecies. However, it is probably much like that of *E. e. onocrepis,*

which has been described by Mount (1963). *Eumeces e. onocrepis* in Levy County, Florida, lays from 3 to 7 eggs once a year in nest cavities constructed in the sand at depths of probably less than a foot. Females remain with the eggs until hatching (31–51 days), presumably offering protection from small predators. Reproductive maturity occurs at the age

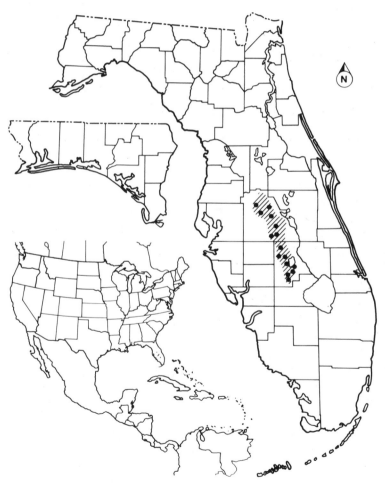

Distribution map of Bluetail Mole Skink (*Eumeces egregius lividus*). Dots indicate known localities.

of one year in the laboratory. Mating takes place in the winter. Mole Skinks eat small invertebrates, especially roaches, spiders, and crickets. *Eumeces egregius* is possibly a gregarious species. Within seemingly suitable habitat, individuals are not dispersed throughout, but rather are concentrated in localized pockets. Apparently they disperse very little. Population densities of *E. e. onocrepis* are sometimes as high as 62.5 adults per ha (25/ac) or even higher, but the Bluetail subspecies appears to be much rarer. In seemingly optimum habitats, with standard collecting techniques (pitfall trapping or raking in the sand), the Sand Skink *(Neoseps reynoldsi)* is encountered about 20 times more frequently than *E. e. lividus.*

SPECIALIZED OR UNIQUE CHARACTERISTICS: *Eumeces e. lividus* is a distinctive, endemic element of Central Florida's Lake Wales Ridge, where it is believed to have persisted since the higher sea level times of previous ages. Mount (1965) considered *lividus* to be closest to the ancestral populations that differentiated in Florida, during periods of higher sea level, to give rise to the other four subspecies. *Eumeces egregius* represents an intermediate step in the evolution of sand-adapted morphology and behavior between the generalized Five-lined Skink *(E. fasciatus)* and the highly specialized sand-swimmer, *N. reynoldsi.*

BASIS OF STATUS CLASSIFICATION: *Eumeces e. lividus* is restricted to the well-drained sandy soils of the Lake Wales Ridge. Most of this area has already been converted to trailer courts, subdivisions, and citrus groves (Peroni and Abrahamson 1985). Agricultural practices destroy the habitat of *lividus,* as does the lawn turf that accompanies residential development. The Bluetail Mole Skink appears to be rare throughout its limited range, even in optimum habitat. Extensive searching in optimum habitat generally yields about 1 *lividus* for every 20 *N. reynoldsi* encountered.

RECOMMENDATIONS: *Eumeces e. lividus* is protected by the federal government and the State of Florida as a Threatened Species. The Florida Natural Areas Inventory lists the Bluetail Mole Skink as a Special Element and maintains a data base of known localities. Bluetail Mole Skinks are in danger of extinction because their required habitat is threatened with extinction. Restrictions against collecting or possessing the Bluetail Mole Skink are probably of little value, and may be counterproductive because they tend to reduce public awareness of the uniqueness, beauty, and irreplaceable nature of Florida Scrub and the distinctive organisms restricted to Florida Scrub. Restrictions against developing the last remnants of Florida Scrub on the Lake Wales Ridge are sorely needed, but have not been forthcoming from development-oriented state and local governments. It remains to be seen if the current Regional Planning Process can reverse these trends. Because *E. e. lividus* is restricted to such a small region and because it appears to be rare even within optimum habitat in that region, we consider it to be an Endangered Species.

Eumeces e. lividus and the Scrub habitat of which it is a part are protected at The Nature Conservancy's recently acquired Saddle Blanket Lakes Scrub Preserve in Polk County and at the privately-endowed Archbold Biological Station in Highlands County. The recent acquisition of the 5400 ha (13,500 ac) Arbuckle Wildlife Management Area in Polk County by Florida's Conservation and Recreational Lands program brings some of the best Florida Scrub and *lividus* habitat still remaining into public ownership. If the Scrubs on the Arbuckle WMA can be managed for natural diversity and protected from vehicular traffic and commercial forestry development, the future for *E. e. lividus* will look much better than it did a decade ago.

To insure the survival of Florida Scrub and the unique plants and animals restricted to it, including *E. e. lividus,* more Scrub preserves are needed. Scrubs have always been, and are now increasingly, isolated, small habitat islands. Unlike most habitat types, in which the larger the preserved tract, the more species can be retained, Scrubs and the unique Scrub biota must be preserved in numerous, isolated, small tracts. No Scrub known contains all the Lake Wales Ridge endemic Scrub plants and vertebrates, for instance. Efforts should be made to locate and protect Scrubs near the northern, southern, and central portions of the distributions of the various endemic Scrub species. A series of perhaps 10 Scrub preserves on the Lake Wales Ridge, each only 16 to 40 ha (40–100 ac) in size, would probably delay the extinction of the Scrub ecosystem and its endemic plants and animals, including the Bluetail Mole Skink, for a very long time.

Selected References

Campbell, H. W., and S. P. Christman. 1982. The herpetological components of Florida Sandhill and Sand Pine Scrub associations. Pp. 163–171 *in* N. J. Scott (ed.). Herpetological communities: A symposium of the Society for the Study of Amphibians and Reptiles and the Herpetologists' League, August, 1977. U.S. Fish and Wildlife Service, Wildl. Res. Rep. 13.

Christman, S. P. 1970. The possible evolutionary history of two Florida Skinks. Quart. J. Fla. Acad. Sci. 33(4):291–293.

Mount, R. H. 1963. The natural history of the Red-tailed Skink, *Eumeces egregius* (Baird). Amer. Mid. Nat. 70(2):365–385.

Mount, R. H. 1965. Variation and systematics of the scincoid lizard, *Eumeces egregius* (Baird). Bull. Fla. St. Mus. 9(5):183–213.

Mount, R. H. 1968. *Eumeces egregius* (Baird). Cat. Amer. Amphib. Rept.:73.1–73.2.

Peroni, P. A., and W. G. Abrahamson. 1985. Vegetation loss on the southern Lake Wales Ridge. Palmetto Fall 1985:6–7.

Smith, C. R. 1982. Food resource partitioning of fossorial Florida reptiles. Pp. 173–178 *in* N. J. Scott (ed.). Herpetological communities: A symposium of the Society for the Study of Amphibians and Reptiles and the Herpetologists' League, August, 1977. U.S. Fish and Wildlife Service, Wildl. Res. Rep. 13.

U.S. Fish and Wildlife Service. 1987. Endangered and threatened wildlife and plants: Proposed Threatened status for two Florida lizards. Fed. Reg. 52(13): 2242–2246.

White, W. A. 1970. The geomorphology of the Florida Peninsula. Geol. Bull. No. 51, Fla. Dept. Nat. Res. 164 pp.

Prepared by: Steven P. Christman, *Department of Natural Sciences, Florida Museum of Natural History, Gainesville, FL 32611.*

Gopher Tortoise

Gopherus polyphemus (Daudin)

FAMILY TESTUDINIDAE

Order Testudines

OTHER NAME: Gopher.

DESCRIPTION: The Gopher Tortoise is a large terrestrial turtle, averaging 23–28 cm (9–11 in) in carapace length. Maximum length is around 38 cm (15 in). The Gopher Tortoise is characterized by stumpy, elephantine hind feet and flattened, shovel-like forelimbs adapted for digging. The carapace is domed and oblong; coloration is generally tan, brown, or gray. The yellowish or mottled plastron has gular scutes which project anteriorly. The plastron of adult males is somewhat concave. Growth annuli may be conspicuous, particularly in juveniles. The head is wide and scaled, with well-developed integumentary glands beneath the chin. Hatchlings are approximately 4.4 cm (1.7 in) in length and are yellowish-orange in color.

RANGE: The Gopher Tortoise occurs in the Southeastern Coastal Plain from extreme eastern Louisiana to southern South Carolina. In Florida, tortoises still occur in all 67 counties; however, their distribution in the southern Peninsula is limited and fragmented by unsuitable habitat and increased urbanization. Populations also occur on coastal islands and on Cape Sable. The species' current stronghold is southern Georgia and the northern and central portions of the Florida Peninsula.

HABITAT: Three environmental conditions are especially important: well-drained loose soil in which to burrow, adequate low-growing herbs for food, and open sunlit sites for nesting. The Gopher Tortoise is primarily associated with Longleaf Pine–Xerophytic Oak Woodlands (sandhills), but it is also found in Sand Pine scrub, coastal strands, Live Oak ham-

Gopher Tortoise, *Gopherus polyphemus* (photograph by B. W. Mansell).

mocks, dry prairies, pine flatwoods, and mixed hardwood–pine communities. Disturbed habitats, such as roadsides, fencerows, clearings, and old fields, often support relatively high densities.

LIFE HISTORY AND ECOLOGY: Gopher Tortoises excavate burrows, averaging 4.5 m (14.8 ft) in length and 2 m (6.6 ft) in depth and wide enough to allow them to turn around at any point. These burrows provide protection from temperature extremes, desiccation, and predators, and serve as refuges for a variety of other animals. Over 300 species of invertebrates, including obligates such as the Gopher Cricket *(Ceuthrophilus* spp.), have been reported from Gopher Tortoise burrows or the accompanying aprons of sand. Burrows also harbor numerous vertebrate species, e.g., the protected Eastern Indigo Snake *(Drymarchon corais couperi),* Florida Mouse *(Podomys floridanus),* Gopher Frog *(Rana capito),* and Florida Pine Snake *(Pituophis melanoleucus mugitus).* The placement and depth of burrows vary with the soil type, geographic location, and ground water levels. An individual tortoise may use more than one burrow and may excavate new burrows at any time during its life. Gopher Tortoise densities and movements are affected by the amount of herbaceous ground cover. Generally, feeding activity is confined to within 50 m of the burrow. Principal foods include grasses, legumes, and grass-like plants of the sedge and aster families. Legumes appear to be particularly important in the diet of juveniles. Fruits such as blackberries, pawpaws, Gopher Apples, and Saw Palmetto berries are also consumed.

The Gopher Tortoise exhibits deferred sexual maturity, low fecundity,

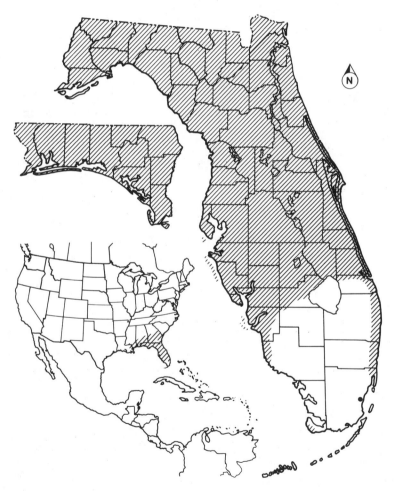

Distribution map of Gopher Tortoise (*Gopherus polyphemus*).

and a long life span. Females reach sexual maturity at 10–20 years of age, depending on latitude. The breeding season is generally considered to be from April to June, but males may attempt to mate throughout the activity season. Nests are usually constructed in the burrow mounds from mid-May to mid-June. Only one clutch is produced annually. Clutch size usually ranges from 3–12, with an average of 6; however, a clutch of 25 eggs has been reported. The incubation period varies latitudinally from about 80–110 days. Predation on nests and hatchlings is heavy. Predators include raccoons, foxes, skunks, armadillos, Coachwhips, Indigo Snakes, and various raptors. Although some hatchlings immediately construct burrows, others may use burrows of adults or merely seek shelter opportunistically under sand or litter. The first years of life are the most critical. Estimated life expectancy is 40–60 years.

SPECIALIZED OR UNIQUE CHARACTERISTICS: The Gopher Tortoise is a key species in Florida's xeric communities. Its burrowing habits not only provide refuges for numerous commensals, but also return leached nutrients to the surface. As it grazes along feeding paths that radiate from the burrow, this reptile serves as a seed dispersal agent for native grasses and forbs.

BASIS OF STATUS CLASSIFICATION: Although still widely distributed in Florida, the Gopher Tortoise has declined and is continuing to decline. Urbanization has severely fragmented populations on the southern coasts. In central Florida, thousands of square kilometers of sandhill habitat have been mined for phosphate or converted to citrus groves or subdivisions. Thickly-planted Slash Pine and Sand Pine monocultures and the lack of prescribed burning have reduced tortoise densities in northern and western Florida. Populations in the Panhandle have been depleted or extirpated as a result of long-term human exploitation. Collection of Gopher Tortoises for races to benefit charitable organizations has also impacted local populations.

RECOMMENDATIONS: Collection of Gopher Tortoises in Florida was prohibited in 1988, and the practice of racing tortoises was banned in 1989. Other conservation measures for this species include establishment of preserves, prescribed burning, protection from illegal harvest, public education, identification of restocking sites, and stronger legislation to protect upland habitats in Florida. Additional studies are needed regarding tortoise use of pine flatwoods and dry prairies.

Selected References

Alford, R. 1980. Population structure of *Gopherus polyphemus* in northern Florida. J. Herpetol. 14:177–182.

Auffenberg, W., and R. Franz. 1982. The status and distribution of the Gopher Tortoise *(Gopherus polyphemus)*. Pp. 95–126 *in* R. B. Bury (ed.). North American tortoises: Conservation and ecology. U.S. Fish and Wildl. Serv., Wildl. Res. Rep. 12.

Auffenberg, W., and J. B. Iverson. 1979. Demography of terrestrial turtles. Pp. 541–569 *in* M. Harless and H. Morlock (eds.). Turtles: Perspectives and research. John Wiley & Sons, New York.

Cox, J., D. Inkley, and R. Kautz. 1987. Ecology and habitat protection needs of Gopher Tortoise *(Gopherus polyphemus)* populations found on lands slated for large-scale development in Florida. Fla. Game and Fresh Water Fish Comm. Nongame Wildl. Program Tech. Rep. No. 4, Tallahassee, Florida. 75 pp.

Diemer, J. E. 1986. The ecology and management of the Gopher Tortoise in the southeastern United States. Herpetologica 42(1):125–133.

Diemer, J. E. 1987. The status of the Gopher Tortoise in Florida. Pp. 72–83 *in* R. Odom, K. Riddleberger, and J. Ozier (eds.). Proc. Third Southeast Nongame and End. Sp. Symp. Ga. Dept. Nat. Resour. Game and Fish Div., Atlanta, Georgia.

Douglass, J. F., and J. N. Layne. 1978. Activity and thermoregulation of the Gopher Tortoise in southern Florida. Herpetologica 34(4):359–374.

Iverson, J. B. 1980. The reproductive biology of *Gopherus polyphemus*. Amer. Midl. Nat. 103:353–359.

Macdonald, L. A., and H. R. Mushinsky. 1988. Foraging ecology of the Gopher Tortoise, *Gopherus polyphemus,* in a sandhill habitat. Herpetologica 44:345–353.

McRae, W. A., J. L. Landers, and J. A. Garner. 1981. Movement patterns and home range of the Gopher Tortoise. Amer. Midl. Nat. 106:165–179.

Taylor, R. W., Jr. 1982. Human predation on the Gopher Tortoise *(Gopherus polyphemus)* in north-central Florida. Bull. Fla. State Mus. Biol. Sci. 28:79–102.

Prepared by: Joan E. Diemer, *Florida Game and Fresh Water Fish Commission, 4005 South Main Street, Gainesville, FL 32601.*

Loggerhead Sea Turtle

Caretta caretta (Linnaeus)

FAMILY CHELONIIDAE

Order Testudines

OTHER NAMES: Caguama (Spanish).

DESCRIPTION: The Loggerhead Sea Turtle is a medium to large turtle adapted to the marine environment. The limbs are modified as flippers, the carapace is streamlined, elongated, and somewhat tapered posteriorly, and the head is large with powerful jaws adapted to crushing mollusks. In Florida, adult carapace lengths range from 70–125 cm (2.3–4.1 ft), and weights reach 70–180 kg (155–400 lb). Adult western Atlantic Loggerheads generally have reddish-brown carapaces with yellow to cream-colored plastrons, whereas hatchlings are brown to reddish-brown dorsally and from buff to gray-black ventrally. The loggerhead can be distinguished from other Florida sea turtles by a combination of characters, including the large size of its head, reddish-brown color, and the presence of two pairs of prefrontal scales on the head and five pairs of pleurals on the carapace.

RANGE: Loggerhead Sea Turtles occur circumglobally. Major nesting grounds are located primarily in temperate and subtropical regions, particularly in the southeastern United States, Mexico, Oman, Australia, South Africa, the Mediterranean, and Japan. In Florida, adult Loggerheads are found in all coastal waters, and subadults frequent the Indian River Lagoon system among other areas. In the United States, most nesting occurs from North Carolina southward around the tip of Florida to the vicinity of Tampa Bay; scattered nesting occurs elsewhere on beaches throughout the Gulf of Mexico. The greatest percentage of Loggerhead nesting in the United States occurs in Florida, primarily from Brevard

Loggerhead Sea Turtle, *Caretta caretta*. Brevard County, Florida (photograph by B. W. Mansell).

County south to Broward County. Nesting concentrations at Jupiter Island/Juno Beach, Hutchinson Island, and in south Brevard County are among the densest in the world, reaching nearly 450 nests per km in some areas. Movement patterns away from the nesting beaches are poorly known, particularly for adult males and juveniles. Hatchlings ride oceanic currents in offshore drift lines in the Atlantic Ocean for several years, and juvenile Florida Loggerheads have been found rafting as far away as the Azores. The overall geographic range of Loggerheads found in Florida waters is extensive and may include many different oceanic habitats, depending on the stage of the life cycle.

HABITAT: The habitat frequented varies as a function of life stage and season. Loggerheads inhabit continental shelves, bays, lagoons, and estuaries in temperate, subtropical, and tropical waters. They occur offshore to the western edge of the Gulf Stream, although most individuals prefer the shallow waters of the continental shelf. In the spring, flotillas rarely are sighted along the outer reefs of the Florida Keys and Cay Sal Bank. Major developmental feeding grounds include large bays, such as Chesapeake Bay in Virginia. Hatchlings and small juveniles are most often associated with floating mats of *Sargassum* in pelagic habitats.

LIFE HISTORY AND ECOLOGY: Nesting in Florida occurs from late April through September. A female deposits an average of 110–120 eggs per nest, and most nest 2–6 times per season at 14-day intervals. Logger-

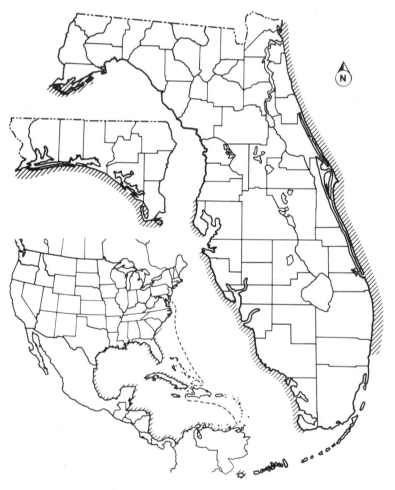

Distribution map of Loggerhead Sea Turtle (*Caretta caretta*). Crosshatching indicates Florida nesting distribution.

heads do not generally nest each year, and most authors ascribe a 2–4 year remigration interval to nesting females. Incubation takes from 50–75 days depending on nest temperature. Hatching most often occurs at night. Hatchlings swim frantically offshore and eventually reach oceanic gyres and drift lines where they raft for several years as juveniles. As sub-adults, they feed in rich coastal developmental habitats, including lagoon-al ecosystems. Sexual maturity is reached at 15–20 years of age depend-ing on growth rate. After nesting, some adults disperse to winter feeding grounds while others remain offshore. Loggerheads also are known to bury into mud in the Canaveral Ship Channel and off West Palm Beach, and this has been termed, perhaps incorrectly, as "hibernation." Logger-heads tagged in Florida have been found in the Bahamas and the Gulf of Mexico, throughout the Caribbean, and as far away as Europe. Little is known of migratory routes or of life history activities away from nesting beaches.

The food of Loggerheads is varied, but consists principally of mol-lusks, crustaceans, and horseshoe crabs. The major predators of nests are raccoons, hatchlings are eaten by ghost crabs, birds, and many marine predators, and adults are preyed upon by sharks.

SPECIALIZED OR UNIQUE CHARACTERISTICS: Loggerhead Sea Turtles nest farther north than any other sea turtle, and they use a wide variety of habitats, both spatially and ecologically, during their long life span. The Florida population is the second largest nesting population in the world, and one of only two that includes some individuals that overwinter by burying in mud. As with other sea turtles, a hatchling's sex is determined by its incubation temperature rather than by genotypic sex determination.

BASIS OF STATUS CLASSIFICATION: As more and more people have moved into Florida, habitat alteration has accelerated along coastal nest-ing beaches. This has resulted in disturbance of nesting females, destruc-tion of nests by off-road vehicles, injuries and death from boat propellers, hatchling disorientation due to bright lights behind beaches, and occa-sional killing of turtles for food, malicious reasons, or in the belief that they compete with or cause problems for fishermen. In marine habitats, thousands of Loggerheads die annually in shrimp trawls (>11,000 per year according to the National Marine Fisheries Service), and such acci-dental drownings, particularly of juveniles, constitute the major imme-diate threat to the species. More long-term threats result from the pollu-tion of the ocean, particularly from petroleum products, and the offshore dumping of refuse, particularly plastics and styrofoam. Loggerheads, especially hatchlings and juveniles, mistake styrofoam and plastic debris, tar balls, and refuse for food. This material clogs the mouth, throat, gut, and nasal passages, and may blind the turtle.

Sea turtle nests are particularly vulnerable to human predation, and poaching continues despite regulations. Although less obvious, the elimination of large mammalian predators and habitat alteration have allowed the proliferation of raccoons in coastal regions. In some areas, the burgeoning raccoon population destroys nearly all sea turtle nests. Nests are also destroyed by natural and human-mediated beach erosion, and by beach cleaning operations. Beach restoration projects may initially inhibit nesting females, but long-term detrimental effects of beach restoration may not be serious if an appropriate sand type is used.

Papillomas, similar to those encountered on Indian River Green Turtles, occasionally occur on Loggerheads in the same area. In addition, a "diseased turtle syndrome" affecting Florida east coast Loggerheads has been identified. The long-term effects of these maladies on Loggerhead populations are unknown.

RECOMMENDATIONS: The single most important conservation measure that can assist Loggerhead survival is the use of turtle excluder devices (TEDS) by shrimp trawlers working off Florida's coastline, particularly in spring and summer months. These lightweight devices fit into the opening of trawl nets and allow trapped turtles and other large by-catch to escape, yet maintain acceptable levels of shrimp catch.

Second, nesting habitat should be acquired, especially beaches supporting large densities of nests. Of particular interest are two beach tracts in Brevard County and Wabasso Beach in Indian River County which are slated for acquisition as part of Florida's Conservation and Recreation Lands (CARL) program.

State and federal regulations regarding protection of sea turtles must be vigorously enforced. In addition, municipalities and county governments should be encouraged to adopt beach lighting ordinances such as have been effectively implemented by a number of local jurisdictions, including the city of Boca Raton and Brevard County. Such ordinances may limit the hours and/or seasons when beach lights may be used, or may require the use of lights that project wavelengths to which hatchling turtles are less sensitive. Restricting off-road vehicle access to beaches during nesting season, requiring beach cleaning operations to use lightweight vehicles or manual pick-up, restoring beaches during winter months prior to nesting, dredging at times when few turtles may be affected, controlling and removing raccoons, and moving eggs to protected hatcheries, especially in areas of high human daytime use, are other measures that can be undertaken to conserve Loggerheads. Because so little time is actually spent on the nesting beach during the course of a Loggerhead's lifetime, increasing emphasis should be placed on protecting habitats away from nesting beaches. Offshore waters used as internesting and feeding habitats, estuaries, ocean rips, convergences, and drift lines, and developmental habitats in bays and lagoons are examples of marine habitats needing particular attention. In Florida, specific regions include the Indian River Lagoon system, Florida Keys, Cedar Keys, and internesting offshore waters of the high density beaches listed above. Marine pollution, including contamination by petroleum products and the indiscriminate dumping of non-biodegradable products, must be eliminated. Offshore oil drilling should not be permitted in sensitive marine ecosystems.

Basic research into Loggerhead movement and activity patterns is required. Research is particularly needed on the life history of all size classes away from nesting beaches, and on males. Coupled with research is the continuing need for education on the biology of Florida's native species and the ecosystems on which they depend. Emphasis should be placed on understanding the biological constraints to conservation, and on the need for ecosystem as well as single-species oriented projects and habitat protection.

Selected References

Carr, A. F. 1952. Handbook of turtles. The turtles of the United States, Canada, and Baja California. Comstock Pub. Assoc., Ithaca, New York. 542 pp.

Carr, A. F. 1986. Rips, FADS, and little Loggerheads. Bioscience 36:92–100.

Carr, A. F. 1987. The impact of nondegradable marine debris on the ecology and survival outlook of sea turtles. Mar. Pollut. Bull. 18(6B):352–356.

Conley, W. J., and B. A. Hoffman. 1987. Nesting activity of sea turtles in Florida, 1979–1985. Fla. Sci. 50:201–210.

Dodd, C. K., Jr. 1988. Synopsis of the biological data on the Loggerhead Sea Turtle *Caretta caretta* (Linnaeus 1758). U.S. Fish and Wildl. Serv., Biol. Rep. 88(14). 110 pp.

Van Meter, V. B. 1983. Florida's sea turtles. Florida Power and Light Company, Miami, Florida. 46 pp.

Weber, M. 1987. TEDS: Salvation for sea turtles? Defenders Mag. 62(1):8–13.

Witzell, W. N. (ed.). 1987. Ecology of east Florida sea turtles. Proc. of the Cape Canaveral, Florida, sea turtle workshop, Miami, Florida, February 26–27, 1985. NOAA Tech. Rep. NMFS 53. 80 pp.

Prepared by: C. Kenneth Dodd, *National Ecology Research Center, U.S. Fish and Wildlife Service, 412 NE 16th Avenue, Room 250, Gainesville, FL 32601.*

Sand Skink

Neoseps reynoldsi Stejneger

FAMILY SCINCIDAE

Order Squamata, Suborder Sauria

OTHER NAMES: Florida Sand Skink.

DESCRIPTION: The Sand Skink is a small, slender, shiny lizard with vestigial, virtually nonfunctional legs and toes. The total length may reach 12.7 cm (5 in), of which about one-half is tail. Sand Skinks are usually some shade of gray or gray-white, or may be light tan colored. The front legs are tiny and have only one toe, and the hind legs are only slightly larger with two toes. During its characteristic "sand-swimming" locomotion, the Sand Skink's front legs are pressed against the body into small grooves, making the animal "snake-like" and facilitating its "swimming" through the sand.

RANGE: The Sand Skink is restricted to central Florida, being known only from Highlands, Polk, Osceola, Orange, Lake, and Marion counties. Sand Skinks reach their greatest abundance in appropriate habitats on the Lake Wales Ridge in Highlands and Polk counties, are common also on the Winter Haven Ridge in Polk County, and are extremely rare and localized in Lake and Marion counties on the Mount Dora Ridge. Sand Skinks have not been found on any of the other central Florida ridges, including the Lakeland, Lake Henry, Brooksville, Orlando, or Bombing Range ridges, nor are they known to occur in adjacent Hardee, Glades, or Sumter counties. The type locality is Fruitland Park in Lake County.

HABITAT: The primary habitat of *Neoseps* is Rosemary Scrub, but it also occurs in Sand Pine Scrub, Oak Scrub, Scrubby Flatwoods, and "Turkey Oak Barrens." The Sand Skink is restricted to microhabitats with loose

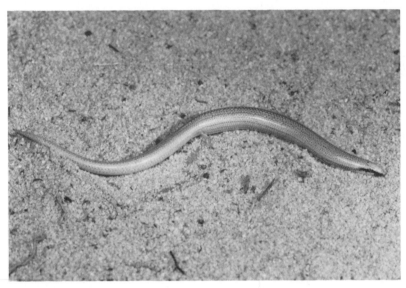

Sand Skink, *Neoseps reynoldsi*. Highlands County, Florida (photograph by B. W. Mansell).

sand and sunny exposures. Because of its restrictive method of locomotion, the Sand Skink cannot live in areas with an abundance of plant
roots, and is absent from High Pine communities except where the native
wiregrass *(Aristida stricta)* has disappeared. In these "Turkey Oak Barrens," *Neoseps* and several other typical scrub species have invaded, no
doubt because the extirpation of the grasses has created soil conditions
similar to those in Scrub. *Neoseps* habitat is characterized by an absence of
ground-covering grasses, an absence of a canopy, and the presence of
scattered shrubs with areas of bare sand (usually white) littered perhaps
with fruticose lichens. Optimum *Neoseps* habitat on the southern Lake
Wales Ridge is a Rosemary Bald within a Scrub community, dominated
by Florida Rosemary *(Ceratiola ericoides)*, scattered Scrub oaks *(Quercus
inopina, Q. chapmanii, Q. geminata)*, and other woody shrubs and peren-
nials, many of which are also endemic to the Central Florida Scrub habitat.

LIFE HISTORY AND ECOLOGY: Sand Skinks spend most of their time 1
to 8 cm (0.5–3.0 in) beneath the surface of the sand, "swimming" up to
surficial plant debris such as palmetto fronds, Spanish Moss, or logs,
where they find their prey, consisting of spiders, ant-lions, termites, bee-
tle larvae, and other small invertebrates. Female *Neoseps* lay two eggs in
the sand, probably under fallen logs in the early summer. Hatchlings

emerge in July at about 2.5 cm (1 in) in length. Sexual maturity may be attained after one year, but this is not known for certain, nor is the normal life span known.

SPECIALIZED OR UNIQUE CHARACTERISTICS: The Sand Skink is the most highly specialized for a fossorial "sand-swimming" existence of any North American lizard, although unrelated lizards in similar habitats in

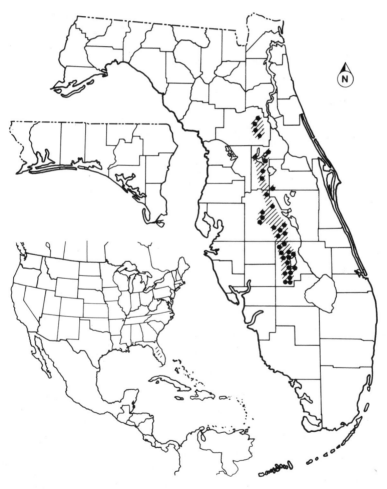

Distribution map of Sand Skink (*Neoseps reynoldsi*). Dots indicate known localities.

Australia, Africa, and India have evolved similar morphology and behavior. The Sand Skink's eyes are greatly reduced; there are no external ear openings; the snout is wedge-shaped, and the lower jaw is countersunk into the upper one. These adaptations allow *Neoseps* to "swim" eel-like through loose sand. *Neoseps* is a characteristic endemic element of the Florida Scrub association. It has no known fossil record, its taxonomic position within the Scincidae (if it is a skink) is unclear, and it is entirely confined to Central Peninsular Florida.

BASIS OF STATUS CLASSIFICATION: *Neoseps* is restricted to the well-drained sandy soils of the Interior Florida Highlands. Most of these areas have already been converted to trailer courts, subdivisions, and citrus groves. *Neoseps* requires loose sand. It cannot tolerate dense ground cover or heavily rooted vegetation. Agricultural practices destroy the habitat of *Neoseps,* as does the lawn turf that accompanies residential development. Although the Sand Skink is still common at many localities, especially in Highlands County, its status may be considered threatened because few of these localities are protected from future development.

RECOMMENDATIONS: *Neoseps* is listed as a Threatened species by the federal government and the State of Florida. The Florida Natural Areas Inventory lists the Sand Skink as a Special Element and maintains a data base of known localities. Sand Skinks are threatened with extinction because their required habitat is threatened with extinction. Within what remnants remain of their habitat, Sand Skinks are often abundant. Restrictions against collecting or possessing the Sand Skink are not only unnecessary, they are in fact counterproductive because they tend to reduce public awareness of the uniqueness, beauty, and irreplaceable nature of Florida Scrub and the distinctive organisms restricted to Florida Scrub. Restrictions against developing the last remnants of Florida Scrub are sorely needed, but have not been forthcoming from development-oriented state and local governments. It remains to be seen if the current Regional Planning Process can reverse these trends.

   Neoseps and the Scrub habitat of which it is a part are protected at The Nature Conservancy's recently-acquired Saddle Blanket Lakes Scrub Preserve in Polk County and at the privately-endowed Archbold Biological Station in Highlands County. The recent acquisition of the 5400 ha (13,500 ac) Arbuckle Wildlife Management Area in Polk County by Florida's Conservation and Recreational Lands program brings some of the best Florida Scrub and *Neoseps* habitat still remaining into public ownership. If the Scrub on the Arbuckle WMA can be managed for natural diversity and protected from vehicular traffic and commercial forestry development, the future for *Neoseps* will look much better than it did a decade ago.

To insure the survival of Florida Scrub and the unique plants and animals restricted to it, including *N. reynoldsi,* more Scrub preserves are needed. Scrubs have always been, and are now increasingly, isolated, small habitat islands. Unlike most habitat types, where the larger the preserved tract, the more species can be retained, Scrubs and the unique Scrub biota must be preserved in numerous, isolated, small tracts. No Scrub known contains all the Lake Wales Ridge endemic Scrub plants and vertebrates, for instance. Efforts should be made to locate and protect Scrubs near the northern, southern, and central portions of the distributions of the various endemic Scrub species. A series of perhaps 10 Scrub preserves on the Lake Wales Ridge, each only 16–40 ha (40–100 ac) in size, would probably delay the extinction of the Scrub ecosystem and its endemic plants and animals for a very long time.

Selected References

Campbell, H. W., and S. P. Christman. 1982. The herpetological components of Florida Sandhill and Sand Pine Scrub associations. Pp. 163–171 *in* N. J. Scott (ed.). Herpetological communities: A symposium of the Society for the Study of Amphibians and Reptiles and the Herpetologists' League, August, 1977. U.S. Fish and Wildlife Service, Wildl. Res. Rep. 13.

Christman, S. P. 1970. The possible evolutionary history of two Florida Skinks. Quart. J. Fla. Acad. Sci. 33(4):291–293.

Myers, C. W., and S. R. Telford. 1965. Food of *Neoseps,* the Florida Sand Skink. Quart. J. Fla. Acad. Sci. 28(2):190–194.

Peroni, P. A., and W. G. Abrahamson. 1985. Vegetation loss on the southern Lake Wales Ridge. Palmetto Fall 1985:6–7.

Smith, C. R. 1982. Food resource partitioning of fossorial Florida reptiles. Pp. 173–178 *in* N. J. Scott (ed.). Herpetological communities: A symposium of the Society for the Study of Amphibians and Reptiles and the Herpetologists' League, August, 1977. U.S. Fish and Wildlife Service, Wildl. Res. Rep. 13.

Telford, S. R. 1959. A study of the Sand Skink, *Neoseps reynoldsi.* Copeia 1959(2): 100–119.

Telford, S. R. 1962. New locality records for the Sand Skink *(Neoseps reynoldsi)* in central Florida, with comments on the habitat. Quart. J. Fla. Acad. Sci. 25(1): 76–77.

Telford, S. R. 1969. *Neoseps reynoldsi* Stejneger. Cat. Amer. Amphib. Rept.:80.1–80.2.

White, W. A. 1970. The geomorphology of the Florida Peninsula. Geol. Bull. No. 51. Fla. Dept. Nat. Res. 164 pp.

Prepared by: Steven P. Christman, *Department of Natural Sciences, Florida Museum of Natural History, Gainesville, FL 32611.*

Florida Scrub Lizard

Sceloporus woodi Stejneger

FAMILY IGUANIDAE

Order Squamata, Suborder Sauria

OTHER NAMES: Scrub Lizard, Rosemary Lizard.

DESCRIPTION: *Sceloporus woodi* is a small, gray or gray-brown, spiny-scaled lizard. This species is sexually dimorphic for adult body size and coloration. Maximum female snout-vent length (SVL) is 63 mm (2.5 in), while that for males is 58 mm (2.3 in). On average, female SVL is 4–5 mm longer than that of males. The dorsal pattern of juvenile lizards consists of two rows of thin, undulating dark bands. This pattern is reminiscent of the pattern found in Eastern Fence Lizards, *Sceloporus undulatus*. Adult female Scrub Lizards retain the juvenile pattern, while the pattern fades in males as they become sexually mature. Adult males possess a bright turquoise patch on both sides of the belly. Along the midline these patches are bordered by black pigmentation. The throat of an adult male is black and has a small turquoise patch on either side at the base. Sometimes faded turquoise patches can be seen on the bellies of adult females. During the breeding season adult females may also exhibit a large diffuse area of orange coloration on the lateral surfaces. A distinguishing characteristic of all Scrub Lizards is the presence of a thick brown dorsolateral stripe running from the neck through the base of the tail.

RANGE: The distribution of the Scrub Lizard is highly disjunct, probably due to the patchy distribution of suitable habitat. Scrub Lizards can be found in many of the extensive Sand Pine *(Pinus clausa)* scrubs in Ocala National Forest (ONF) in north-central Florida. Most of ONF is located in Marion County. There are few records for Scrub Lizards in the southern portion of Putnam County and the northern portion of

141

Florida Scrub Lizard, *Sceloporus woodi*. Highlands County, Florida (photograph by R. W. Van Devender).

Lake County adjacent to the northern and southern borders, respectively, of ONF. In south-central Florida, numerous sites are located in scattered scrub areas located in Polk and Highlands counties. Atlantic Coast populations can still be found in Brevard, Indian River, St. Lucie, Martin, Palm Beach, and Broward counties. Populations of Scrub Lizards along the southwestern Gulf Coast of Florida in Lee and Collier counties may still exist.

HABITAT: This heliothermic lizard prefers open sandy areas bordering Sand Pine scrub and sandhill associations. Like many of its congeners, the Scrub Lizard could be described as a forest edge species. A dense crown of Sand Pine comprises the overstory of scrub habitat. The understory is composed primarily of scrub oaks *(Quercus chapmanii, Q. myrtifolia,* and *Q. virginiana),* while much of the ground is covered with lichen and leaf litter. Sandhill habitats are dominated by Longleaf Pine *(P. palustris)* and Turkey Oak *(Q. laevis).* Wiregrasses *(Aristida, Sporobolus)* are characteristic of this plant association. Rosemary *(Ceratiola)* occurs in both type habitats, especially where fire is uncommon. Both plant associations occur on well drained, deep sand soil.

LIFE HISTORY AND ECOLOGY: A reproductive cycle has been documented for scrub lizards in Ocala National Forest. Females reach sexual maturity around 47 mm (1.9 in) SVL. Male SVL is probably slightly smaller
at maturity. Courtship and mating occur from late March through June.
For females in their second reproductive season, vitellogenesis begins in
March, and oviposition of the first clutch occurs around mid-April.

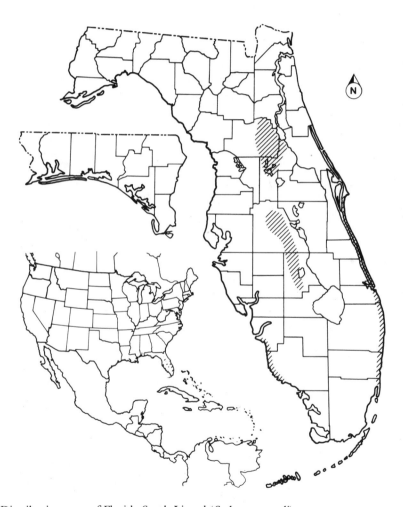

Distribution map of Florida Scrub Lizard (*Sceloporus woodi*).

Smaller females that are in their first reproductive season may begin to yolk follicles somewhat later, in April or May. Females that have not reached maturity by March may mature and yolk a clutch in mid- to late summer. It has been estimated that the largest females could lay up to five clutches in a single reproductive season under optimal conditions; however, three clutches/season is more likely. No females are gravid after August. Average clutch size is 4, and clutches range from 2–8 eggs. Average egg weight at oviposition is 0.30 gm (.01 oz). Hatchlings range from 20–25 mm (0.8–1.0 in) SVL and weigh around 0.40 gm (0.014 oz). Eggs from clutches oviposited in April may take 75 days to develop, but, as ground temperatures get warmer in the summer, eggs from late season clutches probably take less time. Hatching occurs from late June until early November. Hatchlings reach sexual maturity in 10–11 months. Scrub Lizards are sit-and-wait predators that eat ants, beetles, spiders, and other small arthropods. While active, lizards can be found on the ground or low on tree trunks.

SPECIALIZED OR UNIQUE CHARACTERISTICS: Most of the over 50 species in the genus *Sceloporus* seem well adapted to xeric environments, and the Scrub Lizard is no exception. Sand Pine scrub habitat occurs on high, well drained soil, and, although rainfall totals can be quite high, the soil may be very dry. Scrub Lizards, which are found only in Florida, have adapted to this unique plant association.

BASIS OF STATUS CLASSIFICATION: The Committee has changed the status of the Scrub Lizard from Rare to Threatened. This change in status may be most beneficial to coastal populations, which are rapidly disappearing as a result of habitat destruction. Gulf Coast populations are critically threatened at present and may disappear soon.

RECOMMENDATIONS: Very little is known about the demography, life history, ecology, and behavior of *S. woodi*. The large population of lizards found in Ocala National Forest offers excellent opportunities for research in these areas. State agencies should stimulate interest in the study of Scrub Lizards. All research on this species should be regulated and should require submission of a written proposal.

Preservation of important scrub habitats would serve to protect a number of scrub species in addition to *S. woodi*. An immediate effort should be made to prevent the Gulf Coast population from going extinct.

Selected References

DeMarco, V. 1989. Annual variation in the seasonal shift in egg size and clutch size in *Sceloporus woodi*. Oecologia 80:525–532.

Demarco, V. 1992. Embryonic development times and egg retention in four species of sceloporine lizards. Functional Ecol. In press.

Enge, K. M., M. M. Bentzien, and F. Percival. 1986. Florida Scrub Lizard status survey. Technical Report No. 26. Report to the U.S. Fish and Wildlife Service, Jacksonville Endangered Species Office.

Jackson, J. F. 1973. Distribution and population phenetics of the Florida Scrub Lizard, *Sceloporus woodi*. Copeia 1973(4):746–761.

Jackson, J. F., and S. R. Telford. 1974. Reproductive ecology of the Florida Scrub Lizard, *Sceloporus woodi*. Copeia 1974(3):689–694.

Laessle, A. M. 1958. The origin and successional relationship of sandhill vegetation and Sand–Pine scrub. Ecol. Monogr. 28(4):361–387.

Lee, S. D., J. B. Funderburg, and L. R. Franz. 1974. Growth and feeding behavior in the endemic Florida Scrub Lizard, *Sceloporus woodi* Stejneger. Bull. Md. Herp. Soc. 10:16–19.

Prepared by: Vincent DeMarco, *Department of Zoology, 223 Carr Hall, University of Florida, Gainesville, FL 32611.*

Big Pine Key Ringneck Snake

Diadophis punctatus acricus Paulson

FAMILY COLUBRIDAE

Order Squamata, Suborder Serpentes

OTHER NAMES: Ringnecked Snake.

DESCRIPTION: The Big Pine Key Ringneck Snake is a small, black snake usually less than 30 cm (12 in) long. Dorsally, the anterior half is slate gray, giving way to black on the posterior half. The characteristic neck ring is poorly developed or absent in this race. The dorsal surface of the head is grayish brown and spotted. The ventral surface is pale anteriorly and yellow to orange posteriorly. Scales are smooth and the anal plate is divided. Dark pigment on the upper labials is diffuse and not confined to discrete spots as in mainland ringneck snakes.

RANGE: The species is widespread in the eastern United States and is distributed somewhat more sporadically to the Pacific Coast and into Mexico. Seven subspecies occur in the United States. The Lower Keys race has been reported only from Big Pine, Little Torch, and Middle Torch keys. It has been speculated but not documented that populations also exist on the following keys: No Name, Ramrod, Cudjoe, Summerland, and Sugarloaf.

HABITAT: The Big Pine Key Ringneck Snake is found in rocky pine scrub and edges of tropical hardwood hammocks.

LIFE HISTORY AND ECOLOGY: Little information is available on reproduction or microhabitat. A captive specimen was reported to have eaten small frogs and lizards. Specimens have been found crossing roads at night and under flat rocks and boards.

Big Pine Key Ringneck, *Diadophis punctatus acricus*. Big Pine Key, Monroe County, Florida (photograph by S. P. Christman).

SPECIALIZED OR UNIQUE CHARACTERISTICS: This unusual little snake was first described in 1966. It is unique among eastern *Diadophis* in lacking a well-developed neck ring, generally considered characteristic of the species.

BASIS OF STATUS CLASSIFICATION: The snake is apparently neither widespread nor common and could easily become endangered by widespread development of living, recreational, and commercial areas.

RECOMMENDATIONS: There is an urgent need for field work to establish life history parameters of this snake.

Selected References

Carr, A. F. 1940. A contribution to the herpetology of Florida. Univ. Fla. Publ., Biol. Sci. Ser. 3(1):97–98.

Duellman, W. E., and A. Schwartz. 1958. Amphibians and reptiles of southern Florida. Bull. Fla. State Mus. 3(5):181–324.

Lazell, J. D. 1989. Wildlife of the Florida Keys. Island Press, Washington, D. C. 253 pp.

Paulson, D. R. 1966. Variation in some snakes from the Florida Keys. Quart. J. Fla. Acad. Sci. 29(4):295–308.

Prepared by (1978): W. G. Weaver, *Department of Biology, Miami-Dade Community College, Medical Center Campus, 950 NW 20th Street, Miami,*

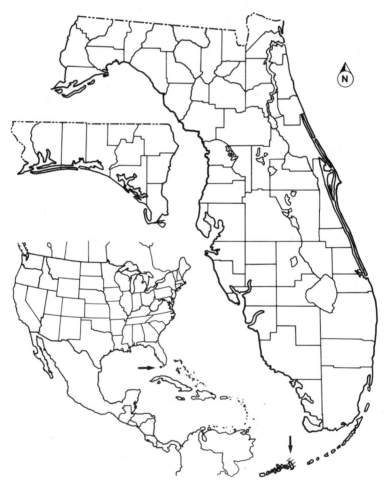

Distribution map of Big Pine Key Ringneck Snake (*Diadophis punctatus acricus*).

FL 33127; and Steven P. Christman, *Department of Natural Sciences, Florida Museum of Natural History, Gainesville, FL 32611.* (1990: Updated by Paul E. Moler, *Florida Game and Fresh Water Fish Commission, 4005 South Main Street, Gainesville, FL 32601.*)

Short-tailed Snake

Stilosoma extenuatum Brown

FAMILY COLUBRIDAE

Order Squamata, Suborder Serpentes

OTHER NAMES: None.

DESCRIPTION: *Stilosoma extenuatum* is a slender, smooth-scaled snake, with a cylindrical body form. The head is not distinct from the body, and the tail tapers abruptly and represents no more than 10% of the body length. The dorsal ground color is a silvery-gray with a series of 50–80 dark brown dorsal blotches separated by yellowish, orange, or red interspaces and with a series of lateral blotches alternating with the dorsal series. The belly is strongly blotched. Although three subspecies were once recognized, the species is now considered to be monotypic. The cylindrical body form, blotched pattern with colored interspaces, and short tail will separate this species from all other Florida snakes.

RANGE: The Short-tailed Snake is endemic to Florida; it occurs from Suwannee and Columbia counties to Hillsborough, Orange, and Highlands counties. The type locality of the species is Lake Kerr, Marion County, Florida.

HABITAT: *Stilosoma extenuatum* is restricted chiefly to Longleaf Pine–Turkey Oak plant associations. It occasionally is found in upland hammock and Sand Pine scrub, but is usually closely adjacent to Longleaf Pine–Turkey Oak stands. Two specimens were dug from a sphagnum bog adjacent to a stand of the typical habitat (Carr 1940 and personal communication).

The ecological factors, other than preferred habitat distribution, which limit the distribution of this species are not known. Preliminary laboratory data indicate that the species selects Norfolk, Blanton fine, and St.

Short-tailed Snake, *Stilosoma extenuatum*. Hillsborough County, Florida (photograph by B. W. Mansell).

Lucie soils over a variety of other types for burrowing when placed in choice situations. The extensive stands of Longleaf Pine–Turkey Oak habitat (now chiefly Turkey Oak) in Marion and Lake counties still maintain populations, and stands of apparently acceptable habitat still exist scattered elsewhere throughout its original range.

LIFE HISTORY AND ECOLOGY: Little is known of the life history and ecology of this species. It is a burrower, seldom seen above ground except in spring and fall (April and October). In captivity it feeds readily on small, smooth-scaled snakes, especially Florida Crowned Snakes *(Tantilla relicta),* but only rarely accepts lizards. Its chief ecological characteristic of concern is its restriction to a rapidly disappearing habitat type.

SPECIALIZED OR UNIQUE CHARACTERISTICS: *Stilosoma* is generically endemic to Florida and monotypic, one of very few such forms. Recent work suggests it is allied with the Kingsnakes (genus *Lampropeltis*). While possessing little aesthetic appeal except to aficionados, its zoogeographic and biosystematic importance to scientists would rate it among the most interesting of North American snakes. Its ecological role in the habitat is unknown but not necessarily insignificant and deserves further study.

BASIS OF STATUS CLASSIFICATION: *Stilosoma extenuatum* is seriously threatened by competition with man for habitat. The well-drained soils on which this species occurs are under intensive development pressure for citrus production and building sites, and the habitat is rapidly being lost. Harvest of the Longleaf Pine and subsequent timber management, or conversion of the habitat to pure Turkey Oak, also appears to severely affect the species. Clearcutting and other timber management programs

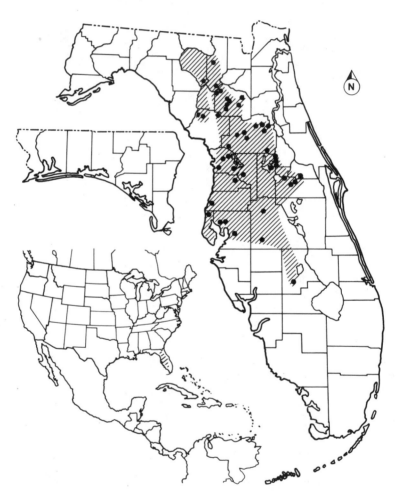

Distribution map of Short-tailed Snake (*Stilosoma extenuatum*). Dots indicate known localities.

in Sand Pine scrub may be of serious concern. Few areas in which this species occurs appear secure from serious threat in the immediate future.

RECOMMENDATIONS: Preservation of the Longleaf Pine–Turkey Oak and Sand Pine scrub habitats is required for *Stilosoma*. The Ocala National Forest currently contains one of the largest blocks of appropriate habitat remaining, and all efforts should be made to prevent degradation of habitat there. Peripheral populations should be protected by habitat acquisition or ecological design of developments in Citrus, Sumter, Hernando, Pasco, and Pinellas counties and Alachua, Columbia, and Suwannee counties. This species appears able to coexist with man as long as development is not too intense. Zoning of developments in critical areas to require one acre homesites which retain the native plant and animal species, or agricultural or industrial developments which provide equal amenities, may provide for the continued existence of this species even in areas subject to necessary development. Care should be taken in such developments to preserve the invertebrate and small vertebrate fauna on which this species probably depends.

Selected References

Allen, R., and W. T. Neill. 1953. The Short-tailed Snake. Fla. Wildlife 6(11):8–9.

Carr, A. F. 1934. Notes on the habits of the Short-tailed Snake. Copeia 1934(2): 138–139.

Carr, A. F. 1940. A contribution to the herpetology of Florida. Univ. Fla. Publ., Biol. Sci. Ser. 3(1):1–118.

Dowling, H. R., and L. R. Maxson. 1990. Genetics and taxonomic relations of the short-tailed snakes, genus *Stilosoma*. J. Zool. 221(1):77–85.

Highton, R. 1956. Systematics and variation of the endemic Florida snake genus *Stilosoma*. Bull. Fla. State Mus. 1(2):73–96.

Highton, R. 1976. *Stilosoma, S. extenuatum*. Cat. Amer. Amphib. Rept.:183.1–183.2.

Mushinsky, H. R. 1984. Observations on the feeding habits of the Short-tailed Snake, *Stilosoma extenuatum* in captivity. Herpetol. Rev. 15(3):67–68.

Woolfenden, G. E. 1962. A range extension and subspecific relations of the Short-tailed Snake, *Stilosoma extenuatum*. Copeia 1962(3):648–649.

Prepared by (1978): Howard W. Campbell (deceased), *National Fish and Wildlife Laboratory, 412 NE 16th Avenue, Room 250, Gainesville, FL 32601.* (1990: Revised by Paul E. Moler, *Florida Game and Fresh Water Fish Commission, 4005 South Main Street, Gainesville, FL 32601.*)

Florida Brown Snake,
Lower Keys population
Storeria dekayi victa Hay
FAMILY COLUBRIDAE
Order Squamata, Suborder Serpentes

OTHER NAMES: DeKay's Snake.

DESCRIPTION: *Storeria dekayi victa* is a spotted brown snake, usually less than 30 cm (11.8 in) long. The dorsal ground color may be various shades of brown. A faint nuchal band is present. The belly is pale, usually with a spot on the lateral edges of each ventral scale. The anal plate is divided and the scales are strongly keeled. The Brown Snakes from the Lower Keys are quite different than those from mainland Florida in several respects. Lower Keys Brown Snakes usually have two preocular scales instead of one. They have less ventral pigment than peninsular Brown Snakes and generally a reduced head pattern.

RANGE: The species lives throughout the eastern United States. The Florida Brown Snake, *S. d. victa*, occurs from southeastern Georgia south into Florida. Specimens are known from the following Lower Keys: Big Pine, Little Torch, Middle Torch, No Name, and Sugarloaf.

HABITAT: On the Lower Keys, Brown Snakes occur in rocky pine forests, in hardwood hammocks, and near aquatic situations, usually under rocks.

LIFE HISTORY AND ECOLOGY: Practically nothing is known about the Lower Keys population. They are smaller than the mainland forms, and decidedly less aquatic than peninsular *S. d. victa*. Although Florida Brown Snakes are often associated with aquatic vegetation, those from the Lower Keys appear to be entirely terrestrial.

Florida Brown Snake, *Storeria dekayi victa*. Big Pine Key, Monroe County, Florida (photograph by S. P. Christman).

SPECIALIZED OR UNIQUE CHARACTERISTICS: In many respects, the Brown Snakes from the Lower Keys are more like those from north Florida than those from the nearby mainland and Everglades regions. This appears to be a relatively common phenomenon, and one which needs more investigation.

BASIS OF STATUS CLASSIFICATION: Massive commercial development in the Lower Keys may result in extinction of this race in that area.

RECOMMENDATIONS: Preservation of selected habitat areas and more study of the Florida Brown Snake are necessary to insure the survival of these populations.

Selected References

Carr, A. F., and C. J. Goin. 1959. Reptiles, amphibians and fresh water fishes of Florida. University of Florida Press, Gainesville. 341 pp.

Duellman, W. E., and A. Schwartz. 1958. Amphibians and reptiles of southern
    Florida. Bull. Fla. State Mus. 3(5):181–324.
Lazell, J. D. 1989. Wildlife of the Florida Keys. Island Press, Washington, D. C.
    253 pp.
Paulson, D. R. 1966. Variation in some snakes from the Florida Keys. Quart. J.
    Fla. Acad. Sci. 29(4):295–308.

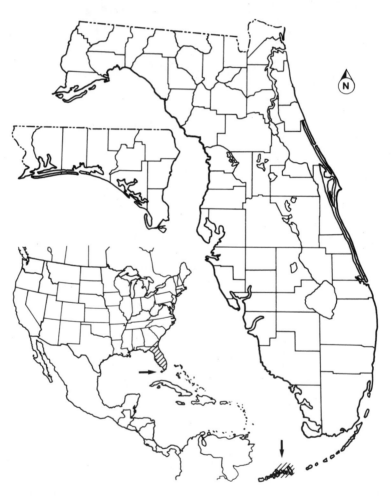

Distribution map of Florida Brown Snake (*Storeria dekayi victa*).
(Lower Keys population only)

Prepared by (1978): W. G. Weaver, *Department of Biology, Miami-Dade Community College, Medical Center Campus, 950 NW 20th Street, Miami, FL 33127;* and Steven P. Christman, *Department of Natural Sciences, Florida Museum of Natural History, Gainesville, FL 32611.* (1990: Updated by Paul E. Moler, *Florida Game and Fresh Water Fish Commission, 4005 South Main Street, Gainesville, FL 32601.*)

Rim Rock Crowned Snake

Tantilla oolitica Telford

FAMILY COLUBRIDAE

Order Squamata, Suborder Serpentes

OTHER NAMES: Miami Crowned Snake, Miami Black-headed Snake.

DESCRIPTION: The Rim Rock Crowned Snake is light brown or tan; the head and nape of the neck are black. The scales are smooth. The maximum length is about 25 cm (10 in). This snake cannot be confused with any other in the Miami–Upper Keys area. Detailed scale and anatomical differences separate it from the more northerly Peninsula Crowned Snake (*Tantilla relicta*); it has more ventral scales and fewer subcaudals, on the average, and has two enlarged basal hooks on the hemipenes instead of one.

RANGE: The Rim Rock Crowned Snake is found in Dade and Monroe counties, Florida, on the Eastern Rock Rim of Miami oolite and on Key Largo, Upper Matecumbe Key, and Grassy Key. A *Tantilla* in the Milwaukee Public Museum (MPM 2596) is reportedly from Key West. Scalation and pattern of this specimen are consistent with those of *T. oolitica* (D. Auth, personal communication), but confirmation of the occurrence of *Tantilla* in the Lower Keys is needed. The type locality is a vacant lot at SW 27th Avenue, near SW 24th Street, Miami, Dade County, Florida.

HABITAT: Although habitat requirements are poorly known, *T. oolitica* is apparently eurytopic. Specimens have been taken in sandy or rocky soils in Slash Pine (*Pinus elliottii*) flatwoods, tropical hammock, and vacant lots and pastures with shrubby growth and scattered Slash Pine.

LIFE HISTORY AND ECOLOGY: Little is known about the life history of this species. It is secretive and a burrower, usually found beneath trash or

Rim Rock Crowned Snake, *Tantilla oolitica*. Key Largo, Monroe County, Florida
(photograph by B. W. Mansell).

rocks or in rotten logs. Other species of *Tantilla* are dietary specialists,
feeding primarily on centipedes and possibly spiders, and the same is
likely true of *T. oolitica.*

SPECIALIZED OR UNIQUE CHARACTERISTICS: *Tantilla oolitica* is
endemic to a small area in southeastern Florida but appears morphologically most similar to *Tantilla coronata* of the southeastern United States,
including the western Florida Panhandle. It is separated from this species
by intervening populations of a related but less similar species, *T. relicta.*
A similar pattern of distribution and relationships is found in only a few
other species and is of considerable biosystematic and zoogeographic interest. Its ecological role in the communities it inhabits is unknown but
not necessarily insignificant.

BASIS OF STATUS CLASSIFICATION: *Tantilla oolitica* is threatened by
rapid loss of habitat throughout its circumscribed range. Its ability to
maintain populations in edificarian situations is to its advantage, but the
rapid habitat modifications underway throughout its range can be expected to soon eliminate even marginally suitable habitat. The increasing

protection of upper Key Largo through Federal (Crocodile Lake National Wildlife Refuge) and State (John Pennekamp Coral Reef State Park, Key Largo Hammocks, Port Bougainville) acquisition will assure at least one large, secure tract of *T. oolitica* habitat remains.

RECOMMENDATIONS: As nothing is known of the limiting factors for this species, it is difficult to make specific suggestions for its survival

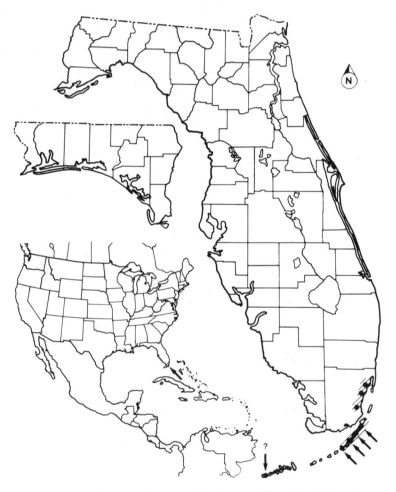

Distribution map of Rim Rock Crowned Snake (*Tantilla oolitica*). Question mark indicates a questionable record.

beyond the preservation of tracts of suitable habitat. It should be noted, however, that the species does appear to tolerate rather severely modified habitat conditions. Thus, the incorporation of environmental considerations into open space design, public parks, and green belts along highways and throughout low-density residential developments, for example, might contribute significantly to its survival. Minimum design criteria should include retaining a maximum of the native plant and animal (especially invertebrate) species in these areas by reducing areas planted in lawns and ornamentals as far as is consistent with primary uses of the areas. Development and subsequent use of the areas should be done to minimize alteration of substrate characteristics by compaction and alteration of the water table. If a reasonably natural complex of plants and invertebrates could be retained over a significant portion of this species' range, it might be able to survive in the face of the urbanization of southeastern Florida.

Selected References

Duellman, W. E., and A. Schwartz. 1958. Amphibians and reptiles of southern Florida. Bull. Fla. St. Mus. 3(5):181–324.

Porras, L., and L. D. Wilson. 1979. New distributional records for *Tantilla oolitica* Telford (Reptilia, Serpentes, Colubridae) from the Florida Keys. J. Herpetol. 13(2):218–220.

Telford, S. R., Jr. 1966. Variation among the southeastern crowned snakes, genus *Tantilla*. Bull. Fla. St. Mus. 10(7):261–304.

Prepared by: Howard W. Campbell (deceased), *National Fish and Wildlife Laboratory, U.S. Fish and Wildlife Service, 412 NE 16th Avenue, Room 250, Gainesville, FL 32601;* and Paul E. Moler, *Florida Game and Fresh Water Fish Commission, 4005 South Main Street, Gainesville, FL 32601.*

Florida Ribbon Snake,
Lower Keys population
Thamnophis sauritus sackeni (Kennicott)
FAMILY COLUBRIDAE
Order Squamata, Suborder Serpentes

OTHER NAMES: Ribbon Snake, Southern Ribbon Snake.

DESCRIPTION: The Florida Ribbon Snake is a small, slender snake with a pair of lateral, longitudinal stripes. Most individuals have well-developed brown, yellow, or orange vertebral stripes bordered by two narrow black stripes. The ventral surface is pale yellow. The scales are keeled and the anal plate is single. The tail is proportionately longer than in mainland ribbon snakes. Although *T. s. sackeni* is usually characterized by having eight supralabials, some specimens from the Lower Keys have only seven.

RANGE: The Florida Ribbon Snake is common in most of Florida. The distinctive Lower Keys population is known only from Big Pine, Cudjoe, Middle Torch, Upper Sugarloaf, and No Name keys.

HABITAT: This species is generally found at the edges of almost any freshwater body. In the Lower Keys, however, the Florida Ribbon Snake inhabits mangrove and spartina habitats as well as freshwater situations.

LIFE HISTORY AND ECOLOGY: The Ribbon Snake is amphibious and a good climber. The Florida Ribbon Snake is known to eat frogs and fish. On the Lower Keys, Ribbon Snakes also eat lizards. Young are born alive in the early summer. Reported clutch sizes are 5–8, small compared to mainland Ribbon Snakes.

SPECIALIZED OR UNIQUE CHARACTERISTICS: The Lower Keys Ribbon Snake is very poorly known. Its biogeographic affinities, like several

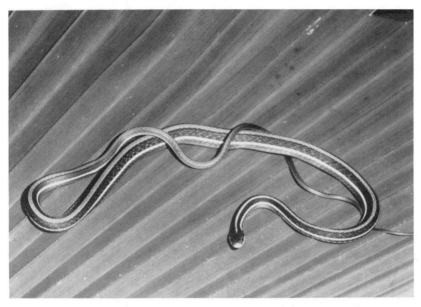

Florida Ribbon Snake, *Thamnophis sauritus sackeni*. No Name Key, Monroe County, Florida (photograph by B. W. Mansell).

other Lower Keys plants and animals, probably lie with more northern populations rather than with populations from southern Florida.

BASIS OF STATUS CLASSIFICATION: Until exploitation and development of the Lower Keys is under better control, most of the unique fauna must be considered Threatened. Although the National Key Deer Wildlife Refuge still remains a sanctuary for Lower Key plants and animals, the remainder of the islands is essentially an "extinction-trap" for much of their flora and fauna.

RECOMMENDATIONS: Preservation of permanent freshwater bodies on the Keys may be necessary for the continued existence of these populations in that area. More study is needed to determine the requirements of these interesting Ribbon Snakes.

Selected References

Carr, A. F. 1940. A contribution to the herpetology of Florida. Univ. Fla. Publ., Biol. Sci. Ser. 3(1):97–98.

Duellman, W. E., and A. Schwartz. 1958. Amphibians and reptiles of southern Florida. Bull. Fla. State Mus. 3(5):181–324.

Lazell, J. D. 1989. Wildlife of the Florida Keys. Island Press, Washington, D. C. 253 pp.

Paulson, D. R. 1966. Variation in some snakes from the Florida Keys. Quart. J. Fla. Acad. Sci. 29(4):295–308.

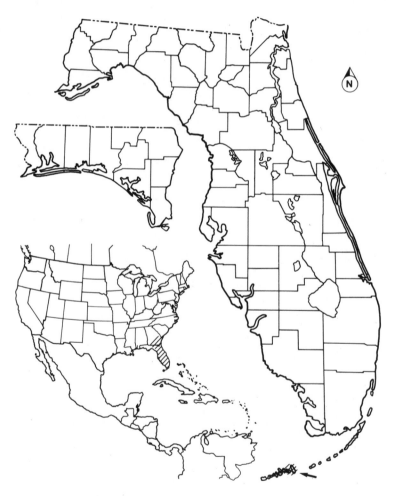

Distribution map of Florida Ribbon Snake (*Thamnophis sauritus sackeni*). (Lower Keys population only)

Prepared by (1978): W. G. Weaver, *Department of Biology, Miami-Dade Community College, Medical Center Campus, 950 NW 20th Street, Miami, FL 33127;* and Steven P. Christman, *Department of Natural Sciences, Florida Museum of Natural History, Gainesville, FL 32611.* (1990: Updated by Paul E. Moler, *Florida Game and Fresh Water Fish Commission, 4005 South Main Street, Gainesville, FL 32601*).

River Cooter

Pseudemys concinna (Le Conte)

FAMILY EMYDIDAE

Order Testudines

OTHER NAMES: Locally known as River Turtle, Suwannee Chicken, Suwannee Cooter, Suwannee Turtle, Mobile Cooter, Mobilian, Slider, Streaky-legs, and Streaky-neck.

DESCRIPTION: A large (up to 40 cm [16 in]) emydid turtle with a relatively smooth, dark, streamlined carapace, somewhat lower than that of similar species and often serrated and slightly flared posteriorly. The ground color of the carapace is brown to black and marked by a faint reticulated pattern. A light yellow posteriorly directed "C" in conjunction with a series of concentric circles or lines on the second costal scute is diagnostic but may be difficult to see unless the shell is wet. The plastron varies from yellow to bright orange and typically bears a dark, seam-following figure that tends to fade in adults. The marginals are generally marked ventrally by large, light-centered dark spots, while an additional dark bar frequently extends across each bridge. Head, neck, and legs are dark with numerous whitish to yellow-orange stripes. Mature males are somewhat smaller than females and possess greatly elongated foreclaws and enlarged tails. Young are marked like adults but brighter, the carapace being greenish; the upper shell of hatchlings is approximately 3.5 to 4.0 cm (about 1.5 in) long.

RANGE: The River Cooter is endemic to the Southeastern Coastal Plain and Piedmont of the United States, where it ranges northward to Virginia and Illinois, southward to central Florida, and westward to Texas and northern Mexico. In Florida, the species is restricted to Gulf Coastal drainages. Traditionally, five subspecies have been recognized rangewide, but recently this has been the subject of considerable scientific disagree-

River Cooter, *Pseudemys concinna*. Wakulla County, Florida (photograph by D. R. Jackson).

ment. Most authorities still recognize *P. c. suwanniensis* as that population from the Tampa Bay region (Alafia River) northwestward to the Apalachicola River. River Cooters in the remainder of the Florida Panhandle are currently considered intergradient with other subspecies. The species is seemingly absent from a number of smaller rivers with headwaters below 7.6 m (25 ft), though this requires confirmation.

HABITAT: In Florida, the River Cooter is restricted to rivers, spring runs, and associated backwaters and impoundments that drain into the Gulf of Mexico. Abundant aquatic vegetation, such as *Naias* and *Sagittaria*, is essential to maintaining healthy populations. Although this turtle has been reported from estuaries, river mouths, and marine grass flats, the salinities at these sites have not been recorded, and the salinity tolerance of the species is poorly known.

LIFE HISTORY AND ECOLOGY: At least in Florida, the River Cooter appears to be almost exclusively herbivorous; it feeds principally on submergent aquatic vegetation such as *Naias*, *Sagittaria*, and *Ceratophyllum*. Rarely venturing onto land except to nest, this turtle spends considerable time basking on logs, rocks, and stumps, from which it warily drops at the slightest approach.

Nesting occurs in late spring and summer; in Florida, most nesting occurs from April through early August. The species shares with its close relative, *P. floridana*, the unique and remarkable habit of digging a nest with three holes instead of the usual one. Clutch size is related to female size and ranges from approximately 10 to 25 eggs. Individual females may nest as many as six times in a single season; however, in at least some

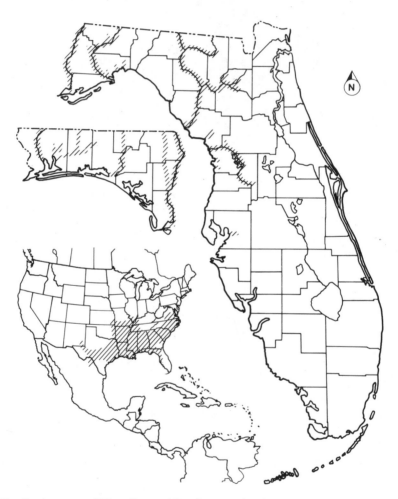

Distribution map of River Cooter (*Pseudemys concinna*).

areas, most nests are destroyed by predators, principally raccoons and Fish Crows. Surviving eggs normally hatch in 70 to 90 days, although the young remain underground for some time before emerging.

SPECIALIZED OR UNIQUE CHARACTERISTICS: *Pseudemys c. suwanniensis* is the largest and darkest of all North American *Pseudemys*. Strongly adapted for a riverine existence, it is perhaps the fastest swimmer among North American emydids. As one moves westward in Florida, the species develops characteristics, such as cusped jaws and a reddish plastron, that are more characteristic of the *rubriventris* group of *Pseudemys*. Elsewhere, considerable difficulty has been encountered in distinguishing the species from *P. floridana*.

BASIS OF STATUS CLASSIFICATION: Although few quantitative data are available, many biologists and other longtime Florida residents believe that population densities of this species are considerably lower in most rivers than they once were. Large numbers of *P. concinna* are known to have been taken in the past for human consumption, which prompted the Florida Game and Fresh Water Fish Commission to establish legal harvest limits for the species. Its habitual use of certain basking and nesting sites makes this turtle extremely vulnerable to collection or wanton destruction, particularly as its riverine habitats are almost completely accessible to man. Several inhabited rivers, including sections of both the Suwannee and Apalachicola systems, have been degraded by dredging, impoundment, mining, and several other forms of pollution, all of which can destroy the turtles' food supplies if not the turtles themselves.

RECOMMENDATIONS: Present population densities and distribution should be established precisely so that baseline data will be available from which to determine future population changes. Inhabited rivers should be protected from habitat degradations resulting from impoundment, dredging, diversion, development within floodplains, and all forms of pollution. Take of the species for personal consumption should be strictly regulated on a statewide basis, with prohibition of any harvest during the nesting season. The use of basking traps and collection for commercial purposes should be banned. Potential river users should be made aware of the protected status of the species by means of strategically placed signs and posters as well as the inclusion of pertinent information within fishing regulation handbooks.

Selected References

Carr, A. F. 1952. Handbook of turtles: Turtles of the United States, Canada and Baja California. Cornell University Press, Ithaca, New York. 542 pp.

Ernst, C. H., and R. W. Barbour. 1972. Turtles of the United States. University Press of Kentucky. 347 pp.

Jackson, C. G., Jr. 1970. A biometrical study of growth in *Pseudemys concinna suwanniensis*. I. Copeia 1970:528–534.

Jackson, C. G., Jr., and M. M. Jackson. 1968. The egg and hatchling of the Suwannee terrapin. Quart. J. Fla. Acad. Sci. 31:199–204.

Marchand, L. J. 1942. A contribution to the knowledge of the natural history of certain freshwater turtles. M. S. thesis, University of Florida, Gainesville. 83 pp.

Ward, J. P. 1984. Relationships of chrysemyd turtles of North America (Testudines:Emydidae). Spec. Publ. Mus. Texas Tech Univ. (21):1–50.

Prepared by: Dale R. Jackson, *Florida Natural Areas Inventory, 1018 Thomasville Road, Suite 200-C, Tallahassee, FL 32303.*

Species of Special Concern

Alligator Snapping Turtle

Macroclemys temminckii (Harlan)

FAMILY CHELYDRIDAE

Order Testudines

OTHER NAMES: Alligator Turtle, Loggerhead, River Loggerhead.

DESCRIPTION: The Alligator Snapping Turtle is a very large freshwater turtle reaching a carapace length of over 50 cm (19.7 in), exceptionally over 75 cm (29.5 in), and a weight of over 50 kg (110 lb), exceptionally over 100 kg (220 lb). The head is very large, and both upper and lower jaws are strongly hooked. The head shape changes with growth, becoming relatively broader and deeper with age; the maximum head width is about 23.7 cm (9.3 in). The head is not fully retractile. The tail is very long, especially in hatchlings. Males reach maturity at a carapace length of about 35 cm (13.8 in), only marginally longer than that of the smallest mature females. However, males ultimately get much larger than females.

The Alligator Snapping Turtle is unlikely to be confused with any other turtle species except the Common Snapper, *Chelydra serpentina*. *Macroclemys* is distinguished from *Chelydra* by the more triangular head; laterally rather than dorsolaterally placed eyes (each of which is surrounded by elongate fleshy papillae); larger size (*Chelydra* does not commonly exceed 40 cm [15.7 in] or 20 kg [44 lb]); the presence of about 4 (1 to 5) extra scutes on each side of the carapace between the marginals and the large lateral or costal scutes; the much rougher shell, which is tricarinate throughout life; and the presence of a bifurcated, wormlike "fishing lure" on the upper surface of the tongue.

RANGE: In Florida, the Alligator Snapping Turtle is found only in Gulf river drainages from the Santa Fe and Suwannee rivers northwest through the Panhandle. It occurs in the Okefenokee, but not in the St. Marys or St. Johns rivers. The species has not been recorded from most of the

Alligator Snapping Turtle, *Macroclemys temminckii*. Liberty County, Florida (photograph by B. W. Mansell).

smaller rivers of the Florida Panhandle, such as the Steinhatchee, Fenholloway, Econfina, Aucilla, and St. Marks, but there are important populations in the Ochlockonee. There are no records for the New River of Franklin and Liberty counties, but the Apalachicola/Chipola system, including Lake Seminole, is one of the most important in the nation for *Macroclemys*. There are no records for the Econfina River of Bay County, but there is evidence of at least low densities of *Macroclemys* in the Choctawhatchee River, Rocky Creek, the Yellow and Blackwater rivers, and the Escambia and Perdido rivers.

Outside Florida, the species is widespread in the lower Mississippi, with isolated records into Kansas, Illinois, and Indiana. The western boundary of the range is represented by southeastern Kansas, most of Oklahoma except the extreme west, and eastern Texas.

HABITAT: Typically, the Alligator Snapping Turtle is found in deep rivers and canals, but it is also found in lakes and swamps, especially those located near deep running water. Occasionally it is found in brackish water. This turtle is highly aquatic, rarely emerging from the water except for nesting purposes, and this may account for its failure to colonize apparently suitable habitat in the small, Panhandle rivers mentioned above.

Unlike most Florida turtles, it is rarely found on highways. It is more of a bottom-walker than a swimmer. There is only one published record of aerial basking (Ewert 1976). Although often very sedentary, these turtles may progressively move upstream many kilometers over periods of many years, and this may account for the occasional discovery of very large specimens in the upper reaches of the Mississippi River system. Dams

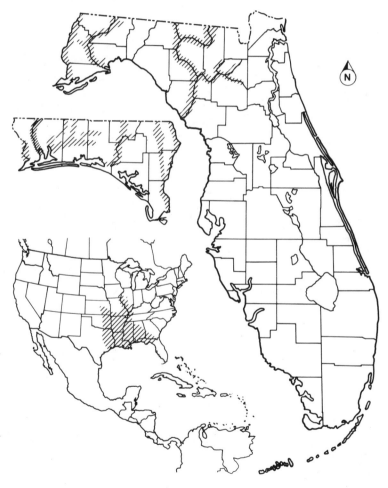

Distribution map of Alligator Snapping Turtle (*Macroclemys temminckii*).

and impoundments probably have a major effect upon the natural movements of the species. However, impoundments sometimes attract good concentrations of Alligator Snapping Turtles, although, since these may also concentrate the attentions of turtle trappers, it would be inappropriate to consider dams and impoundments to enhance the carrying capacity or habitat of the species.

LIFE HISTORY AND ECOLOGY: Mating occurs in February, March, and April in Florida, but presumably later in the more northern parts of the range. Nesting in Florida has been recorded from April to June and usually occurs on relatively steep river banks, not far from the water. In the Apalachicola, most nesting apparently occurs during the first two weeks of May. Apparently only a single clutch is deposited annually, and indeed some females appear to nest only in alternate years. The eggs are buried in a flask-shaped cavity in the soil and may number from 9 to 61; the average is 24.5 in Louisiana (Dobie 1971). Larger females tend to lay larger clutches. Six Apalachicola nests contained from 31 to 40 eggs each (average: 34.2). Growth is rather slow, and first maturity in both sexes is thought to be reached after 11–13 years in Louisiana (Dobie 1971), and possibly after a somewhat longer time further north.

The species "angles" for fish, holding the mouth wide open to expose the "lure" on the tongue. Adults are less inclined to use the lure, which loses its strikingly contrasting coloration with growth, and in much of the eastern part of the range, heavy-shelled molluscs make up much of the diet, although other dietary items from musk turtles to acorns may also be taken, as well as carrion of all kinds. In the western parts of the range, waters are more acidic and less productive of molluscs, and there the turtles eat fish, crawfish, crabs, waterfowl, and sometimes such vegetable matter as tupelo and palmetto berries.

SPECIALIZED OR UNIQUE CHARACTERISTICS: The Alligator Snapping Turtle is remarkable in many ways. It is the largest freshwater turtle in North America, and one of the largest in the world. Certain tropical turtles, including *Chitra indica, Pelochelys bibroni,* or *Podocnemis expansa* may on occasion approach or exceed *Macroclemys* in carapace length, but they lack the huge head and impressive mien of the latter. The largest Alligator Snapping Turtle seen by the writer (from White Springs, Hamilton County, Florida) had a maximum straight-line carapace length of 80.0 cm (31.5 in) and a maximum head width of 23.7 cm (9.3 in). The largest Alligator Snapping Turtles weigh over 110 kg (240 lb).

In addition to the remarkable size, the species is noteworthy for the ambush-type feeding behavior, especially of the young, prey being lured by means of the vermiform appendage on the floor of the mouth. The extensive development of the skin flaps and barbels in the Alligator Snapper may serve to help detect the presence of prey in muddy waters.

The South American Matamata Turtle (*Chelus fimbriatus*) may be an ecological replacement for the Alligator Snapping Turtle in the Amazon and Orinoco river systems. Although having a completely different head and neck structure and being a representative of the other suborder of living turtles, the Matamata shares with the Alligator Snapper the features of large size, extremely roughened, tuberculated carapace, skin excrescences and fringes on the head and neck, piscivorous diet, and sedentary mode of life. Prey ingestion, however, is accomplished by generating a vigorous inrush of water (and prey) into the mouth and throat, rather than by a powerful bite.

BASIS OF STATUS CLASSIFICATION: As a large, highly edible, slow-breeding, and slow-growing species, the Alligator Snapping Turtle may be considered intrinsically vulnerable. Its population dynamics are based upon the very long-term survival of adults, which have few natural enemies, and curtailment of the long life expectancy of adults by significant levels of human predation could be expected to cause rapid population decrease. Moreover, because of extensive interstate commerce in Alligator Snappers, the range-wide status of the species and the out-of-state market demand for Alligator Snapping Turtles must both be considered in evaluating the stresses on the Florida populations.

A great deal of circumstantial evidence suggests that the Alligator Snapping Turtle has been commercially exterminated throughout much of its range, and that the Louisiana markets, that once were supplied almost entirely from in-state sources, now rarely handle a turtle from Louisiana, the trappers having become dependent upon locating untrapped areas of Arkansas, Mississippi, and Florida for supplies. (For a detailed consideration of status outside Florida, see Pritchard 1990.) Moreover, it appears that a given area is "trapped out" after two or three seasons' effort, and will not be worth trapping again for years (possibly about a decade).

Florida responded rapidly to industrial-scale capture of Alligator Snapping Turtles in Panhandle rivers in the early 1970s, by passing regulations establishing a bag limit of one animal, and banning any commercialization of the species, or export from the state. Nevertheless, clandestine take continues, for example in Lake Seminole, where turtles are generally landed on the Georgia side of the lake. However, the present level of trapping remains unquantified.

Although the legal protection offered the Alligator Snapping Turtle in Florida is commendable and reasonably comprehensive, it would be naive to believe that this alone will result in the elimination of exploitation or stress on the species in Florida even as it becomes progressively depleted in other states. The river systems inhabited by the species in Florida are all shared with other states. Although the species is now fully protected in Alabama, commercial exploitation remains legal in Georgia, and as long as the species continues to fetch high—and rising—prices in Louisiana, no population can be considered safe.

RECOMMENDATIONS: This species needs protection from trapping for at least a decade in order to allow populations to recover. This may require federal action, in view of the nearly complete lack of regulatory control of harvest in the principal market states. Current regulations of the Florida Game and Fresh Water Fish Commission may be adequate to protect the species in Florida, but the regulations are not easy to enforce as long as legal markets exist in neighboring states.

It goes without saying that a survey of populations of this species by qualified biologists would be highly desirable. But such a study should not be used as an excuse to take no action to protect the species for years to come.

Selected References

Allen, E. R., and W. T. Neill. 1950. The Alligator Snapping Turtle, *Macroclemys temminckii*, in Florida. Spec. Publ. Ross Allen's Rept. Inst. 4:1–15.

Dobie, J. L. 1971. Reproduction and growth in the Alligator Snapping Turtle, *Macroclemys temminckii* (Troost). Copeia 1971(4):645–658.

Ewert, M. A. 1976. Nests, nesting, and aerial basking of *Macroclemys* under natural conditions, and comparisons with *Chelydra* (Testudines:Chelydridae). Herpetologica 32(2):150–156.

Hall, H. H., and H. M. Smith. 1947. Selected records of reptiles and amphibians from southeastern Kansas. Trans. Kansas Acad. Sci. 49:447–454.

Minton, S. A., and M. R. Minton. 1973. Giant reptiles. Charles Scribner's Sons, New York. 345 pp.

Pritchard, P. C. H. 1990. The Alligator Snapping Turtle. Biology and conservation. Milwaukee Public Museum Publications, Milwaukee, Wisconsin. 104 pp.

Smith, P. W. 1961. The amphibians and reptiles of Illinois. Illinois Nat. Hist. Surv. Bull. 28:1–298.

Wickham, M. M. 1922. Notes on the migration of *Macroclemys lacertina*. Oklahoma Acad. Sci. n.s., 247, Univ. Studies 15:20–22.

Prepared by: Peter C. H. Pritchard, *Florida Audubon Society, 1101 Audubon Way, Maitland, FL 32751.*

Florida Keys Mole Skink

Eumeces egregius egregius (Baird)

FAMILY SCINCIDAE

Order Squamata, Suborder Sauria

OTHER NAMES: Striped Red-tailed Skink, Red-tailed Skink.

DESCRIPTION: This is a small, shiny, brownish skink with a pair of dorsolateral light lines on the body and a pinkish tail. The ground color may be some shade of gray-brown to a darker brown. The tail may be salmon, pink, or orange. The dorsolateral lines remain parallel throughout their length and do not widen as in other subspecies of *E. egregius*. The Florida Keys Mole Skink reaches a length of 12.7 cm (5 in), of which approximately two-thirds is tail.

RANGE: This lizard is found in the Dry Tortugas and the Lower Florida Keys. Individuals have been recorded from the Tortugas, Key West, Stock Island, Middle Torch Key, Big Pine Key, Key Vaca, Grassy Key, Upper Matecumbe Key, Indian Key, and Key Largo. Those from the Upper Keys usually show characteristics intermediate between this race and the mainland form, *E. egregius onocrepis*. It is not known whether this lizard still occurs at the type locality on Indian Key. Other subspecies of *E. egregius* range throughout Florida and northward into southern Georgia and southeastern Alabama.

HABITAT: The Florida Keys Mole Skink is found in sandy areas, usually near the shoreline, but not always. It has been recorded from "under stones on sand in the shade" (Duellman and Schwartz 1958). This lizard also occurs frequently under driftwood and tidal wrack along shorelines. It probably requires a fairly loose soil, in which it burrows in the characteristic "sandswimming" manner.

LIFE HISTORY AND ECOLOGY: Little is known about the life history and ecology of this animal. Much of what follows is based on a study by Mount (1963) of the related *E. egregius onocrepis*, in north-central Florida. The species lays from 3 to 7 eggs once a year under debris, usually in nest cavities constructed in the sand. Females remain with the eggs until hatching (31 to 51 days), presumably offering protection from small predators. Reproductive maturity occurs at the age of one year in the la-

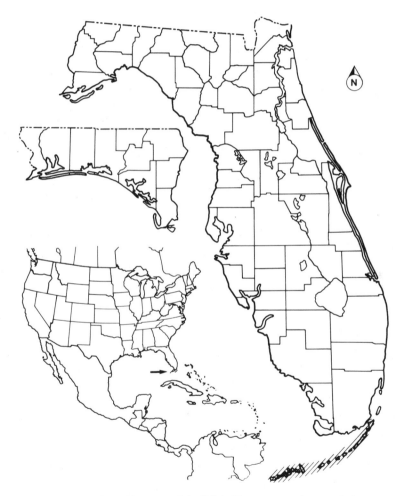

Distribution map of Florida Keys Mole Skink (*Eumeces egregius egregius*).

boratory. Mating takes place in March. Mole Skinks eat small invertebrates, especially spiders, roaches, and crickets. Nowhere in the Keys
does this lizard seem to be very abundant. Unlike other subspecies of *E.
egregius*, the Florida Keys race does not seem to be especially gregarious.

SPECIALIZED OR UNIQUE CHARACTERISTICS: *Eumeces e. egregius* is
another element of the distinctive isolated fauna of the Lower Florida
Keys. Its closest relative is apparently not the adjacent subspecies *onocrepis*, but rather the north Florida form *E. e. similis*. Several other examples
of this interesting north-south disjunction between the Lower Florida
Keys and North Florida are known. The species *E. egregius* is interesting
also because of the intermediate evolutionary position it seems to occupy
between the generalized cursorial skinks and the highly specialized fossorial "sand-swimmer," *Neoseps reynoldsi*.

BASIS OF STATUS CLASSIFICATION: The Lower Florida Keys are presently undergoing tremendous development and human population pressures. Continuation of these trends will result in the extirpation of much
of the unique fauna of these islands, including the Keys Mole Skink.

RECOMMENDATIONS: The National Key Deer Wildlife Refuge remains
a bright ray of hope on a dim horizon for the Keys. Anything that can be
done to add additional land to the refuge should be done. Collecting on
the refuge has not been restricted. Although in general, habitat destruction not collecting is the main enemy of the lower vertebrates, amateur
collecting on the National Key Deer Wildlife Refuge should be controlled.

Selected References

Duellman, W. E., and A. Schwartz. 1958. Amphibians and reptiles of southern
    Florida. Bull. Fla. State Mus. 3(5):181–324.
Mount, R. H. 1963. The natural history of the Red-tailed Skink, *Eumeces egregius*
    Baird. Amer. Mid. Nat. 70(20):356–385.
Mount, R. H. 1965. Variation and systematics of the scincoid lizard, *Eumeces
    egregius* Baird. Bull. Fla. State Mus. 9(5):183–213.
Mount, R. H. 1968. *Eumeces egregius* Baird. Cat. Amer. Amphib. Rept.:73.1–73.2.

Prepared by: Steven P. Christman, *Department of Natural Sciences, Florida
Museum of Natural History, Gainesville, FL 32611.*

Eastern Indigo Snake

Drymarchon corais couperi (Holbrook)

FAMILY COLUBRIDAE

Order Squamata, Suborder Serpentes

OTHER NAMES: Gopher Snake, Blue Indigo Snake, Blue Bull Snake.

DESCRIPTION: The Eastern Indigo is the longest North American snake, with a maximum recorded length of 2.63 m (8.6 ft). The coloration is iridescent black, but the throat is typically red, coral, or white. Both the color of the throat and the extent of this coloration are extremely variable. In some individuals, especially in south Florida, a bright red covers the face and throat and may extend several inches onto the belly. In much of north Florida, Indigo Snakes show only a light pinkish blush on the throat. In some northern populations (e.g., Gulf Hammock) there is no red; snakes from these populations are solid black with the exception of a central, white throat patch. The scales of the Indigo Snake are smooth, although adult males typically show a partial anterior keel on the scales of the middorsal 3–5 scale rows. The anal scale is undivided in this species.

The only snake commonly confused with the Eastern Indigo Snake is the Black Racer (*Coluber constrictor*). The Black Racer is a smaller snake, seldom exceeding 1.2 m (4 ft) in Florida; it is dull black in coloration, with white (brown in some areas) on the throat and lower labial scales. Unlike the Indigo Snake, the Black Racer has a divided anal scale.

RANGE: The Eastern Indigo Snake occurs in most of Florida and much of southern Georgia, although populations in Georgia and the Panhandle of Florida may be very localized. There are old records for southeastern Mississippi, extreme southern Alabama, and southern South Carolina, but Indigo Snakes may no longer occur naturally in those states.

There are seven other subspecies of the Indigo Snake, collectively extending from southern Texas to northern Argentina. The Eastern Indigo

181

Eastern Indigo Snake, *Drymarchon corais couperi*. Florida (photograph by B.W. Mansell).

Snake is isolated from the Texas Indigo Snake, the nearest of the other Indigo Snakes, by a distance of approximately 1000 km (600 mi).

HABITAT: In peninsular Florida, the Indigo Snake may be found in habitats ranging from mangrove swamps and wet prairies to xeric pinelands and scrub. In the northern parts of its range, it typically winters in Gopher Tortoise (*Gopherus polyphemus*) burrows on the higher sand ridges, although it may forage in more hydric habitats during the warmer months.

LIFE HISTORY AND ECOLOGY: This species feeds on virtually any vertebrate small enough for it to overpower. Prey includes fish, frogs, toads, lizards, snakes, small turtles, birds, and small mammals. It does not hesitate to attack and eat venomous snakes. The Indigo Snake is not a constrictor, and its prey is usually swallowed alive.

Indigo Snakes are completely diurnal. They actively search for prey, especially favoring the edges of wetlands, where frogs and snakes abound. During the warmer months, they range widely, individuals utilizing activity areas of 50–100 ha (125–250 ac) or more. Males are territorial, at least during the breeding season, and confrontations sometimes lead to combat or cannibalism. During the winter months, Indigo Snakes usually

stay fairly close to some sort of deep shelter (e.g., Gopher Tortoise burrow, stump hole, land crab burrow). Activity area during this period is
usually less than 10 ha (25 ac). Shedding occurs with surprising frequency in this species, about every 30–45 days. Indigo Snakes typically
become inactive for a period of 10–14 days immediately prior to shedding.

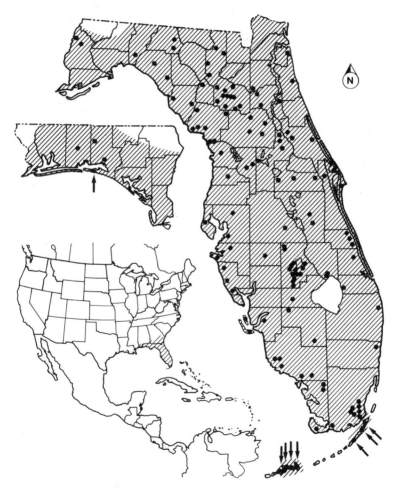

Distribution map of Indigo Snake (*Drymarchon corais couperi*). Dots indicate
museum records.

Breeding occurs November–April. Eggs, which are laid during May or June, are large and relatively few in number (5–10). The resulting hatchlings are 45.7–60.9 cm (18–24 in) in length. Indigo Snakes are apparently capable of long term sperm storage; there is a report of a female laying fertile eggs after more than four years in isolation.

SPECIALIZED OR UNIQUE CHARACTERTISTICS: The Eastern Indigo is the longest of North American snakes. The species to which it belongs is primarily tropical in distribution; the Eastern Indigo ranges into the warm temperate zone by using deep refugia to avoid the worst of winter cold. The disjunct distribution of the Eastern Indigo Snake makes it a prime candidate for the study of speciation and genetic divergence.

BASIS OF STATUS CLASSIFICATION: The Eastern Indigo Snake was formerly collected heavily for the pet trade. Although undoubtedly some illegal collecting continues, the federal Threatened listing of the Eastern Indigo Snake has largely curtailed the commercial collecting of this species. Also, Indigo Snakes are known to be killed as a result of "gassing" of Gopher Tortoise burrows, a technique once used widely for collecting rattlesnakes. "Gassing" is now illegal in Florida, but given the increasing demand for rattlesnakes in the curio and specialty leather trade, this practice probably still continues.

The most insidious and far reaching threat to the survival of this species is habitat loss or degradation. Especially in the northern portions of its range, the Indigo Snake is critically dependent upon the availability of appropriate winter refugia. In xeric habitats, such retreats are required during hot dry weather as well, because the Indigo is vulnerable to the desiccating heat of summer. Historically, these refugia were most often provided by Gopher Tortoise burrows and stump holes. However, Gopher Tortoises are now rare in much of the Florida Panhandle, and hundreds of thousands of "lightered" stumps have been removed by the resinous wood industry. The combined effect has been a drastic reduction in the availability of winter refugia in portions of northern Florida.

Elsewhere, the Indigo Snake has suffered from the increasing fragmentation of its habitat. Indigo Snakes are large, highly visible, and wide-ranging. Whereas some species of snakes are secretive and able to survive in small woodlots, Indigo Snakes require relatively large tracts of suitable habitat. Even very low density development, e.g., 8 ha (20 ac) "ranchettes," can seriously impact populations of Indigo Snakes, since the activity area of an individual snake may be divided among 20–50 properties.

In such situations, Indigo Snakes are especially vulnerable to vehicles, domestic dogs, and insensitive landowners.

RECOMMENDATIONS: Habitat protection intended to benefit the Indigo Snake should be focused on large tracts of land, generally of at least 1000 ha (2500 ac). Small, isolated habitat tracts have little potential for sustaining populations of Indigo Snakes long-term. When Indigo Snake habitat is unavoidably to be eliminated as a result of development activities, mitigation funds should be pooled in "mitigation land banks" in order to accumulate adequate funds to allow for the acquisition of preserves of adequate size.

In xeric habitats, especially those in north Florida, the future status of the Indigo Snake is closely tied to that of the Gopher Tortoise. The Indigo Snake will benefit from efforts to rebuild Gopher Tortoise populations. This may require a combination of tortoise restocking and active habitat management (primarily through prescribed fire). Existing prohibitions against the "gassing" of tortoise burrows should be strongly enforced.

Selected References

Allen, R., and W. T. Neill. 1952. The Indigo Snake. Fla. Wildlife 6(3):44–47.

Bogert, C. M., and R. B. Cowles. 1947. Moisture loss in relation to habitat selection in some Floridian reptiles. Amer. Mus. Nov. 1358:1–34.

Diemer, J. E. 1983. The distribution of the Eastern Indigo Snake, *Drymarchon corais couperi,* in Georgia. J. Herpetol. 17(3):256–264.

Layne, J. N., and T. M. Steiner. 1984. Sexual dimorphism in occurrence of keeled dorsal scales in the Eastern Indigo *(Drymarchon corais couperi).* Copeia 1984(3):776–778.

Moler, P. E. 1985. Distribution of the Eastern Indigo Snake, *Drymarchon corais couperi,* in Florida. Herpetol. Rev. 16(2):37–38.

Moler, P. E. 1985. Home range and seasonal activity of the Eastern Indigo Snake, *Drymarchon corais couperi,* in northern Florida. Final Performance Rpt., Study No. E-1-06, III-A-5, Florida Game and Fresh Water Fish Commission, Tallahassee, Florida.

Mount, R. H. 1975. The reptiles and amphibians of Alabama. Agric. Exp. Station, Auburn University. 347 pp.

Speake, D. W., and J. A. McGlincy. 1981. Response of indigo snakes to gassing of their dens. Proc. Ann. Conf. SE Assoc. Fish and Wildl. Agencies 35:135–138.

Speake, D. W., J. A. McGlincy, and T. R. Colvin. 1978. Ecology and management of the Eastern Indigo Snake in Georgia: A progress report. Pp. 64–73 *in* R. R. Odom and L. Landers (eds.). Proc. Rare and Endangered Wildl. Symposium, Ga. Dept. Nat. Res., Game and Fish Div., Tech. Bull WL4.

Steiner, T. M., O. L. Bass, Jr., and J. A. Kushlan. 1983. Status of the Eastern Indigo Snake in southern Florida national parks and vicinity. Report SFRC-8 3/01, South Florida Res. Ctr., Everglades Nat. Park, Homestead, Florida.

Prepared by: Paul E. Moler, *Florida Game and Fresh Water Fish Commission, 4005 South Main Street, Gainesville, FL 32601.*

Species of Special Concern

Red Rat Snake,
Lower Keys population
Elaphe guttata guttata (Linnaeus)

FAMILY COLUBRIDAE

Order Squamata, Suborder Serpentes

OTHER NAMES: Corn Snake, Pink Rat Snake, Rosy Rat Snake.

DESCRIPTION: These medium-sized snakes can grow to nearly 1.2 m (4 ft) in length but are more commonly seen as juveniles or individuals about 0.9 m (3 ft) long. The back is marked by a series of poorly defined pink blotches bordered by slightly darker pigment. The pale red or pinkish ground color is similar in hue to the blotches. The belly is yellow to orange and is only faintly marked by the black, checkerboard pattern characteristic of peninsular populations.

The lateral edges of the first blotch extend forward to the head, where they unite behind the eyes. Juveniles are strongly blotched and have a dark stripe from eye to neck on each side. Scales are keeled and the anal plate is divided.

RANGE: The species is fairly common in the southeastern and Atlantic coastal states. It occurs throughout Florida, where it undergoes a decided color change in the Lower Keys. The pale insular populations were once given subspecific status, but subsequent work showed the color pattern of these populations to exist within color variations of *E. g. guttata*. Specimens have been collected from the following keys: Bahia Honda, Big Pine, Big Torch, Key Vaca, Key West, Indian, Little Pine, Little Torch, Middle Torch, Ramrod, Saddlebunch, Stock Island, Sugarloaf, and Summerland. They also have been reported from the Marquesas Keys.

Red Rat Snake, *Elaphe guttata guttata*. Key West, Monroe County, Florida (photograph by B. W. Mansell).

HABITAT: Lower Keys populations live in pine woods, mangrove forest, and in edificarian situations.

LIFE HISTORY AND ECOLOGY: These chiefly nocturnal snakes hide under rocks and logs and will burrow into loose sand. They are also found in conjunction with Australian Pine, wooden planking, and under wooden bridges. The snake is often found under the bark of Jamaica dogwood trees. Carr (1940) reported declining populations long before the recent keys development. However, at present, populations appear to be stable and locally abundant. The snake is an accomplished climber and subsists on rodents, birds, and lizards.

SPECIALIZED OR UNIQUE CHARACTERISTICS: The edificarious habit of this species suggests that it is highly adaptable to change.

BASIS OF STATUS CLASSIFICATION: The paucity of field work makes estimates of population size questionable. These snakes are threatened to the extent that most vertebrate populations of the Lower Keys are threatened by development. The distinctively colored Lower Keys specimens of the Red Rat Snake are especially in demand in the pet trade.

RECOMMENDATIONS: Increased field work is needed to gain accurate data about the life history of Lower Keys populations of the Red Rat Snake.

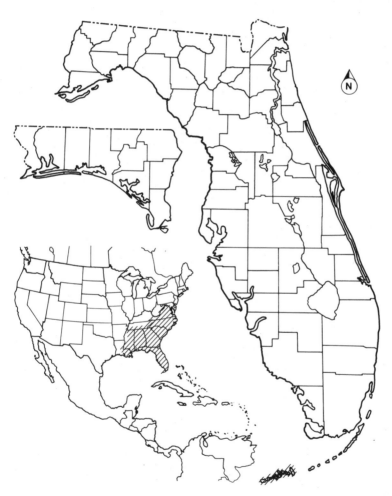

Distribution map of Red Rat Snake (*Elaphe guttata guttata*). (Lower Keys population only)

Selected References

Carr, A. F. 1940. A contribution to the herpetology of Florida. Univ. Fla. Publ., Biol. Sci. Ser. 3(1):97–98.

Duellman, W. E. and A. Schwartz. 1958. Amphibians and reptiles of southern Florida. Bull. Fla. State Mus. 3(5):181–324.

Lazell, J. D. 1989. Wildlife of the Florida Keys. Island Press, Washington, D. C. 253 pp.

Mitchell, J. C. 1977. Geographic variation of *Elaphe guttata* (Reptilia: Serpentes) in the Atlantic Coastal Plain. Copeia 1977(1):33–41.

Prepared by (1978): W. G. Weaver, *Department of Biology, Miami-Dade Community College, Medical Center Campus, 950 NW 20th Street, Miami, FL 33127;* and Steven P. Christman, *Department of Natural Sciences, Florida Museum of Natural History, Gainesville, FL 32611.* (1990: Updated by Paul E. Moler, *Florida Game and Fresh Water Fish Commission, 4005 South Main Street, Gainesville, FL 32601).*

Spotted Turtle

Clemmys guttata (Schneider)

FAMILY EMYDIDAE

Order Testudines

OTHER NAMES: None.

DESCRIPTION: The Spotted Turtle has a small, dark brown to black carapace covered with a scattering of small, round, yellow or white spots, which may be lost in old adults on rare occasion. It never exceeds 12.7 cm (5 in) in total shell length. The carapace is smooth and oval in outline. The plastron is unhinged and is yellow to orange in ground color with large black blotches on each scute. The skin is black with a scattering of yellow spots and a large yellow or orange blotch in the tympanic region. The chin is white to orange in color. Males have brown eyes and a long tail with the anal opening near the tip. Females have yellow or orange eyes and a short tail with the anal opening under the rear margin of the shell. Spotted Turtles can be distinguished from all other turtles by their small size and dark carapace and skin covered by many small, regular, round, yellow spots.

RANGE: The Spotted Turtle is restricted to eastern North America from northern Michigan and northern Illinois across northern Indiana and Ohio and southern Ontario and Quebec to the Atlantic Coastal Plain from southern Maine to central Florida. Its distribution in Florida is spotty and may be disjunct from populations in Georgia. There are records from the eastern Panhandle in Wakulla, Suwannee, and Lafayette counties and in the northern and central Peninsula in Baker, Columbia, Duval, Putnam, St. Johns, Alachua, Marion, and Polk counties. The southernmost records require some discussion (see comments).

HABITAT: This turtle is an inhabitant of shallow woodland ponds and

Spotted Turtle, *Clemmys guttata* (photograph by R. W. Van Devender).

meandering streams and sloughs in fresh or mildly brackish water. They prefer slow moving or still waters with a soft bottom and abundant aquatic vegetation. They are relatively terrestrial at certain times of year and are often seen moving overland. Most Florida specimens have been found crossing roads in areas of wet pine flatwoods.

LIFE HISTORY AND ECOLOGY: Very little is known of the life history of the Spotted Turtle in Florida. Elsewhere in its range, it is a diurnally active, opportunistic feeder, eating both plant and animal food. Home ranges are about 0.5 ha (1.3 ac). Spotted Turtles prefer cooler temperatures than most turtles. A population in southeastern Pennsylvania appears to cease all activity at temperatures over 32°C (90°F), and most activity occurs at temperatures below 25°C (77°F). Feeding is initiated when temperatures reach 15°C (59°F). If these physiological requirements remain constant for the species throughout its range, its activity period in Florida must be short and limited to winter and early spring.

Mating occurs in early spring and may involve many copulating pairs in a small area. Three to five elliptical eggs are laid in early summer in a flask-shaped nest dug by the female in well-drained soil. Hatchlings emerge in late summer and are just over 2.5 cm (1 in) in length.

Spotted Turtles are typically quite secretive and are not easily approached. Extensive overland migration often occurs in spring, and it is during this period that it is most often collected.

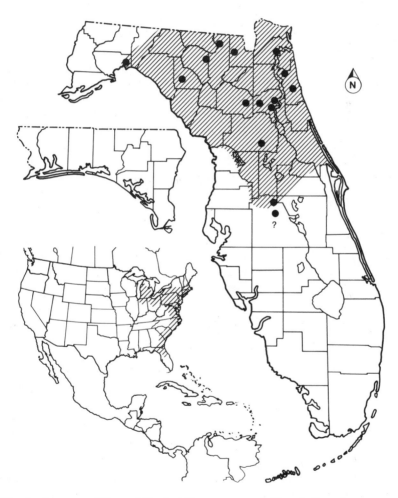

Distribution map of Spotted Turtle (*Clemmys guttata*). Dots indicate known localities. Question mark indicates an unsubstantiated record.

SPECIALIZED OR UNIQUE CHARACTERISTICS: Spotted Turtles were once quite common in the pet trade. Although they are less commonly sold today, they are still available through reptile dealers for about $40. Most specimens in the pet trade are said to come from North Carolina. The extreme rarity of this species in Florida makes it unlikely that individuals from this state are sold in the pet trade.

BASIS OF STATUS CLASSIFICATION: In spite of regular field work, including several major surveys of the herpetofauna of northern Florida, the Spotted Turtle remains a remarkably elusive species. It is only within the last 15 years that enough material on this species has been collected in Florida to assure skeptics that it is in fact native to the state. It appears to be due to the relative increase in numbers of trained biologists and other interested parties who have the occasional encounters with this species that we know more of its distribution in Florida. It is impossible to estimate current or past population sizes for this species in Florida. However, it seems highly likely that any adverse impact on Florida's wooded wetlands will have an adverse effect on this species.

Florida populations of Spotted Turtles appear to be small and isolated and occur at the edge of the range of the species. Therefore, they are likely candidates for extinction.

RECOMMENDATIONS: This species is so rare in Florida that direct study of its biology would be extremely difficult. Protection of the species will best be accomplished by preserving the diversity and water quality of wooded wetlands in northern and central Florida. The number of specimens found in southern Putnam County, in the Oklawaha drainage, in the last 10 years suggests that this is an important area for this species in Florida. Restoration and protection of this drainage would improve the chances for survival of this species within the state.

COMMENTS: Although all recent authors agree that the Spotted Turtle is native to the state of Florida, some questions remain about the southernmost records. There are vouchers for the Lake Weir, Marion County, record and that from the northern edge of Polk County (SR 557, 2.3 km [1.4 mi] N I-4). An additional specimen was reported from Lake Weir by Wilfred Neill, but no specimen exists. The SR 557 specimen was collected with one live individual, which was released, and one badly smashed DOR, which was unfortunately discarded. The southernmost record, Winter Haven, Polk County, remains unsubstantiated. Extensive collecting in the area of Winter Haven by Sam Telford over the last 40 years suggests that this species probably does not occur in the immediate vicinity of Winter Haven. However, this city is just 16.7 km (10 mi) S of the SR 557 locality, and the specimen reported by Neill as coming from Winter Haven may have come from this same region.

Selected References

Banicki, L. H. 1981. New records of the Spotted Turtle, *Clemmys guttata*, in northern Florida. Fla. Sci. 44:253–254.

Berry, J. F., and C. S. Gidden. 1974. The Spotted Turtle in Florida and southern Georgia. Fla. Sci. 36:198–200.

Ernst, C. H. 1967. A mating aggregation of the turtle *Clemmys guttata*. Copeia 1967:473–474.

Ernst, C. H. 1970a. Home range of the Spotted Turtle, *Clemmys guttata* (Schneider). Copeia 1970:391–393.

Ernst, C. H. 1970b. Reproduction in *Clemmys guttata*. Herpetologica 26:228–232.

Ernst, C. H. 1972. *Clemmys guttata*. Cat. Amer. Amphib. Rept. 124.1–124.2.

Ernst, C. H. 1976. Ecology of the Spotted Turtle, *Clemmys guttata* (Reptilia, Testudines, Testudinidae) in southeastern Pennsylvania. J. Herpetol. 10:25–33.

Ernst, C. H. 1982. Environmental temperatures and activities in wild Spotted Turtles, *Clemmys guttata*. J. Herpetol. 16:112–120.

Iverson, J. B. 1986. A checklist with distribution maps of the turtles of the world. Privately printed. Richmond, Indiana.

Iverson, J. B., and C. R. Etchberger. 1989. The distribution and zoogeography of the turtles of Florida. Fla. Sci. 52(2):119–144.

Lovich, J. E. 1988. Geographic variation in the seasonal activity cycle of Spotted Turtles, *Clemmys guttata*. J. Herpetol. 22:482–485.

Neill, W. T. 1954. Ranges and taxonomic allocations of amphibians and reptiles in the southeastern United States. Publ. Res. Div. Ross Allen's Rept. Inst. 1(7): 75–96.

Vliet, K. A. 1983. Geographic distribution: *Clemmys guttata*. Herp. Review 14(4): 123.

Prepared by: James F. Berry, *Department of Biology, Elmhurst College, Elmhurst, IL 60126;* and Peter A. Meylan, *Department of Biology, University of South Florida, Tampa, FL 33620.*

Barbour's Map Turtle

Graptemys barbouri Carr & Marchand

FAMILY EMYDIDAE

Order Testudines

OTHER NAMES: Barbour's Sawback Turtle.

DESCRIPTION: There is a considerable size difference between male and female Barbour's Map Turtles. The male is the smaller of the sexes, rarely exceeding 12.7 cm (5 in). The female commonly reaches 20 to 28 cm (8–11 in) and may occasionally exceed 30 cm (12 in) in length. The olive-green carapace has light yellow markings which form a U-shape on each of the lateral scutes. These markings fade with age, and the older turtles may be considerably darker than the young. The head has an olive-green background with a large yellow blotch behind the eyes and an extensive pattern of yellow lines. The head of the female is massive, containing large crushing jaws, while the head of the male is much smaller. Young map turtles have a very prominent dorsal keel, thus giving rise to the name sawback.

RANGE: Originally described in 1941 from specimens collected from the Chipola River in Jackson County, the species is confined to the Apalachicola drainage system. This includes the Chipola and Apalachicola rivers in Florida and the Chattahoochee and Flint rivers in Georgia. Several small streams that enter these rivers also contain map turtles.

HABITAT: Rivers are the preferred habitat of this turtle. Areas of the river that contain considerable exposed limestone and a strong current are preferred.

LIFE HISTORY AND ECOLOGY: The feeding habits of Barbour's Map

Barbour's Map Turtle, *Graptemys barbouri*. Jackson County, Florida (photograph by B. W. Mansell).

Turtles differ according to the sex and the size of the turtle. The diet of males and small females consists mainly of caddisfly larvae. Other aquatic insects, small snails, and occasionally plants are included in their diet. The large females feed almost exclusively on snails and the bivalve *Corbicula*, which they crush with their massive jaws.

The usual clutch size varies from 4 to 11 white, oval eggs, with several clutches being laid in a season. The males become sexually mature in 3 to 4 years, while the females take approximately 12 years to reach sexual maturity.

These turtles are often found congregated in areas containing exposed limestone. The home range of adult turtles remains relatively constant year after year. Dispersal over land, common in many aquatic turtles, is unknown. Hatchlings show limited dispersal during their first year. Dispersal is more pronounced during periods of extreme high water.

SPECIALIZED OR UNIQUE CHARACTERISTICS: Sexual dimorphism in Barbour's Map Turtle is more pronounced than that found in other species of turtles. As a result of this dimorphism, differences in behavior and ecology exist between the sexes.

BASIS OF STATUS CLASSIFICATION: The restricted geographic range of this species makes it vulnerable. Collecting of large female map turtles for food in the Chipola River by divers threatens long term survival of this population. The increased urbanization along the Chipola River, along with escalating clearing of land for agriculture, could result in decreased water quality and reduction in suitable nesting habitat for

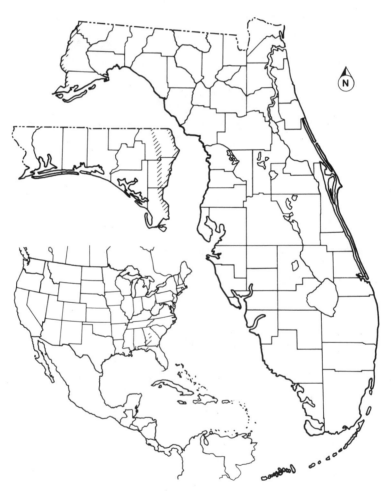

Distribution map of Barbour's Map Turtle (*Graptemys barbouri*).

this species. Commercialization of the Apalachicola River also poses a potential threat to this species.

RECOMMENDATIONS: Protection of the river system from ecological destruction is necessary in order to preserve the habitat of this species. Collection of map turtles for food and pets should be prohibited. Education of the people in the Chipola and Apalachicola rivers area should be provided in order to discourage the use of this turtle for food and increase awareness of the unique characteristics of this river system. Limited collecting should be allowed only for scientific research that will add to knowledge of this species.

Selected References

Cagle, F. R. 1952. The status of turtles *Graptemys pulchra* Baur and *Graptemys barbouri* Carr and Marchand, with notes on their natural history. Copeia 1952(4): 223–234.

Carr, A. F. 1952. Handbook of turtles. The turtles of the United States, Canada, and Baja California. Comstock Publ. Assoc., Ithaca, New York. 542 pp.

Carr, A. F. and L. J. Marchand. 1942. A new turtle from the Chipola River, Florida. Proc. New England Zool. Club 20:95–100.

Dobie, J. L. 1972. Correction of distribution records for *Graptemys barbouri* and *Graptemys pulchra*. Herp. Rev. 4(1):23.

Ernst, C. H., and R. W. Barbour. 1972. Turtles of the United States. University Press of Kentucky, Lexington. 347 pp.

Sanderson, R. A. 1974. Sexual dimorphism in the Barbour's Map Turtle, *Malaclemys barbouri* (Carr and Marchand). Master's thesis, University of South Florida. 94 pp.

Sanderson, R. A., and J. E. Lovich. 1988. *Graptemys barbouri* Carr and Marchand. Cat. Amer. Amphib. Rept. 421.1–421.2.

Wahlquist, H., and G. W. Folkerts. 1973. Eggs and hatchlings of Barbour's Map Turtle, *Graptemys barbouri* Carr and Marchand. Herpetologica 29(3):236–237.

Wharton, C. H., T. French, and C. Ruckdeschel. 1973. Recent range extensions for Georgia amphibians and reptiles. HISS News-Journal 1(1):22.

Prepared by: Roger A. Sanderson, *Department of Medical Oncology, University of South Florida, Tampa, FL 33620.*

Alabama Map Turtle

Graptemys pulchra Baur

FAMILY EMYDIDAE

Order Testudines

OTHER NAMES: None.

DESCRIPTION: (The following description applies specifically to Florida populations.)

The shell is triangular in cross section. The highest point of the shell is slightly more than one-third the upper shell length from the front edge. The rear edge of the upper shell is saw-toothed. Females may reach 28 cm (11 in) and have large skulls and broad jaws. Males may reach 12.7 cm (5 in) and have small heads, longer tails, and lack long front toenails. The upper shell is greenish with faint yellowish reticulations and is bordered by short, yellow, vertical bands. The ridge of the upper shell has a longitudinal black stripe or blotches over the projecting tips of the scutes. The lower shell is immaculate and yellowish-white in adults; the rear edge of the scutes are bordered with black in young individuals. The neck, legs, and tail are black with broad yellow or orange stripes. There is a broad yellow or orange blotch behind each eye and one between the eyes. Hatchlings are more brightly colored than adults and are about 4.4 cm (1.75 in) in length.

RANGE: The species is found from northern Mississippi and Alabama to southeastern Louisiana and northwestern Florida. In Florida, it is confined to the Escambia River and Yellow River drainages.

HABITAT: The species is most abundant in the Escambia River, where nesting areas and food species are most available. Although frequently found in small streams, it is most abundant in large rivers. It is absent where freshwater snails and clams are not found, as in the Perdido River

Alabama Map Turtle, *Graptemys pulchra*. Escambia County, Alabama (photograph by M. A. Bailey).

and Blackwater River. Apparently tolerant of organic pollution, the species maintains stable populations in areas contaminated by sewage. Salt water is avoided to the extent that individuals are rarely found within the mile upstream of a river mouth.

LIFE HISTORY AND ECOLOGY: Young individuals and males feed primarily on insects. Adult females feed almost exclusively on small freshwater clams and snails.

Individuals normally remain within several hundred yards of a favorite basking site. They can return to the home range after being displaced 15 miles upstream or downstream.

Sexual maturity is reached in about 14 years in females and in about 3 years in males. Maximum size is reached in females in about 23 years, and natural longevity probably exceeds 50 years. Predators, particularly raccoons and crows, destroy over 90% of the natural nests. Once hatched, minor mortality occurs among young individuals. Most adult deaths are caused by man and possibly the Alligator Snapping Turtle.

Nesting occurs from May through July on sandy beaches adjoining home streams. Six to 13 elliptical, flexible-shelled eggs are deposited in flask-shaped nests above 12.7 cm (5 in) in depth. Most females produce several nests per season.

SPECIALIZED OR UNIQUE CHARACTERISTICS: Females, with their broad jaws, are well adapted for feeding on thick-shelled clams. The introduction of the imported Oriental Mussel to the Escambia River has probably resulted in local population expansion in this turtle.

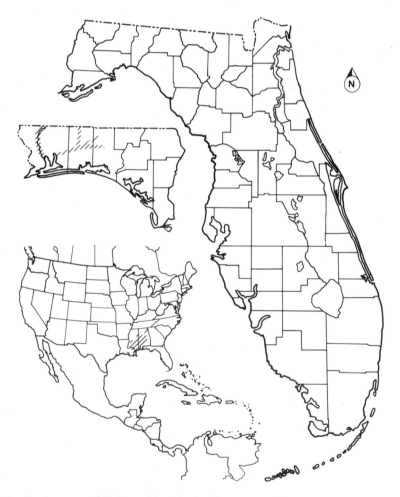

Distribution map of Alabama Map Turtle (*Graptemys pulchra*).

BASIS OF STATUS CLASSIFICATION: Although relatively abundant in restricted areas, the species is confined in Florida to only two rivers. Any substantial modification to these drainages, such as stream channelization or heavy metal pollution, could reduce populations radically. The common practice of shooting basking turtles, if increased, may reduce numbers in some areas.

RECOMMENDATIONS: The quality of natural waters should be maintained and, in many areas, improved. A survey of population densities should be made to determine any future population changes in this species.

Selected References

Cagle, F. R. 1952. The status of the turtles *Graptemys pulchra* Baur and *Graptemys barbouri* Carr and Marchand, with notes on their natural history. Copeia 1952(4):223–234.

Conant, R. 1975. A field guide to reptiles and amphibians of eastern and central North America. Houghton Mifflin Co., Boston. 429 pp.

Shealey, R. M. 1973. The natural history of the Alabama Map Turtle, *Graptemys pulchra* Baur in Alabama. Ph.D. diss., Auburn University, Alabama. 120 pp.

Shealey, R. M. 1976. The natural history of the Alabama Map Turtle, *Graptemys pulchra* Baur in Alabama. Bull. Fla. State Mus. Biol. Sci. 21(2):97–111.

Prepared by: Robert M. Shealey, *Biology Department, Pensacola Junior College, Pensacola, FL 32504.*

Mangrove Terrapin
Malaclemys terrapin rhizophorarum Fowler

FAMILY EMYDIDAE

Order Testudines

OTHER NAMES: Diamondback Terrapin, Keys Terrapin.

DESCRIPTION: Nearly a century ago, Fowler (1906) described the Mangrove Terrapin on the basis of a single specimen found in the southern Florida Keys. The type locality is the island of Boca Grande, now part of Key West National Wildlife Refuge.

In subsequent years, only a few additional specimens, all from the Upper Keys, were referred to this subspecies. This small and widely dispersed sample formed the basis for a generally accepted characterization of Mangrove Terrapins (striped necks and bold vertical stripes on the hind legs; e. g., Conant 1975, Behler and King 1979) which is, unfortunately, inaccurate.

There appear to be two morphologically distinct terrapin populations in the Florida Keys. One—the true Mangrove Terrapin—is restricted to the lower half of the Florida Keys, south of Marathon Key. A second, clearly different population occurs in the northern Keys, especially on the islands of Florida Bay, and may represent a previously unrecognized subspecies.

Fowler's original description of the Mangrove Terrapin was simply a lengthy enumeration of a wide variety of characters without any real differential diagnosis. On the basis of several hundred specimens observed during the course of field work over the past decade, however, it is now possible to stipulate a suite of distinctive characters for Mangrove Terrapins. These include: all plastral scute seams bordered by black bands of varying and irregular width; hind legs uniformly gray or sometimes speckled with black; neck and forelimbs typically a uniform light gray color; carapace uniformly colored a dull brown to almost black; margins of the

Mangrove Terrapin, *Malaclemys terrapin rhizophorarum*. Barracouta Key, Monroe County, Florida (photograph by R. C. Wood).

jaws pale colored. In some adult specimens, concentric grooves and ridges are present on the carapace scutes; in others, the surface of the carapace scutes is completely smooth.

RANGE: The Mangrove Terrapin's range is limited to the southern Florida Keys. It does not occur north of the Seven Mile Bridge on U. S. Highway 1. Specimens have been found as far west as the Marquesas Keys. No terrapins occur farther westward on the Dry Tortugas.

HABITAT: *Malaclemys t. rhizophorarum* populations are concentrated primarily on the mangrove-covered islands of Key West National Wildlife Refuge, where they are most often encountered among the intertidal pneumatophores at the base of Black Mangroves (*Avicennia germinans*) or in shallow ponds sometimes found in the interior of these islands. Mangrove Terrapins are rarely seen on any of the islands linked by the highway (U. S. 1) extending the length of the Keys. Much of the prime mangrove habitat which once existed in this part of the Keys, and which may well have supported a considerable terrapin population, has been destroyed by human activities.

LIFE HISTORY AND ECOLOGY: Very little is known about the life history of Mangrove Terrapins. A few hatchlings have been seen in the wild, and, therefore, there must be some successful reproduction. But no obviously suitable nesting habitat has yet been identified anywhere within the known range of this subspecies. The only parts of most islands where Mangrove Terrapins are found that are consistently above high tide (and, therefore,

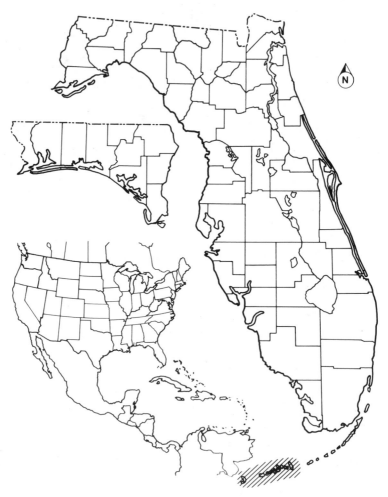

Distribution map of Mangrove Terrapin (*Malaclemys terrapin rhizophorarum*).

suitable for nests) are the berms that often ring the perimeters of islands at the ecotone between the fringing Red Mangroves (*Rhizophora mangle*) and the more interiorly located Black Mangroves. Invariably, these berms are so densely riddled with land crab burrows that it seems unlikely that terrapins could successfully nest here.

Marked sexual dimorphism exists, as is true for all *Malaclemys* subspecies. Adult males are substantially smaller (carapace midline length up to 12.5 cm) than females (carapace length up to 19.5 cm), but have much longer and fatter tails than do females. Female heads are proportionately broader than those of males, and female shells are likewise proportionately deeper dorsoventrally. There is a strongly skewed adult sex ratio, females invariably being more common than males. The actual sex ratio varies considerably from one island to another, ranging upwards from a minimum of 4:1.

Like all Diamondback Terrapins, *M. t. rhizophorarum* is carnivorous. A significant component of its diet consists of small bivalves and tiny, elongate snails, which are everywhere abundant. In addition to being active predators, they also appear to be scavengers; a terrapin on the Marquesas was observed feeding on a small dead fish (Red Snapper) under water.

Direct evidence of predation on Mangrove Terrapins does not yet exist. However, there is considerable evidence of predation on nearby terrapin populations. Bald Eagles (*Haliaeetus leucocephalus*) habitually prey upon subadult terrapins. Terrapin remains were identified in the stomach of an American Crocodile (*Crocodylus acutus*) from Biscayne Bay. An adult terrapin shell was recovered from the stomach of a shark caught in the Indian River on the east coast of Florida. Undoubtedly this is only a partial list of the actual number of predator species.

Mangrove Terrapins are characterized by extremely cryptic behavior. During the day they are often found partly to completely buried in mud. Fresh trackways (which often lead to buried terrapins) plowed across the muddy bottoms of very shallow ponds on some of the mangrove islands suggest that these turtles may forage primarily at night, while during the day they bury themselves to escape the heat and, perhaps also, potential predators.

Black Mangrove forests appear to have denser concentrations of terrapins than do the adjacent Red Mangroves. The pneumatophores of the Black Mangroves are often so closely bunched that terrapins must tilt their bodies 90 degrees from their normal horizontal position and pull themselves sideways through the pneumatophore thickets in what is undoubtedly a unique form of locomotion among all living turtles.

The density of Mangrove Terrapin populations varies considerably from one island to another. Barracouta Key, despite having once been a Navy bombing range for many years, supports a relatively large population. Other keys, which differ in no obvious way from Barracouta, have few or in some cases no terrapins.

Although Diamondback Terrapins typically reside in brackish waters throughout most of their range, Mangrove Terrapins are frequently found in hypersaline water in the interior of the islands where they occur, ranging from 45 to over 100 ppt. Moreover, unlike most other terrapin subspecies, Mangrove Terrapins remain active throughout the year and do not hibernate during the winter.

SPECIALIZED OR UNIQUE CHARACTERISTICS: Mangrove Terrapins are restricted in their distribution to the southern half of the Florida Keys. They are the southernmost of all Diamondback Terrapins, and, as such, are of considerable ecological and biogeographical interest. They tolerate greater salinity than any other terrapin subspecies yet studied, and, unlike more northern populations, they do not hibernate. They have developed a unique form of locomotion in order to negotiate through dense concentrations of Black Mangrove pneumatophores.

BASIS OF STATUS CLASSIFICATION: Mangrove Terrapins are considered Rare by virtue of their very limited geographic range and probably small total population. Much of the suitable habitat within the range of the subspecies has been destroyed by human activities along the U. S. Highway 1 corridor. Only occasional anecdotal sightings of Mangrove Terrapins have been reported from southern Keys connected by the highway. Viable populations exist still on some of the islands within Key West National Wildlife Refuge. Human incursions do not seem to be frequent or prolonged in these areas, and as long as this situation continues the remaining Mangrove Terrapin populations should survive.

RECOMMENDATIONS: A significant area of Mangrove Terrapin habitat lies within the boundaries of federally protected wildlife refuges. This fact, coupled with the inconspicuous habits of the terrapins themselves, suggests that this subspecies is in no immediate danger of extinction. However, it is imperative that the habitats of known and suspected populations continue to be rigorously protected. In addition, further field studies are needed, both to monitor the status of known populations and to attempt to locate additional populations in areas that have not yet been extensively surveyed. Moreover, better knowledge of the life histories of these turtles would undoubtedly facilitate their protection in the future.

Selected References

Behler, J. L. and F. W. King. 1979. The Audubon Society field guide to North American reptiles and amphibians. Alfred A. Knopf, New York. 743 pp.

Carr, A. F. 1946. Status of the Mangrove Terrapin. Copeia 3:170–172.

Carr, A. F. 1952. Handbook of turtles. The turtles of the United States, Canada and Baja California. Comstock Pub. Assoc., Ithaca, New York. 542 pp.

Conant, R. 1975. A field guide to reptiles and amphibians of eastern and central North America. Houghton Mifflin Co., Boston. 429 pp.

Fowler, H. W. 1906. Some cold-blooded vertebrates of the Florida Keys. Proc. Acad. Nat. Sci. Philadelphia 58(1):77–113, pl.4.

Johnson, W. R. 1952. Range of *Malaclemys terrapin rhizophorarum* on the west coast of Florida. Herpetologica 8(3):100.

Pritchard, P. C. H. 1979. Encyclopedia of turtles. TFH Publications, Inc., Jersey City. 895 pp.

Schwartz, A. 1955. The Diamondback Terrapins (*Malaclemys terrapin*) of peninsular Florida. Proc. Biol. Soc. Washington 68:157–164.

Wood, R. C. 1981. The mysterious mangrove terrapin. Fla. Nat. 54(3):6–7.

Prepared by: Roger C. Wood, *Faculty of Science and Mathematics, Stockton State College, Pomona, NJ 08240.*

Gulf Coast Smooth Softshell

Apalone mutica calvata Webb

FAMILY TRIONYCHIDAE

Order Testudines

OTHER NAMES: Chicken.

DESCRIPTION: The Gulf Coast Smooth Softshell is a rather small turtle, usually less than 23 cm (9 in) in carapace length (record for the subspecies is a 28.7 cm [11.3 in] female from Dallas County, Alabama), with the typical characteristics of the soft-shelled family (broad, very flat, soft, scuteless carapace, only three claws on each foot, and elongate tubular snout). The species *mutica* is distinguished from the sympatric *Apalone spinifera* by the absence of ridges on the nasal septum and by the absence of spines or tubercles on the anterior part of the carapace. The subspecies *calvata* is distinguished by the juvenile pattern of large, often ocellate, circular spots; the absence of stripes on the dorsal surface of the snout; the pattern of fine, poorly contrasting markings on the dorsal surfaces of the limbs; and the presence of thick black borders around the pale post-ocular stripes.

RANGE: *Apalone mutica* is widely distributed in the Mississippi Valley. The subspecies *calvata*, however, is only known from the Pearl River and Tombigbee River in Mississippi; from Washington and East Baton Rouge parishes in Louisiana; from the Alabama River in Dallas, Elmore, and Macon counties and the Conecuh River in Escambia County in Alabama; and from the vicinity of Century on the Escambia River in Escambia County, Florida. It is possible that *calvata* has a more extensive range in the Florida Panhandle than this.

Gulf Coast Smooth Softshell, *Apalone mutica calvata*. Macon County, Alabama (photograph by R. M. Mount).

HABITAT: This species is highly aquatic and typically found in rivers and streams but may also be expected in lakes and impoundments.

LIFE HISTORY AND ECOLOGY: No detailed studies on this subspecies have been reported. Fresh nests have been found in sandbars on the Escambia River on June 1.

BASIS OF STATUS CLASSIFICATION: The classification is not based upon a thorough study of the status of this subspecies in Florida, but rather upon the peripheral nature of the range of the form in the state. More data are needed to evaluate the status of the subspecies properly.

RECOMMENDATIONS: A survey should be carried out to determine the complete range and survival outlook of the turtle.

Selected References

Mount, R. H. 1975. The reptiles and amphibians of Alabama. Auburn Univ. Agric. Exp. Stn. 347 pp.

Plummer, M. V. 1977a. Activity, habitat, and population structure in the turtle *Trionyx muticus*. Copeia 1977(3):431–40.

Plummer, M. V. 1977b. Reproduction and growth in the turtle *Trionyx muticus*. Copeia 1977(3):440–47.

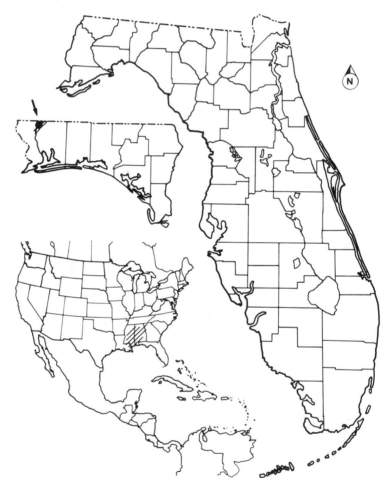

Distribution map of Gulf Coast Smooth Softshell (*Apalone mutica calvata*). Dot indicates the only known locality.

Webb, R. G. 1962. North American recent soft-shelled turtles (Family Trionychidae). Univ. Kansas Publ. Mus. Nat. Hist. 13(10):429–611.

Prepared by: Peter C. H. Pritchard, *Florida Audubon Society, P.O. Drawer 7, Maitland, FL 32751.*

Leatherback Turtle

Dermochelys coriacea (Vandelli)

FAMILY DERMOCHELYIDAE

Order Testudines

OTHER NAMES: Trunk Turtle, Trunkback Turtle, Leathery Turtle, Luth.

DESCRIPTION: This is the largest of all marine turtles; adults weigh 295–590 kg (650-1300 lb). The scutes, limb and head scales, and claws typical of nearly all other turtle species are absent, although hatchlings are covered with bead-like scales that disappear within a few months, and on rare occasions may have a rudimentary claw on each forelimb also. The overall color of the dorsal surface is black, with very variable white spotting. The underside is white or pinkish, with some, sometimes much, dark infuscation. The shell as a whole has a total of 12 longitudinal wavy or tuberculate ridges. The beak is strongly cusped at all ages, and in adult females there is a pink blaze on the crown of the head. Specimens between hatchling size and a carapace length of about 120 cm (47 in) are very rarely encountered.

RANGE: This extremely wide-ranging species nests on tropical, usually mainland shores of the Atlantic, Indian, and Pacific oceans, whilst non-breeding animals range far into temperate and even sub-polar waters, with many records from the British Isles and the Maritime Provinces of Canada, possibly as far north as Baffin Island. To the south, the species reaches to the Cape of Good Hope and to Argentina, and the latitudinal range is at least as great in the Pacific. No subspecies are currently recognized, although various authors in the past (e.g., Carr 1952) have restricted the nominal subspecies to the Atlantic Ocean, with *Dermochelys coriacea schlegeli* in the Indo-Pacific region (see Pritchard and Trebbau [1984] for a detailed discussion).

Nesting by the Leatherback occurs regularly, but by no means abun-

Leatherback Turtle, *Dermochelys coriacea* (photograph by P. C. H. Pritchard).

dantly, in Florida. Most nesting records are for the Atlantic Coast in the mid-peninsula area, with perhaps more nestings on Hutchinson Island than elsewhere on this coast. Harris et al. (1984) reported 18 Florida nestings in 1979, 9 in 1980, 39 in 1981, 45 in 1982, and 31 in 1983. Some nesting occurs as far south as Broward County; the latitudinal extremes are represented by Flagler County and Dade County. North of Florida, there are only two (Georgia) nesting records. On the Gulf Coast, there is a single record of hatchlings on the beach between Phillips Inlet (Walton County) and Destin (Okaloosa County).

Considerably greater numbers of Leatherbacks have been spotted in the course of pelagic surveys. These observations suggest a summer concentration of Leatherbacks in waters near Cape Canaveral, most over water 20–40 m (66–132 ft) in depth. Fritts et al. (1983) reported only 7 of 47 animals in water over 100 m (330 ft) in depth.

LIFE HISTORY AND ECOLOGY: By nesting in the tropics but feeding in temperate or even sub-polar waters, the Leatherback is committed to long distance movements. Philopatry (i. e., precise return to the site of hatching or earlier nestings) is probably less precise than in most other marine turtles, and Leatherbacks in some parts of their range may rapidly occupy very newly-formed nesting habitat. Growth rates in the wild are uncertain but may be extremely rapid, with the possibility of maturity after only three years. Feeding is at the surface or in the water column rather than benthic, and the bulk of the diet consists of jellyfish. Nesting occurs in the spring and early summer months in the North Atlantic (but in the winter months on the Pacific Coasts of Mexico and Central Amer-

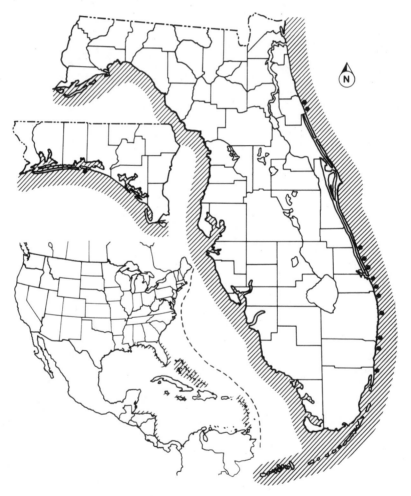

Distribution map of Leatherback Turtle (*Dermochelys coriacea*). Dots indicate nesting records.

ica). Nests include, on average, 80–85 "normal" eggs, with the invariable addition of smaller, yolkless, and often deformed eggs, for the most part laid toward the end of the clutch, and usually a few dozen in number. Preferred nesting beaches have a reefless approach, with deep water close to land; post-nesting dives to as deep as 475 m (1568 ft) have been recorded. As many as 10 nestings may occur in a season, at mean intervals of about 10.5 days, but nesting rarely occurs in successive seasons, and often two non-breeding seasons will intervene between nesting seasons.

SPECIALIZED OR UNIQUE CHARACTERISTICS: The Leatherback is the largest of all living turtles (terrestrial, freshwater, or marine). Moreover, its morphology is unique, especially as regards the integument, the shell structure (which normally includes a neomorphic layer of thousands of bones forming a continuous mosaic, and underlain by a layer of oily connective tissue about 4 cm [1.6 in] thick), and the paedomorphic nature of the skeleton. Physiologically the species is unique among turtles in showing a substantial degree of endothermy, facilitated by such anatomical features as counter-current heat exchange mechanisms in the shoulder region, to allow the forelimbs to cool to close to ambient temperatures without losing significant deep-body heat. The diving ability of the Leatherback is unmatched by any other reptile.

BASIS OF STATUS CLASSIFICATION: Worldwide, the Leatherback is more abundant than has often been thought, with an estimated world population (breeding females only) of 136,000, and Atlantic nesting populations may possibly be on the increase in some areas (e. g., Trinidad). Whether or not the U. S. Department of Interior and CITES categorizations of the Leatherback as "endangered" (or "Appendix I") are justified is arguable. Only in southeast Asia have population declines been clearly demonstrated; but stresses remain on many of the Atlantic populations (e. g., excessive egg collecting in Central America; or extensive beach slaughter of nesting females in Guyana and the Antilles, especially Trinidad). The Florida nesting records are few and peripheral, and contribute negligibly to overall Atlantic populations of the Leatherback. Bearing in mind that a Leatherback may nest 10 times in a season, the approximately 10–40 nests recorded per year in Florida may have been laid by as few as 1–4 individuals.

RECOMMENDATIONS: The Leatherback is fully protected by law in Florida, as are all sea turtle species throughout the United States. Moreover, deliberate take of the species, or its eggs, probably occurs only rarely in the state. Nevertheless, steps need to be taken to minimize accidental mortality, e. g., by capture in shrimp trawls, entanglement in lobster lines, or ingestion of plastic refuse in the ocean. The first of these problems is now being addressed by means of the TED (Turtle Excluder Device), but solutions to the other two mentioned will not be easy or quick.

The future of the Leatherback in the Atlantic rests primarily in the hands of other nations. International commerce in Leatherback products is negligible, but the pressure on both the turtles and their eggs on many of the tropical nesting grounds is clearly excessive.

Selected References

Allen, E. R., and W. T. Neill. 1957. Another record of the Atlantic Leatherback, *Dermochelys c. coriacea*, nesting on the Florida coast. Copeia 1957(2):143–144.

Carr, A. F. 1952. Handbook of turtles. Comstock Publ. Assoc., Ithaca, New York. 542 pp.

Fritts, T. H., A. B. Irvine, R. D. Jennings, L. A. McCollum, W. Hoffman, and M. A. McGehee. 1983. Turtles, birds, and mammals in the northern Gulf of Mexico and nearby Atlantic waters. U. S. Fish and Wildlife Service, Minerals Management Service. FWS OB–82–85. 455 pp.

Harris, B. A., W. J. Conley, and J. A. Huff. 1984. The status of Florida's nesting sea turtle populations from 1979 through 1983. Florida DNR and Inst. Oceanogr., St. Petersburg. 26 pp.

Nichols, V. A., and C. H. du Toit. 1983. A Leatherback returns to Flagler County: A new northern nesting record for the U. S. Atlantic Coast. Herp. Review 14(4):107.

Pritchard, P. C. H. 1980. *Dermochelys coriacea*. Cat. Amer. Amphib. Rept.: 238.1–238.4.

Pritchard, P. C. H. and P. Trebbau. 1984. The turtles of Venezuela. Soc. Study Amphib. Rept., Spec. Publ. 403 pp.

Ruckdeschel, C., L. Ellis, and C. R. Shoop. 1982. *Dermochelys coriacea* (Leatherback Sea Turtle) nesting. Herp. Review 13(4):126.

Schroeder, B. A., and N. Thompson. 1987. Distribution of the Loggerhead Turtle, *Caretta caretta*, and the Leatherback Turtle, *Dermochelys coriacea*, in the Cape Canaveral, Florida, area: Results of aerial surveys. Pp. 44–45 *in* W. Witzell (ed.). Ecology of east Florida sea turtles. NMFS, NOAA Technical Report NMFS 53.

Yerger, R. W. 1965. The Leatherback Turtle on the Gulf Coast of Florida. Copeia 1965(3):365–366.

Prepared by: Peter C. H. Pritchard, *Florida Audubon Society, 1101 Audubon Way, Maitland, FL 32751.*

Southern Coal Skink

Eumeces anthracinus pluvialis Cope

FAMILY SCINCIDAE

Order Squamata, Suborder Sauria

OTHER NAMES: None.

DESCRIPTION: The Southern Coal Skink is a medium-sized (about 12.7 cm [5 in] in total length), ground-dwelling lizard having a brown or sometimes light green dorsal stripe (often with faint dark lines or rows of spots in it); laterally, a pair of broad white or greenish-white lines run the length of the body and onto the tail. These two light lines enclose a rich brown or black lateral band; the uppermost light line passes over the eye through the supraocular scales, while the lowermost includes all the supralabial scales along the upper lip (usually 7, with dark pigment in spaces between scales) and passes through the ear opening. Around midbody are 24–30 scale rows. There are no postnasal scales, a single postmental scale, and the legs usually overlap when appressed. The juveniles are noteworthy for being lustrous black with no light lines on the body. The chin and area about the eyes in juveniles are white.

RANGE: The geographic distribution of this species (containing two subspecies) is somewhat unusual because of the absence of a central continuous "core." The range of the species is fragmented, with populations occurring from the Appalachians westward to the eastern margin of the Great Plains, and from Lake Ontario in the north to Panhandle Florida. Most of the range of the Southern Coal Skink occurs in two disjunct areas, one west of the Mississippi River from Kansas and Missouri south to Louisiana and eastern Texas and the other on the east side of the Mississippi River from the Florida parishes of Louisiana continuously to about the Ochlockonee River in Panhandle Florida. In Florida the Southern Coal Skink now is known from Santa Rosa, Okaloosa, Walton,

Southern Coal Skink, *Eumeces anthracinus pluvialis* juvenile. Walton County, Florida (photograph by B. W. Mansell).

Holmes, Gulf, Liberty, and Franklin counties, and probably also is found in other counties west of the Apalachicola River.

HABITAT: Throughout its range, this skink is noted to prefer *humid* habitats near water. Panhandle Florida localities all seem to be acid wetlands of various sorts. Some are margins of swampy stream courses in piney flatwoods. The vegetation in these particular low-lying areas is dominated by titis (*Cliftonia monophylla, Cyrilla racemiflora*), Sweet Bay Magnolia (*Magnolia virginiana*), and sometimes Black Gum (*Nyssa sylvatica* var. *biflora*) and Pond Cypress (*Taxodium ascendens*). Other localities are more properly described as bogs or seeps on lower hillsides at the margin of stream courses, and are dominated by sphagnum mosses and other acid wetland plants in the ground cover and titis and other evergreen shrub species in the overstory. Other specimens have been taken from a crayfish burrow in a roadside ditch and from the edge of shallow water along the shoulder of a highway where it cut through a swampy flatwoods stream.

LIFE HISTORY AND ECOLOGY: Very little is known concerning the life history and ecology of the Southern Coal Skink. From scanty information available in notes on geographic distribution, it is possible to speculate that Florida populations mate in early spring and females lay about

4–6 oval, leathery eggs that they brood. Young probably hatch 4–6 weeks later, sometime from late May to early July. The diet most likely consists mainly of small terrestrial and arboreal insects and other arthropods. This species is noted for its peculiar behavior among North American lizards of retreating from danger into shallow water where it hides under rubble on the bottom.

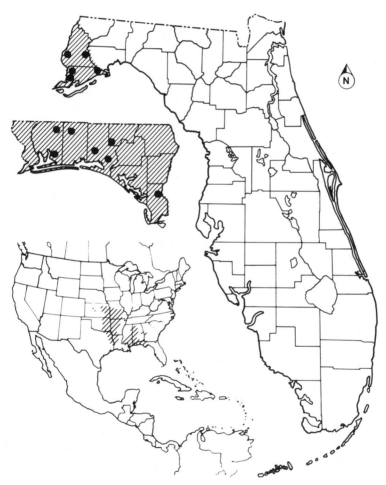

Distribution map of Southern Coal Skink (*Eumeces anthracinus pluvialis*). Dots indicate known localities.

SPECIALIZED OR UNIQUE CHARACTERISTICS: Because of its discontinuous geographic distribution, the Coal Skink is important to the study of biogeography. Its extensive latitudinal range makes it potentially valuable to the study of race formation and comparative demography.

BASIS OF STATUS CLASSIFICATION: The habitat of the Southern Coal Skink is common in Panhandle Florida, but only about 11 localities are known for it. This may be partly due to the secretive nature of this diminutive lizard and to the lack of systematic zoological field work carried out in such habitats. Because of its apparent fragmentary distribution throughout its range, and the low number of known localities in Florida, its status is here considered to be Rare.

RECOMMENDATIONS: A basic knowledge of any species is necessary in order to first judge whether its existence is threatened, and second to understand what can be done to preserve it. There is a critical need to know more about the occurrence, life history, and ecology of the Southern Coal Skink in Florida. Study of local populations of this lizard should be encouraged and financially supported wherever possible.

Selected References

Cope, E. D. 1880. On the zoological position of Texas. Bull. U. S. Natl. Mus. 17:19.

Mount, R. H. 1975. The reptiles and amphibians of Alabama. Alabama Agr. Exp. Sta., Auburn. 347 pp.

Seibert, H. C. 1964. The Coal Skink in Florida. J. Ohio Herp. Soc. 4:79.

Smith, P. W., and H. M. Smith. 1952. Geographic variation in the lizard *Eumeces anthracinus*. Univ. Kansas Sci. Bull. 34(2):679–694.

Stevenson, H. M. 1969. Records of the Coal Skink in Florida. Quart. J. Fla. Acad. Sci. 31(3):205–206.

Prepared by: D. Bruce Means, *Coastal Plains Institute, 1313 North Duval Street, Tallahassee, FL 32303.*

Cedar Key Mole Skink

Eumeces egregius insularis Mount

FAMILY SCINCIDAE

Order Squamata, Suborder Sauria

OTHER NAMES: Brown Red-Tailed Skink, Red-Tailed Skink.

DESCRIPTION: This is a small, shiny, brown lizard with a pair of dorso-lateral light stripes running the length of the body. The ground color is some shade of brown or gray-brown, and the tail is light pink or salmon. This is the largest of the subspecies of *E. egregius*, approaching a total length of 15 cm (5.9 in), with the tail accounting for two-thirds of this. The legs are small but well-developed.

RANGE: This lizard is confined to the islands in the vicinity of Cedar Key, Levy County, Florida. It has been found on Seahorse Key, Cedar Key, Airstrip Island, and probably also occurs on the other larger islands near Cedar Key. Other subspecies of *E. egregius* occur throughout Florida, and northward into southern Georgia and southeastern Alabama. The type locality on Airstrip Island still supports a population of this lizard, although it has been very much reduced in recent years.

HABITAT: *Eumeces e. insularis* is usually found under driftwood and tidal wrack ("sea weed") along the shore. On Seahorse Key it also occurs farther inland in loose sand at the bases of trees. It probably requires a loose sand, in which it burrows in its characteristic "sand-swimming" manner.

LIFE HISTORY AND ECOLOGY: Nothing is known concerning the life history of the race, but it is probably similar to that described by Mount (1963) for the mainland race, *Eumeces egregius onocrepis*. *Eumeces egregius* lays from 3 to 7 eggs once a year under debris, usually in a nest cavity

Cedar Key Mole Skink, *Eumeces egregius insularis*. Cedar Key, Levy County, Florida
(photograph by B.W. Mansell).

constructed in the sand. Females remain with the eggs until hatching
(31–51 days), presumably offering protection from small predators. Reproductive maturity occurs at the age of one year in the laboratory, and
mating takes place in the winter. The Cedar Key Mole Skink eats mainly
marine amphipods, which are exceedingly abundant under tidal wrack
and driftwood. In some areas, the Cedar Key Mole Skink appears to be
very abundant.

SPECIALIZED OR UNIQUE CHARACTERISTICS: *Eumeces e. insularis* is a
distinctive race of an almost endemic Florida lizard. The affinities of this
subspecies are not well understood. Like many island endemics, the Cedar
Key Mole Skink is larger than its mainland relatives. *Eumeces egregius* is
interesting because of the intermediate evolutionary position it seems to
occupy between the generalized cursorial skinks, such as the Five-lined
Skink (*Eumeces fasciatus*), and the highly specialized "sand-swimming"
skinks, such as *Neoseps reynoldsi*, the Sand Skink.

BASIS OF STATUS CLASSIFICATION: This lizard was once extremely

abundant on Airstrip Island near Cedar Key. Intense collecting by amateur reptile fanciers has drastically reduced its numbers there over the
past 15 years. The Cedar Keys National Wildlife Refuge, which includes
Seahorse Key, should be a haven for this lizard, if collecting there could
be reduced.

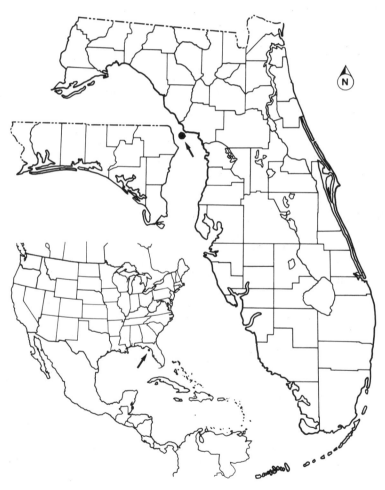

Distribution map of Cedar Key Mole Skink (*Eumeces egregius insularis*).

RECOMMENDATIONS: Limiting collecting on the Cedar Keys National Wildlife Refuge would protect this subspecies.

Selected References

Mount, R. H. 1963. The natural history of the Red-tailed Skink, *Eumeces egregius* Baird. Amer. Mid. Nat. 70(2):356–385.

Mount, R. H. 1965. Variation and systematics of the scincoid lizard, *Eumeces egregius* Baird. Bull. Fla. State Mus. 9(5):183–213.

Mount, R. H. 1968. *Eumeces egregius* Baird. Cat. Amer. Amphib. Rept.:73.1–73.2.

Prepared by: Steven P. Christman, *Department of Natural Sciences, Florida Museum of Natural History, Gainesville, FL 32611.*

Mole Snake

Lampropeltis calligaster rhombomaculata (Holbrook)

FAMILY COLUBRIDAE

Order Squamata, Suborder Serpentes

OTHER NAMES: Brown King Snake.

DESCRIPTION: This medium-sized kingsnake (adults about 76–101 cm [30–40 in] long) is light brown to brown dorsally with about 45 to 55 rounded, reddish-brown blotches down the back; a similar number of reddish-brown, small vertical bars occurs along both sides, usually spaced alternately between the lateral edges of the dorsal blotches. Both the blotches and the bars are thinly edged with black. The belly is white to beige or yellowish and is checkered with alternating squares of dark brown color. The undersurface of the tail may be similar to the belly, but in one Florida juvenile, it is yellowish-brown with two parallel darker stripes. Old adults may be uniformly brown dorsally. The head is proportionately small, and not clearly set off from the neck. All scales are smooth, and the anal plate is undivided. The Mole Snake is easily confused with the Corn Snake, especially when young, but the latter two characteristics separate these species.

RANGE: The range of the Mole Snake is primarily the southeastern United States from Maryland to central Florida, then west to western Mississippi. Continuing west, this species is called the Prairie Kingsnake (*Lampropeltis calligaster calligaster*). Florida specimens are known from Bay, Calhoun, Liberty, Gulf, and Walton counties in the Panhandle and from Brevard and Okeechobee counties in mid-peninsular Florida. Records from Madison County and the St. Johns River indicate that the secretive Mole Snake may range continuously throughout Florida from Pensacola to the northern edge of Lake Okeechobee.

Mole Snake, *Lampropeltis calligaster rhombomaculata*. North Carolina (photograph by B. W. Mansell).

HABITAT: In the Florida Panhandle, a number of specimens have been taken crossing roads in the western half of the Apalachicola National Forest in Liberty County. The native habitat along one such road collection was a recently burned Longleaf Pine flatwoods with Bracken Fern and Wiregrass, but no Saw Palmetto. Other sites included planted Slash Pine stands in early growth stages following site-preparation logging. Three specimens from Okeechobee County were collected on a grassy road shoulder in a subdivision, on a paved road in a residential area surrounded by open pastureland, and from a paved parking lot in front of a convenience store. Fallow lands seem to figure prominently in the present-day habitat preferences of this species. More thorough knowledge of preferred native habitats awaits future study.

LIFE HISTORY AND ECOLOGY: Throughout its range, the Mole Snake is known to be fossorial; it is commonly turned up from fallow fields by plowing. Florida specimens have been collected crossing roads at all hours from early morning until dusk during spring and early summer (and in November). Ken Richmond (personal communication) encountered three different individuals crossing roads up to two hours after dark. In Alabama, adjacent to Panhandle Florida, individuals are often taken on black-topped roads on warm nights after dark. The sex-ratio of specimens taken in this manner is strongly skewed toward males, suggesting that they are moving about in search of females. Populations may be greater in size and more common than is reflected by road encounters.

Little is known about the life cycle, food habits, or population biology of this species in Florida. The following information is deduced from

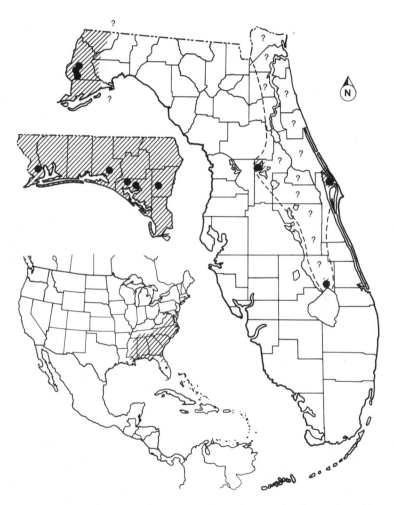

Distribution map of Mole Snake (*Lampropeltis calligaster rhombomaculata*). Dots indicate known localities. Question marks indicate area of possible but undocumented occurrence.

scattered literature on both subspecies. A clutch of about 6 to 10 white, leathery eggs is laid in late spring or early summer; they hatch in late summer. Individuals probably reach maturity by their second or third spring after hatching. Food consists of shrews and moles, small rodents and young rabbits, frogs, lizards, small snakes, small birds, eggs, and some insects.

SPECIALIZED OR UNIQUE CHARACTERISTICS: It is probable that this secretive snake is an inhabitant of burrows made by other animals, especially those forming its diet, such as shrews, moles, and rodents. A predator on small mammals in fallow and cultivated fields, this kingsnake may have locally high economic value as a partial biological control on agricultural pests. Florida peninsular populations are at the southern end of a widely ranging subspecies that is relatively rare throughout its distribution. Florida populations represent the endpoint of clinal variation in several morphological variables, and one student of the Mole Snake has suggested that the Okeechobee population might merit subspecies distinction.

BASIS OF STATUS CLASSIFICATION: The Mole Snake is considered to be Rare in Florida because specimens are seldom seen and are known from fewer than 15 localities over the entire state. In addition, the subspecies is rare over most of its range outside Florida.

RECOMMENDATIONS: Studies of the life history, ecology, population biology, and habitat management are needed for this species in order to more properly assess whether it may be Threatened rather than Rare, and to assess its role in the vertebrate food webs of Floridian environments.

Selected References

Ashton, R. E., Jr., and P. S. Ashton. 1981. Handbook of reptiles and amphibians of Florida. Part 1. The snakes. Windward Publ. Inc., Miami, Florida. 176 pp.

Blaney, R. M. 1978. *Lampropeltis calligaster*. Cat. Amer. Amphib. Rept.:229.1–229.2.

Hamilton, W. J., Jr., and J. A. Pollack. 1956. The food of some colubrid snakes from Fort Benning, Georgia. Ecology 37(3):519–526.

Layne, J. N., T. J. Walsh, and P. Meylan. 1986. New records for the Mole Snake, *Lampropeltis calligaster,* in peninsular Florida. Fla. Sci. 49(3):171–175.

Mount, R. H. 1975. The reptiles and amphibians of Alabama. Auburn Univ. Agr. Exp. Sta. 347 pp.

Wright, A. H., and A. A. Wright. 1957. Handbook of snakes of the United States and Canada. Comstock Publ. Assoc., Ithaca, New York. Vol. 1. 564 pp.

Prepared by: D. Bruce Means, *Coastal Plains Institute, 1313 North Duval Street, Tallahassee, FL 32303.*

Eastern Common Kingsnake,
Apalachicola population
Lampropeltis getula (Linnaeus)
including *L. g. goini* Neill and Allen
FAMILY COLUBRIDAE
Order Squamata, Suborder Serpentes

OTHER NAMES: Chipola Kingsnake, Blotched Kingsnake, "Goini."

DESCRIPTION: Uniquely patterned individuals of the Eastern Common Kingsnake, *L. getula*, are referred to here as Apalachicola populations pending publication of a taxonomic review study in progress (Means, in preparation). These populations include specimens with the characteristics of *L. g. goini* Neill and Allen and individuals that are striped, totally speckled, or broad-banded. These distinctive populations are located in the coastal lowlands adjacent to the lower Apalachicola River valley of central Panhandle Florida. Adults either (1) have all dorsal scales bicolored (light yellow, dark brown) with no pattern of light crossbands separated by darker interspaces, or (2) have light crossbands at least two or more scales wide middorsally that are separated by darker interband scales, each centered with a light spot. Crossband scales are usually dark posteriorly and light basally with a sharp line of demarcation between colors midway down each scale. Interband scales are always light in the center and usually completely fringed by darker pigment. Occasional specimens have patterns arranged in longitudinal hatching or long stripes.

These are medium-sized snakes (adults from 0.9 to 1.7 m [3–5.5 ft] long) usually possessing an undivided anal scale, about 47 divided subcaudals, 215 ventrals, 21 middorsal scale rows, and about 18 (14–20) light crossbands (when present). The color pattern alone distinguishes these kingsnakes. Ventral color is dark brown or chocolate arranged either entirely across the base of each ventral scale (in speckled individuals with no discernible crossbands) or as a double series of squarish blotches alternating with tan or light brown pigment. Juveniles are similar to adults in the arrangement of light crossbands or stripes, but usu-

Apalachicola Common Kingsnake, *Lampropeltis getula* "goini." Liberty County, Florida (photograph by D. B. Means).

ally possess very dark interband spaces that become lighter colored during growth to maturity.

RANGE: Entirely speckled (all dorsal scales with an equal amount of light and dark pigment) or striped specimens occur mostly in Liberty and Franklin counties between the Apalachicola and Ochlockonee rivers on the west and east, respectively, and between Telogia Creek on the north and the Gulf of Mexico on the south. Within this region kingsnakes may also possess broad bands greater than 2 scales wide middorsally, but, if so, the interband areas are almost always composed of dark scales with light centers. Intermediates (interband areas becoming darker, crossband width decreasing to 2 scales or less) are common both west of the Apalachicola River to Bay County (including the type locality of *L. g. goini* near Wewahitchka, Gulf County) and east of the Ochlockonee River to

Jefferson County. The occurrence of these phenotypes ceases abruptly north of Telogia Creek in northern Liberty County, being replaced there by the nominate race, *Lampropeltis getulus getula*.

HABITAT: These kingsnakes live in the flatwoods of the Gulf Coastal Lowlands, primarily along wetland margins of bayheads, creek swamps, acid bogs, savannahs, roadside ditches, dwarf cypress stands, and ever-

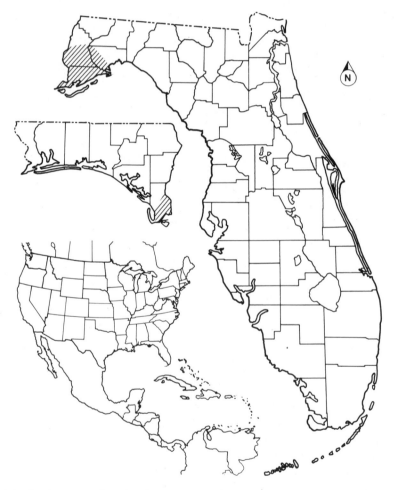

Distribution map of Apalachicola Common Kingsnake (*Lampropeltis getula* "goini").

green shrub communities. Occasionally individuals wander into the adjacent Longleaf Pine flatwoods. They have been found at the freshwater marsh zone fringing the Apalachicola River and Bay estuary, and in freshwater wetlands immediately behind the beachfront in Franklin County.

LIFE HISTORY AND ECOLOGY: Little is known concerning the life history and ecology of these particular populations, except that their food probably consists chiefly of snakes, amphibians, eggs of ground-nesting birds and turtles, and possibly small rodents. Courtship occurs from March to May; eggs are laid in early summer (June–July) and hatch sometime in July or August after an incubation period of about 60 days. Sexual maturity probably is reached in the third spring after hatching at a size of about 0.9 m (3 ft) long. Activity is greatest in mid-morning hours, with a second peak in late afternoon, although occasional individuals are found in midday; rarely, juveniles are observed moving after dark.

SPECIALIZED OR UNIQUE CHARACTERISTICS: The unique light pattern of these kingsnakes suggests an adaptation to some special environmental feature that may be similar to conditions in south peninsular Florida and in Duval and Baker counties, where other lightly patterned kingsnakes are known (but which differ in the details of their patterns and other characters). The distinctive Apalachicola populations occur in a geographic area that is noted for its endemism of plants and other animals. Apalachicola populations comprise a true Floridian form found exclusively in this state and probably evolved locally.

BASIS OF STATUS CLASSIFICATION: An intense collecting pressure has been focused on these populations by private and commercial snake collectors, some of whom advertise and pay local residents for specimens. Specimens have appeared on price lists of the snake pet trade for $200–$300 apiece. The small geographic range of these populations and the declining encounter rate experienced by biologists in the past decade warrant consideration of these pattern variants as Rare.

RECOMMENDATIONS: Considering the apparent decline of the Apalachicola populations and the fact that site-preparation silviculture alters many of their habitats, a ban on the taking and sale of specimens should be implemented by the Florida Game and Fresh Water Fish Commission until thorough study of the natural history and ecology of these populations is accomplished. The development and implementation of a successful management plan for these populations is necessary to insure their survival. Protection of these populations should be a high priority of the U. S. Forest Service, because the bulk of the range lies within the western half of the Apalachicola National Forest.

Selected References

Blaney, R. M. 1971. Systematics of the Common Kingsnake, *Lampropeltis getulus* (Linnaeus). Tulane Stud. Zool. Bot. 19(3–4):47–104.

Loftin, H. L. 1962. A new record of the Florida Panhandle Kingsnake, *Lampropeltis getulus goini.* Herpetologica 18:138–139.

Means, D. B. 1977. Aspects of the significance to terrestrial vertebrates of the Apalachicola River drainage basin, Florida. Pp. 23–67 *in* R. J. Livingston and E. A. Joyce, Jr. (eds.). Proc. of the Conference on the Apalachicola Drainage System. Fla. Mar. Res. Publ. 26.

Neill, W. T. 1963. Polychromatism in snakes. Quart. J. Fla. Acad. Sci. 26(1): 194–216.

Neill, W. T., and R. Allen. 1949. A new kingsnake (genus *Lampropeltis*) from Florida. Herpetologica 5:101–106.

Prepared by: D. Bruce Means, *Coastal Plains Institute, 1313 North Duval Street, Tallahassee, FL 32303.*

Gulf Salt Marsh Snake

Nerodia clarkii clarkii (Baird & Girard)

FAMILY COLUBRIDAE

Order Squamata, Suborder Serpentes

OTHER NAMES: Clark's Water Snake, Striped Water Snake, Salt Marsh Water Snake.

DESCRIPTION: The Gulf Salt Marsh Snake is a relatively slender, longitudinally-striped water snake with strongly-keeled scales. The dorsum is patterned with two dark-brown stripes along each side of the body, separated by lighter stripes of a yellowish to pale olive coloration. The belly is reddish-brown to black with a large central row of whitish or yellowish spots and often a smaller row along each side. Adults average approximately 61 cm (2 ft) in total length, but females can be up to 91.4 cm (3 ft) long.

RANGE: The Gulf Salt Marsh Snake occurs in saline habitats along the Gulf Coast from near Corpus Christi, Texas, to the vicinity of Cedar Keys, Levy County, Florida. Two other subspecies (*Nerodia clarkii compressicauda* and *Nerodia clarkii taeniata*) continue southward along the Florida Gulf and northward along the Atlantic Coast to Volusia County, Florida, including the Florida Keys and the north coast of Cuba. The type locality of *N. c. clarkii* is in Texas.

The Gulf Salt Marsh Snake intergrades with the Mangrove Salt Marsh Snake *(N. c. compressicauda)* along the west coast of central Florida, in a long coastal strip between Cedar Keys and Tampa Bay. Intergrades from this area often have a dorsal pattern combining stripes, blotches, and crossbands, closely resembling the Atlantic Salt Marsh Snake *(N. c. taeniata)* of the Florida east coast.

HABITAT: Coastal salt marshes supporting Cordgrass *(Spartina)*, Black-

Gulf Salt Marsh Snake, *Nerodia clarkii clarkii.* Cedar Key, Levy County, Florida (photograph by B. W. Mansell).

rush *(Juncus roemerianus),* and other halophytes are the typical habitat of the Gulf Salt Marsh Snake, but mangrove swamps are also utilized at the southern end of its Florida range. Although *N. c. clarkii* can survive for long periods in full-strength seawater, habitat salinities are normally much lower. This snake is usually found along the grassy edges of brackish creeks and ponds, where salinity may fluctuate daily due to tidal influence.

LIFE HISTORY AND ECOLOGY: The Gulf Salt Marsh Snake appears to be most active at night and is often found foraging in shallow water during low tidal stages. It feeds primarily on small fishes that become trapped in the shallows and is known to corral its prey by enclosing a small area of water within a loop of its body. *Nerodia c. clarkii* gives birth to live young, usually in July and August. Litter size ranges from 1 to 16, averaging 7, and tends to increase with female size. Mating probably occurs in early spring.

SPECIALIZED OR UNIQUE CHARACTERISTICS: Salt Marsh Snakes *(N. clarkii* ssp.) are among the few North American reptiles uniquely adapted to estuarine environments. They are characterized by a suite of physiological, morphological, and behavioral attributes that clearly differentiate them from related freshwater species. Survival in seawater is facilitated by a low dehydration rate and minimal sodium uptake, but there is no evidence of a salt gland. Even when dehydrated, Salt Marsh Snakes will not drink seawater. Instead, they require periodic access to fresh water presumably available from rain, dew, and tidal changes, as well as body fluids of prey animals and possibly their own metabolic water.

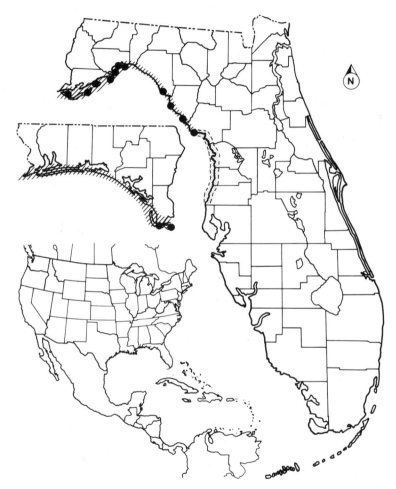

Distribution map of Gulf Salt Marsh Snake (*Nerodia clarkii clarkii*). Stippling indicates zone of intergradation with Mangrove Water Snake (*N. c. compressicauda*). Dots indicate known localities.

Salt Marsh Snakes are reproductively compatible with a closely related freshwater species, the Southern Water Snake *(N. fasciata)* and hybridize at many brackish localities. Consequently, some systematists consider Salt Marsh Snakes to be subspecies of *N. fasciata*. However, genetic introgression between freshwater and saltwater populations is normally minimal.

BASIS OF STATUS CLASSIFICATION: The habitat of the Gulf Salt Marsh Snake is limited to a very narrow and fragile strip of estuarine wetlands that is discontinuous along the upper Gulf Coast of Florida, especially in the western Panhandle. Throughout much of its Florida range, *N. c. clarkii* occurs as disjunct, local populations that are vulnerable to extirpation from habitat disturbance. In addition to direct habitat loss from coastal development, Salt Marsh Snakes are also susceptible to more subtle perturbations. Wetland alteration, such as draining, diking, and impounding, can promote hybridization and genetic swamping by the Southern Water Snake, an adjacent freshwater species. Chemical pollution from insecticides and industrial wastes may adversely affect Salt Marsh Snakes, especially if pollutants are concentrated in the tissues of their prey.

RECOMMENDATIONS: The Gulf Salt Marsh Snake ranges along a relatively undeveloped portion of the Florida coast and is protected, at least indirectly, on a number of coastal refuges, preserves, and sanctuaries. Although habitat protection now appears ensured along the Big Bend coast (Levy County through Wakulla County), populations farther west throughout the Panhandle remain vulnerable and would benefit from expansion of coastal sanctuaries in this region.

Selected References

Dunson, W. A. 1980. The relation of sodium and water balance to survival in sea water of estuarine and freshwater races of the snakes *Nerodia fasciata, N. sipedon* and *N. valida. Copeia* 1980(2):268–280.

Lawson, R., A. J. Meier, P. G. Frank, and P. E. Moler. 1991. Allozyme variation and systematics of the *Nerodia fasciata-Nerodia clarkii* complex of water snakes (Serpentes:Colubridae). *Copeia* 1991(3):638–659.

Pettus, D. 1956. Ecological barriers to gene exchange in the Common Water Snake *(Natrix sipedon)*. Ph.D. diss., University of Texas, Austin. 87 pp.

Pettus, D. 1958. Water relationships in *Natrix sipedon. Copeia* 1958(3):207–211.

Pettus, D. 1963. Salinity and subspeciation in *Natrix sipedon*. Copeia 1963(3): 499–504.

Prepared by: Howard I. Kochman, *U.S. Fish and Wildlife Service, National Ecology Research Center, 412 NE 16th Avenue, Room 250, Gainesville, FL 32601;* and Steven P. Christman, *Florida Museum of Natural History, University of Florida, Gainesville, FL 32611.*

Southern Copperhead

Agkistrodon contortrix contortrix (Linnaeus)

FAMILY CROTALIDAE

Order Squamata, Suborder Serpentes

OTHER NAMES: Highland Moccasin, Pilot Snake.

DESCRIPTION: The Southern Copperhead is a medium-sized pit viper with a coppery colored head and a handsome body pattern of 16–21 dark brown hourglass-shaped bands on a light brown, tan, or rusty ground color. The distinctive bands are broad along the sides of the snake, becoming pinched into a dumbbell shape middorsally, or sometimes failing to meet altogether. The overall pattern is often very pleasing to the eye, appearing delicate and resembling the earth tones of leaf litter, against which the copperhead is perfectly camouflaged. The ventral pattern is white or cream-colored with square to roundish brown blotches aligned in two rows, one on each side of the midventral line. Young are lighter colored than adults and possess a conspicuously yellow tail-tip, which is wriggled to lure prey. The triangular-shaped head is distinct from the neck and has a facial pit on each side between the eye and nostril. The front of each side of the upper jaw is equipped with a moveable, recurved fang, and the pupils of the eye are elliptical.

The species ranges from newborn which are about 25 cm (10 in) long to maximum-sized adults up to 132 cm (52 in) in length; Florida adults range from about 66.0 to 81.3 cm (26–32 in). The dorsal scales are keeled and are in 25 rows at midbody; the anal scale is undivided and the subcaudals are typically undivided except near the tip.

RANGE: The Copperhead is restricted in Florida along the northern borders of Escambia, Okaloosa, and possibly other counties west of the Choctawhatchee River, and to the vicinity of the upper Apalachicola River from the town of Chattahoochee to some unknown distance south

Southern Copperhead, *Agkistrodon contortrix contortrix*. Calhoun County, Florida (photograph by B. W. Mansell).

of the level of Bristol and Blountstown, possibly as far as Scott's Ferry. A record for the Ochlockonee River drainage exists in southern Gadsden County near where Ocklawaha Creek drains into Lake Talquin.

HABITAT: Specimens have been taken from mature hardwood floodplain forests and from the beech-magnolia association or mixed pine-oak-hickory forest on the steep slopes of the high eastern valley wall along the Apalachicola River from Chattahoochee to Bristol. The species seems not to wander far eastward from the Apalachicola escarpment in spite of the steep-walled valleys running east into the uplands. Records from roads traversing the escarpment face at Chattahoochee and Bristol and from the main entrance to Torreya State Park are common, but no records exist more than about 0.8 km (1/2 mi) east of the escarpment. Frequently specimens are encountered in mixed bottomland hardwood forests (composed of *Carya aquatica, Celtis laevigata, Quercus laurifolia, Quercus lyrata,*

Liquidambar styraciflua, and others) on higher elevations in the floodplain of the Apalachicola River from Torreya State Park to the vicinity of Sutton's Lake south of Florida Road 20 on the west side of the main river channel.

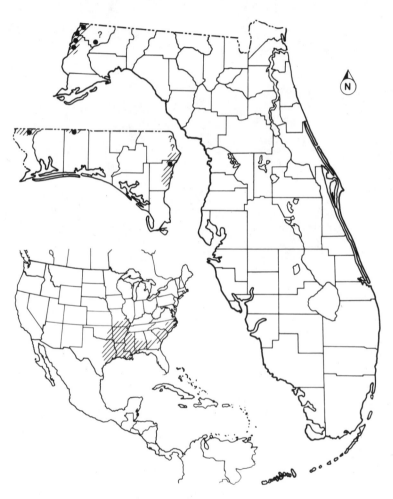

Distribution map of Southern Copperhead (*Agkistrodon contortrix contortrix*). Dots indicate known localities. Question marks indicate area of possible but uncertain occurrence.

LIFE HISTORY AND ECOLOGY: In spring and fall, Copperheads are active in the morning and evening, but during hot weather they are chiefly nocturnal. Copulation has been observed mostly in April and May. After a gestation period of about 105 days, an average of about 5 or 6 young per female are born in August or September. Males in Kansas become sexually mature in their second summer, and females produce their first litters at 3 years of age, and thereafter in alternate years. Individuals are capable of living to 15 years or more, but most die before that age. Food consists of small vertebrates and certain insects such as cicadas and caterpillars. Voles, shrews, and white-footed mice *(Peromyscus spp.)* are important in the diet of adults, whereas more frogs, small snakes, and lizards are eaten by the young.

Copperheads spend most of their time in a characteristic coil awaiting prey. Individuals spend their lives in a home range that was calculated to be 9.8 ha (24.5 ac) for males and 3.4 ha (8.5 ac) for females in Kansas, but of course these figures may be different for Florida animals. In other parts of the country, Copperheads are known to migrate to communal dens in the fall, where they spend the winter with numerous other individuals. It is not known whether Florida Copperheads do this.

SPECIALIZED OR UNIQUE CHARACTERISTICS: The Southern Copperhead is a wide-ranging species in the eastern United States whose geographic distribution for some unknown reason does not include much of Florida, in spite of the fact that the species reaches the Gulf Coast in Louisiana and Texas. The Apalachicola River population represents a narrow tongue of the distribution of the species that juts southward from southern Georgia probably because the floodplain and high relief provide a suitably large band of hardwood forest habitat.

BASIS OF STATUS CLASSIFICATION: Because of its highly restricted range in the Panhandle, the Southern Copperhead merits Rare status.

RECOMMENDATIONS: Research to develop more precise understanding of the distribution and life history of the Copperhead in Florida is needed, particularly regarding its occurrence below Bristol and in the lower Chipola River valley. Presently some portion of the species range in Florida is protected by Torreya State Park, Three Rivers State Park, The Nature Conservancy Bluffs and Ravines Preserve, and by the sovereign lands underlying the floodplain of the Apalachicola and Chipola rivers.

Selected References

Carr, A. F. 1940. A contribution to the herpetology of Florida. Univ. Fla. Publ. Biol. Sci. Ser. 3:1–118.

Carr, A. F., and C. J. Goin. 1955. A guide to the reptiles, amphibians and freshwater fishes of Florida. University of Florida Press, Gainesville. 341 pp.

Fitch, H. S. 1960. Autecology of the Copperhead. Univ. Kansas Publ. Mus. Nat. Hist. 13:85–288.

Mount, R. H. 1975. The reptiles and amphibians of Alabama. Auburn Univ. Agric. Exp. Stn., Alabama. 347 pp.

Neill, W. T. 1957. Historical biogeography of present-day Florida. Bull. Fla. State Mus. 2(7):175–220.

Prepared by: D. Bruce Means, *Coastal Plains Institute, 1313 North Duval Street, Tallahassee, FL 32303.*

Mimic Glass Lizard

Ophisaurus mimicus Palmer

FAMILY ANGUIDAE

Order Squamata, Suborder Sauria

OTHER NAMES: None.

DESCRIPTION: The Mimic Glass Lizard is one of four Florida species of long, slender, legless lizards belonging to the genus *Ophisaurus*. They can be distinguished from snakes by the presence of movable eyelids, external ear openings, and ventral scales not modified into enlarged transverse plates. Glass lizards have very long tails—about 2/3 of total length, but the tail is easily broken in most species. Most of the body is covered by heavy scales which form a semirigid "exoskeleton." A lateral fold along each side allows for expansion of the body to accommodate respiration and feeding. The Mimic Glass Lizard and the Island Glass Lizard, *Ophisaurus compressus,* have fewer than 96 scale rows along the lateral fold; other Florida glass lizards have more than 98. The Island Glass Lizard has a single, wide, dark line along each side of the tail, whereas the Mimic Glass Lizard has several narrow dark lines. The Mimic Glass Lizard is the smallest of Florida's glass lizards, with a maximum known snout-vent length of 181 mm (7 1/8 in).

RANGE: This species is found in the lower Coastal Plain from southeastern North Carolina to northern Florida, thence west to southeastern Mississippi. It does not appear to occur in the Florida Peninsula. There is a specimen from Duval County, Florida, but all other Florida records are from the Panhandle west of and including Apalachicola National Forest. Panhandle counties from which specimens are known are Escambia, Santa Rosa, Okaloosa, Walton, Bay (imprecise locality—not mapped), Liberty, and Wakulla. (There is a questionable record from Everglades National Park.)

Mimic Glass Lizard, *Ophisaurus mimicus.* Liberty County, Florida (photograph by B.W. Mansell).

HABITAT: Most specimens of this species have come from areas of Longleaf Pine *(Pinus palustris)* flatwoods with Wiregrass *(Aristida stricta)* as the predominant ground cover. This habitat type was once widespread in the southeastern Coastal Plain, but has now been drastically reduced in extent.

LIFE HISTORY AND ECOLOGY: As with other Florida glass lizards, *O. mimicus* appears to be primarily diurnal to crepuscular in activity. A Mississippi specimen contained 11 enlarged ova. One Florida specimen was being eaten by a Black Racer when collected. Nothing else is known about the natural history of this species. In other Florida glass lizards, the diet consists primarily of insects, arachnids, and earthworms, and this is likely true of the Mimic Glass Lizard as well.

SPECIALIZED OR UNIQUE CHARACTERISTICS: The distribution of the Mimic Glass Lizard overlaps those of the Eastern Glass Lizard *(Ophisaurus ventralis)* and the Eastern Slender Glass Lizard *(Ophisaurus attenuatus longicaudus),* but there is little or no overlap with the range of the Island Glass Lizard. Thus the group as a whole provides interesting examples of both ecological niche partitioning and geographic, ecological replacement.

BASIS OF STATUS CLASSIFICATION: This species was only described recently. Only about 67 specimens are known, of which 28 (41.8%) are from north Florida. The principal habitat, Longleaf Pine–Wiregrass flatwoods, was once widespread in the lower Coastal Plain but has been largely converted to pine plantations and other agricultural uses.

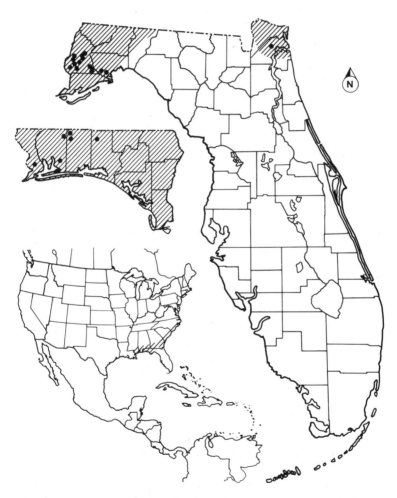

Distribution map of Mimic Glass Lizard (*Ophisaurus mimicus*). Dots indicate known localities.

RECOMMENDATIONS: Large tracts of habitat for this species are today more or less limited to state and national forests and a few military reservations. Elsewhere, extensive wiregrass ground cover has been largely eliminated through silvicultural or other agricultural conversion or habitat succession as a consequence of fire exclusion. The Longleaf Pine-Wiregrass flatwoods and savannahs are maintained by frequent fire. Intensive, mechanical silvicultural site preparation tends to eliminate the Wiregrass ground cover. The Mimic Glass Lizard will benefit from forestry management practices which include frequent fire, especially during the growing season, and minimize mechanical site preparation.

Selected References

Palmer, W. M. 1987. A new species of glass lizard (Anguidae: *Ophisaurus*) from the southeastern United States. Herpetologica 43(4):415–423.

Prepared by: Paul E. Moler, *Florida Game and Fresh Water Fish Commission, 4005 South Main Street, Gainesville, FL 32601.*

South Florida Rainbow Snake

Farancia erytrogramma seminola Neill

FAMILY COLUBRIDAE

Order Squamata, Suborder Serpentes

OTHER NAMES: Seminole Rainbow Snake.

DESCRIPTION: Rainbow Snakes are iridescent, glossy black above, with three red stripes. The venter is red and/or yellow with three rows of black spots. In the South Florida Rainbow Snake, the ventral black spots coalesce to render the venter predominately black, except on the throat, and the middorsal red stripe is reduced to a dotted line due to invasion of black pigment. The largest of three South Florida Rainbow Snakes reported was 131 cm (51.5 in) in length, but elsewhere the species is known to reach lengths in excess of 152 cm (5 ft).

RANGE: The South Florida Rainbow Snake is known only from Fisheating Creek, Glades County, Florida, which lies approximately 250 km (150 mi) south of the nearest area known to support other Rainbow Snakes. Intensive collecting at Rainey Slough, a western tributary of Fisheating Creek, did not produce any Rainbow Snakes (S. Godley, personal communication).

HABITAT: Elsewhere in Florida, Rainbow Snakes are strongly aquatic in habit, seldom wandering far from water. The two South Florida Rainbow Snakes for which data are available were both collected in the water at night. The only known locality, Fisheating Creek, is a sluggish, small to moderate sized stream which flows through a well developed cypress strand. During periods of drought, it is typically reduced to a series of disconnected lakes.

LIFE HISTORY AND ECOLOGY: Rainbow Snakes are oviparous and have been reported to lay clutches of 22–50 eggs. Adults feed primarily upon eels *(Anguilla rostrata)*, but aquatic amphibians may also be eaten. Nothing is known about the specific ecology of the South Florida Rainbow Snake.

SPECIALIZED OR UNIQUE CHARACTERISTICS: The Rainbow Snake and the related Mud Snake *(Farancia abacura)* are specialized to feed upon

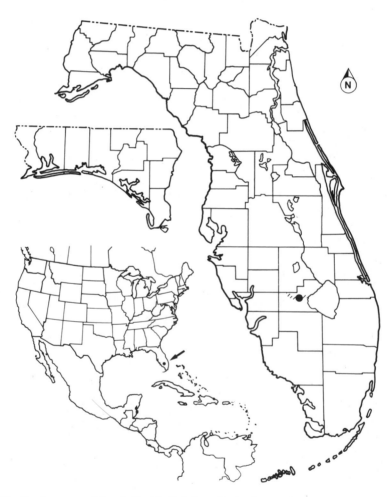

Distribution map of South Florida Rainbow Snake (*Farancia erytrogramma seminola*). Dot indicates the only known locality.

elongate, slippery prey. The stout tip of the Rainbow Snake's tail may be used to help restrain the eels upon which it feeds.

BASIS OF STATUS CLASSIFICATION: The South Florida Rainbow Snake was described on the basis of three specimens collected between 1949 and 1952; no additional specimens are known.

RECOMMENDATIONS: Fisheating Creek is currently one of the most pristine systems in southern Florida. Continued protection would assure the survival of the South Florida Rainbow Snake as well as a diverse assemblage of other species. Surveys are needed to determine the status and distribution of this snake, and a study of its ecology should be initiated if an adequate population can be located.

Selected References

Gibbons, J. W., J. W. Coker, and T. M. Murphy, Jr. 1977. Selected aspects of the life history of the rainbow snake *(Farancia erytrogramma)*. Herpetologica 33:276–281.

Neill, W. T. 1964. Taxonomy, natural history, and zoogeography of the rainbow snake, *Farancia erytrogramma* (Palisot de Beauvois). Amer. Midl. Nat. 71(2):257–295.

Wright, A. H., and A. A. Wright. 1957. Handbook of snakes of the United States and Canada. Comstock Publ. Assoc., Ithaca, New York. Vol. 1, 564 pp.

Prepared by: Paul E. Moler, *Florida Game and Fresh Water Fish Commission, 4005 South Main Street, Gainesville, FL 32601.*

Florida Pine Snake

Pituophis melanoleucus mugitus Barbour
FAMILY COLUBRIDAE
Order Squamata, Suborder Serpentes

OTHER NAMES: Southern Pine Snake.

DESCRIPTION: The Florida Pine Snake is a large, stocky snake with dark brown to reddish dorsal blotches on a light gray to sandy colored background. The belly is pale, and the darker dorsal blotches intrude onto the upper portions of the ventral scales. Its head and snout are conical in shape, an adaptation to the snake's burrowing habits. The snake is attributed with a bad temper and an awful hiss. Adults range in size from 91 to 228 cm (36–90 in).

RANGE: This snake is restricted to the Atlantic and Gulf Coastal Plains, from southeastern South Carolina to south Florida, west to the Florida Panhandle. Specimens from northern Escambia County in the extreme western Panhandle begin to show features of the Black Pine Snake *(Pituophis melanoleucus lodingi;* P. Moler, personal communication). Based on museum records, the distribution of this snake in south Florida is spotty, although further investigations may prove it to be more widely distributed. There are no records from the Florida Keys.

HABITAT: The Florida Pine Snake occupies xeric sites, including Longleaf Pine–xerophytic oak woodlands, Sand Pine scrub, pine flatwoods on well drained soils, and old fields on former sandhill sites. Radio-telemetry studies in sandhill habitats in northern Florida indicate that this species prefers High Pine (Longleaf Pine–Turkey Oak association) and old fields over Sand Live Oak hammocks and other forest types with heavy canopies. Under drought conditions, Pine Snakes seek open habitats surrounding wetlands. Two radio-tracked females exhibited home ranges of 11

Florida Pine Snake, *Pituophis melanoleucus mugitus*. Duval County, Florida (photograph by B. W. Mansell).

and 12 ha (27.5 and 30 ac) each, while 3 males used areas 2–8 times larger in size. The Florida Pine Snake is extremely fossorial, particularly seeking out the tunnel systems of pocket gophers and, to a lesser extent, the burrows of Gopher Tortoises. Radio-tracked snakes were observed to dig open pocket gopher mounds using methods described by Carpenter (1982) for the closely related Bullsnake *(Pituophis melanoleucus sayi)*. Radio-tracked snakes were active between March and October but showed their greatest activity in May, June, July, and October. During these months, they made the greatest numbers of moves and travelled the greatest distances.

LIFE HISTORY AND ECOLOGY: Florida Pine Snakes lay 4–8 (average 5.6) large, white eggs, probably underground, from June to August. Eggs hatch in September and October, based on reported incubation times of 67–72 days. The average length of hatchlings is 59.5 cm (23.4 in). The Florida Pine Snake is reported to eat ground-dwelling birds and their eggs, mice, and pocket gophers *(Geomys pinetis)*. A recent study found that immature Cottontail and Marsh Rabbits, Woodrats, Old Field Mice, and Florida Mice are also important foods (R. Franz, unpub. data).

SPECIALIZED OR UNIQUE CHARACTERISTICS: The Florida Pine Snake and other eastern subspecies are adapted to life in open sandy habitats. These snakes are uniquely modified for burrowing. Their conical-shaped heads and muscular bodies allow them to push their way into loosely-

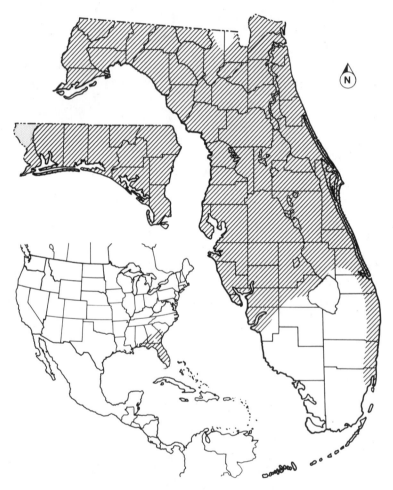

Distribution map of Florida Pine Snake (*Pituophis melanoleucus mugitus*). Stippling in Escambia County indicates zone of intergradation with Black Pine Snake (*P. m. lodingi*).

packed sand or into the burrows of rodents and reptiles. The eastern Pine Snakes are probably remnants of a xeric adapted fauna (which included horses, camels, rhinoceroses, Spadefoot Toads, Gopher Tortoises, and giant tortoises) that extended into the southeastern United States from western North America, via a Gulf Coast Corridor, in the Miocene or Pliocene.

BASIS OF STATUS CLASSIFICATION: According to some herpetologists, there have been serious declines in the numbers of Florida Pine Snakes in the last 20 years. It is believed that this has resulted from excessive collecting, road mortality, and habitat alteration. In response to this concern, the Florida Game and Fresh Water Fish Commission has listed this snake as a Species of Special Concern, with a possession limit of one snake per person.

RECOMMENDATIONS: The Florida Pine Snake should be protected from commercial collecting. The protection provided by the existing regulations is probably sufficient at this time. The state should continue to use fire as a major management tool on upland sites on public lands in order to insure the survival of upland faunas and floras of which this snake is a member. Research into all aspects of the Pine Snake's biology should be encouraged.

Selected References

Allen, R., and W. T. Neill. 1952. The Southern Pine Snake. Fla. Wildlife 5(10):18–19.

Ashton, R. E., Jr., and P. S. Ashton. 1981. Handbook of reptiles and amphibians, Part I. Snakes. Windward Publ., Inc. Miami, Florida. 176 pp.

Carpenter, C. C. 1982. The Bullsnake as an excavator. J. Herpetol. 16(4):394–401.

Carr, A. F. 1940. A contribution to the herpetology of Florida. Univ. Fla. Publ., Biol. Ser. 3(1):1–118.

Franz, R. 1986. The Florida Gopher Frog and the Florida Pine Snake as burrow associates of the Gopher Tortoise in northern Florida. Pp. 16–20 *in* D. R. Jackson and R. J. Bryant (eds.). The Gopher Tortoise and its community. Proc. 5th Ann. Mtg. Gopher Tortoise Council.

Iverson, J. B. 1978. Reproductive notes on Florida snakes. Fla. Sci. 41:201–207.

Lee, D. S. 1967. Eggs and hatchlings of the Florida Pine Snake, *Pituophis melanoleucus mugitus*. Herpetologica 23:241–242.

Neill, W. T. 1951. Eggs and young of the Southern Pine Snake, *Pituophis melanoleucus mugitus*. Publ. Ross Allen Rept. Inst. 1(5):56–57.

Wright, A. W., and A. A. Wright. 1957. Handbook of snakes of the United States and Canada. Cornell University Press, Ithaca, New York. Vol. 2, 551 pp.

Prepared by: Richard Franz, *Florida Museum of Natural History, Gainesville, FL 32611.*

Contributors

Writers

Paul E. Moler, Florida Game and Fresh Water Fish Commission, 4005 South Main Street, Gainesville, FL 32601

Ray E. Ashton, Jr., Water and Air Research, Inc., 6821 SW Archer Road, Gainesville, FL 32602

James F. Berry, Department of Biology, Elmhurst College, Elmhurst, IL 60126

Howard W. Campbell (deceased), National Fish and Wildlife Laboratory, U. S. Fish and Wildlife Service, 412 NE 16th Avenue, Gainesville, FL 32601

Steven P. Christman, Department of Natural Sciences, Florida Museum of Natural History, Gainesville, FL 32611

Vincent DeMarco, Department of Zoology, 223 Carr Hall, University of Florida, Gainesville, FL 32611

Joan Diemer, Florida Game and Fresh Water Fish Commission, 4005 South Main Street, Gainesville, FL 32601

C. Kenneth Dodd, National Ecology Research Center, U. S. Fish and Wildlife Service, 412 NE 16th Avenue, Room 250, Gainesville, FL 32601

W. A. Dunson, Department of Biology, The Pennsylvania State University, University Park, PA 16802

Llewellyn M. Ehrhart, Department of Biological Sciences, University of Central Florida, P.O. Box 25000, Orlando, FL 32816

Richard Franz, Department of Natural Sciences, Florida Museum of Natural History, Gainesville, FL 32611

J. Steve Godley, Biological Research Associates, Inc., 3819 East 7th Avenue, Tampa, FL 33605

Dale R. Jackson, Florida Natural Areas Inventory, 1018 Thomasville Road, Suite 200-C, Tallahassee, FL 32303

Howard I. Kochman, U. S. Fish and Wildlife Service, National Ecology Research Center, 412 NE 16th Avenue, Room 250, Gainesville, FL 32601

D. Bruce Means, Coastal Plains Institute, 1313 North Duval Street, Tallahassee, FL 32303

Anne Meylan, Florida Marine Research Institute, 100 Eighth Avenue, SE, St. Petersburg, FL 33701–5095

Peter A. Meylan, Eckerd College, P.O. Box 12560, St. Petersburg, FL 33733

Larry H. Ogren, National Marine Fisheries Service, Panama City Laboratory, 3500 Delwood Beach Road, Panama City, FL 32408

Peter C. H. Pritchard, Florida Audubon Society, P.O. Drawer 7, Maitland, FL 32751

Roger A. Sanderson, Department of Medical Oncology, University of South Florida, Tampa, FL 33620

Robert M. Shealey, Box 155, Moore, SC 29369

Joseph Travis, Department of Biological Science, Florida State University, Tallahassee, FL 32306-2043

W. G. Weaver, Department of Biology, Miami-Dade Community College, Medical Center Campus, 950 NW 20th Street, Miami, FL 33127

Blair E. Witherington, Department of Zoology, University of Florida, Gainesville, FL 32611

Roger C. Wood, Faculty of Science and Mathematics, Stockton State College, Pomona, NJ 08240

Photographers

C. L. Abercrombie, Department of Sociology, Wofford College, Spartanburg, SC 29301

R. D. Babb, 851 North Senate Street, Chandler, AZ 85225

M. A. Bailey, Alabama Natural Heritage Program, ADCNR-Lands Division, 64 North Union Street, Montgomery, AL 36130

S. P. Christman, Department of Natural Sciences, Florida Museum of Natural History, Gainesville, FL 32611

D. R. Jackson, Florida Natural Areas Inventory, 1018 Thomasville Road, Suite 200-C, Tallahassee, FL 32303

B. W. Mansell, 2826 Rosselle Street, Jacksonville, FL 32205

D. B. Means, Coastal Plains Institute, 1313 Duval Street, Tallahassee, FL 32303

A. Meylan, Florida Marine Research Institute, 100 Eighth Avenue, SE, St. Petersburg, FL 33701-5095

R. M. Mount, Department of Zoology, Auburn University, Auburn, AL 36849

P. C. H. Pritchard, Florida Audubon Society, P.O. Drawer 7, Maitland, FL 32751

R. W. Van Devender, Department of Biology, Appalachian State University, Boone, NC 28608

R. C. Wood, Faculty of Science and Mathematics, Stockton State College, Pomona, NJ 08240

Index

Library of Congress Cataloging-in-Publication Data

Rare and endangered biota of Florida.

   Includes bibliographical references and index.
   Contents: v. 1. Mammals / edited by Stephen R.
Humphrey —   — v. 3. Amphibians and reptiles /
edited by Paul E. Moler.
    1. Rare animals—Florida.   2. Endangered species—
Florida.   3. Rare plants—Florida.   4. Endangered
plants—Florida.   I. Ashton, Ray E.   II. Humphrey,
Stephen R.
QL84.22.F6R37   1992   591.52′9′09759   91-36368
ISBN 0-8130-1127-2 (v. 1 : alk. paper)
ISBN 0-8130-1128-0 (v. 1 : pbk. : alk. paper)